CABLE COWBOY

JOHN MALONE
AND THE
RISE OF THE
MODERN CABLE BUSINESS

MARK ROBICHAUX

JOHN WILEY & SONS, INC.

For Mary

CONTENTS

INTRODUCTION

On the night of June 24, 1998, a corporate jet streaked through the inky skies over the Midwest toward Denver, unofficial capital of the cable television industry in the United States. Inside, John Malone, chairman of Tele-Communications, Incorporated (TCI), sank deeper into a creamy soft leather seat. He was delighted to leave New York. The city was basting in a heat wave, and at every stop the cable TV baron had made in Manhattan on that steamy day, throngs of photographers and reporters had jostled to get closer to him.

Now, 35,000 feet aloft in the polished teak interior of the jet, Malone was surrounded only by a few loyal lieutenants and this writer. Despite the long eventful day, concluding a week of clandestine meetings, he was affable and refreshed. Even with a head of gray hair, his wide grin, chiseled jaw, and intense brown eyes endowed Malone with rugged good looks that made him appear younger than his 59 years. He was, in fact, almost giddy, fueled not by champagne—they hadn't uncorked any—but by adrenaline. Hours earlier, Malone had pulled off the biggest coup in an illustrious and controversial career: selling TCI, the world's largest and most powerful cable concern, to AT&T, one of the world's largest telephone titans and the heart of the once mighty Ma Bell.

Although he had answered questions effortlessly in the press conference earlier that afternoon, even Malone, the cerebral cable billionaire, hadn't yet fully grasped the implications of what he had just done—a $48 billion deal, one of the largest media mergers in history, that promised to blanket millions of homes with a panoply of interactive digital services that Malone had dreamed of for years. TCI's coaxial cable wires could deliver data and Internet traffic at speeds unmatched by the nation's telephone companies, making them crucial to the expansion of the Internet. The deal would accelerate the changes already silently roiling American culture: how we get our news, entertain ourselves, teach our children, buy our stocks, and plan our vacations.

Combined, TCI and AT&T would serve one of the biggest customer bases ever assembled. News of the deal had been carried to every corner of the globe by CNN, which happened to be one of more than two dozen cable channels in which Malone owned an interest. The White House had learned of the deal only the night before it went down, when Malone's camp had alerted, among others, Vice President Al Gore, Malone's public nemesis.

To buy up TCI's 622 million shares, AT&T had agreed to pay a premium of more than 30 percent over TCI's price on the Nasdaq stock market at the time. Just as he had done for two decades at the helm of the cable TV industry, Malone had come out on top of the AT&T merger. Or had he? Over the next three hours, Malone basked in the moment, launching a nonlinear lecture of sorts, veering from industry issues to arcane topics, such as the molecular makeup of his diet and how the body breaks down carbohydrates. He repeated ancient stories about TCI characters long since gone, and in the easy, confident manner that had attracted so many investors big and small, Malone mapped out where new fortunes awaited them.

More than halfway home on the flight back to Denver, the banter in the TCI jet's cabin had given way to the soft hum of the engines. In the faint light, Malone glanced out the window into the black sky, thought about the partner with whom he had started it all, the late Bob Magness, and muttered to no one in particular, "Bob would have loved this one."

That night on the TCI jet, as Malone started to toy with ideas for a post-AT&T life, how could he and the others know that by the summer of 2002, the world as they had planned would be such a radically different place?

Two years down the road, the TCI merger would spark another landmark accord: America Online's $165 billion deal to buy media powerhouse Time Warner, the richest transaction ever. Each suitor sought the same thing: a new nervous system for the digital age, with miles and miles of copper coaxial TV cable reaching into millions of homes. A parade of companies would follow the template set in the AT&T deal, merging, investing, and chasing the grand vision of offering consumers a nonstop stream of information and entertainment—and many would fall short. Just weeks after AOL and Time Warner merged, the Internet bubble burst, sending values of online firms tumbling. The terrorist attacks of September 11, 2001, further accelerated a recession that battered media stocks in nearly every sector. Synergies and savings were elusive. By 2002, AOL–Time Warner would lose more than $100 billion in shareholder value since the merger announcement, amid rumors the behemoth might be dismantled. Vivendi, a French water utility that remade itself into a global media giant with the purchase of Seagram Company's Universal Studios and other properties, nearly choked in the process, losing half its stock value. Walt Disney stock would deflate, first because of its ill-fated Internet plunge, then by weak ratings at its ABC network. Hardly anyone was immune to the weak economy and morose ad market. And unthinkable as it was that evening for the TCI clan flying across the heartland, AT&T itself would cease to exist in a few short years.

I had studied the bumpy odyssey of the industry for 6 of my 12 years at the *Wall Street Journal,* fascinated by the cast of underfunded cowboys who had wanted merely to make a buck by building a rural antenna service. Their vision always seemed just beyond their grasp, and they often stumbled in running to reach it. Now this same spider's web of copper lines across the country was suddenly the single fastest route to the Internet, promising a stunning array of services; it would be unmatched in capacity and speed—the most sophisticated wired network in the world. The tapestry of events that led to cable's dominance was connected by a single thread: John Malone.

After the sale of TCI to AT&T, some had expected John Malone to disappear from the scene, weary from 25 years of near-death experiences in building TCI with his partner, Bob Magness. But instead of receding, Malone would reconstitute his old power overseas, and in the process, reconstruct a truly global empire. When he rode away from the AT&T deal, he hung on to Liberty Media Corporation, which held choice programming pieces of the old TCI empire, and immediately began striking deals. When AT&T stumbled with its strategy to remake Ma Bell into a cable powerhouse, Malone agitated for change. He stirred intrigue with his 4 percent stake in entertainment giant AOL Time Warner, sparking rumors that he and his old buddy Ted Turner might stage a takeover. And in the years that followed, Malone struck more deals, assembling a global cable operation bigger than the realm he had built with Magness.

Why should it be any different now? Malone had held center stage in the pantheon of cowboys, gamblers, and debt-riddled deal makers who had built the digital nervous system of the nation. Malone clearly wasn't one of them; he had been reared in Connecticut, educated at Yale, and steeled in the storied research ranks of Bell Labs—yet he had grown into one of them, parlaying his quicksilver mind, financial agility, and public persuasion into an irresistible force in pursuit of the dreams they all held. They were entrepreneurs whose infamy often negated the need for last names.

But Malone symbolized a much more ominous side of business to critics, consumers, and competitors. They saw a monopoly run by a rapacious, Machiavellian bully who lived up to his many nicknames, including Darth Vader, Genghis Khan, and The Godfather. He had skated perilously close to securities law violations, and like industrial powers Andrew Carnegie or J. P. Morgan before him, had extracted a price for the progress he offered. As his power grew in the world of television, he decided which cable networks survived, he defied regulators, and he crushed competitors. And all of this he did openly, brazenly. He seemed to provoke his critics, relishing their many barbs. Yet, for all of his influence, Malone remained a stranger to many in the cable industry, and few outside it had even heard of him.

TCI's story was a classic American entrepreneurial tale, and it reflected the slapdash, bootstrap history of the cable industry itself. TCI was born in the scrubland of western Texas in 1952 when Bob Magness, a part-time rancher with a weakness for whisky and gambling, gleaned from a couple of hitchhikers a nifty investment idea that almost bankrupted him. He sought help from Malone, and by 1990, Malone had expanded TCI's reach and assets more than 10-fold, making nearly 500 acquisitions in that time, an average of one deal every two weeks. The structures of his deals were exotic, and his financial alchemy often befuddled Wall Street and investors. The flurry of complex mergers, acquisitions, stock dividends, and spin-offs clouded the picture of the company's true performance, which was phenomenal by the one measure that counts in almost all business: shareholder value. Despite its reputation as a risky play, through 1997, TCI outperformed every other stock in the market. A single share of TCI, purchased at the 1974 low of 75 cents, was worth $4,184 by the end of 1997—a 5,578-fold increase.[1] And in each of these deals, one outcome was certain: No one benefited more than Magness and Malone. Still, he saw no need to apologize for the creation of wealth. His shareholders got rich along with him. For Malone it was a noble, if not moral, achievement, the fruit of his enormous capacity to deduce and strategize. As Malone ascended to power, the cable television industry, too, had transformed itself.

The same cable wires that today light up more than 70 million TV homes in the United States trace their beginnings to an antenna service for folks in the shadow of the mountain in the late 1940s. Over time, these wires had inspired multi-billion-dollar deals, raised false hopes for futuristic services, ignited fights over access to information, and sparked endless accusations of rate gouging and monopoly misdeeds. Now this thicket of copper tendrils, which would spawn hundreds of new networks, had suddenly emerged as a key part of the fabled information superhighway. Now the work of so many cable cowboys had evolved into the neural network of the twenty-first century, and it was finally coming to life.

Malone was still not ready to hang up his holsters.

LICENSE TO STEAL

In the autumn of 1972, in a conference room in a squat, brown converted warehouse on the outskirts of south Denver, executives of Tele-Communications, Incorporated (TCI), most of them clad in Western-style shirts and boots or off-the-rack polyester suits, were winding down their day with libations. They often did this, but this day was nonetheless special: They were about to meet TCI's new president, John Malone, and his wife, Leslie. It was after five o'clock in the afternoon, and the Malones should have shown up by now.

But the Malones had been liberated from a long wait at LaGuardia Airport in New York only an hour earlier, after a delay caused by ominous thunderclouds. From the moment their flight was called, they had worried that the tardy departure was forcing the TCI executives out West to sit around waiting. Before long, though, the flight was Denver-bound, and John Malone began to ponder his fate with the new company. Weeks earlier Malone, who had run the cable TV division of a big company called General Instrument Corporation, had spurned a far more lucrative job offer in New York, the world's business capital from Steve Ross, the legendary chairman of Warner Communications, to head up Warner's budding cable TV operations. Ross saw cable as a direct pipeline for delivering Warner Bros.

movies to home viewers. Ross had promised the 29-year-old Malone a limo and a $150,000 salary, even pledging to relocate the new cable headquarters to Connecticut, where Malone lived, to shorten the young executive's commute.

Instead of accepting those cushy terms, Malone had chosen hardship—to take a pay cut and join TCI, an obscure cable company that had lurched from crisis to crisis for the preceding 20 years. Instead of hustling in the bustle of the Big Apple for the charismatic Steve Ross, Malone had elected to work in a western cow town for Bob Magness, a former cottonseed salesman and cattle rancher. Magness had used a wobbly foundation of brinkmanship, bald-faced gambles, and abundant debt to build TCI into the fourth largest cable provider in the United States—although it still reached fewer than 1 million homes. Malone had picked TCI because Magness, fatigued and running out of luck, was ready to relinquish power and let a new man run the entire show—and because, if Malone could make it work, he might become extremely wealthy. TCI, which had become a publicly owned company in 1970, might be a diamond in the rough.

In his visits to cable clients in Denver in the preceding year as president of Jerrold Electronics, the General Instrument division that acted as a lender and supplier of cable boxes and other equipment to cable systems, Malone had taken a liking to the informal Western setting there. Colorado was scenic and unhurried, a world away from New York. Malone had first fixed his sights on Bob Magness after watching the elder executive haggle with Jerrold's best two salespeople in a meeting one day. Magness had deftly outfoxed Malone's men in negotiating the terms for building and financing yet another TCI cable system. Impressed, Malone had quickly grown fond of the slow-talking, quick-witted rancher, and soon they were eating steak dinners together in the Magness home in Denver. In successive meetings, Magness, with his signature brevity, captured a little bit more of Malone's imagination. Eager in his persuasion, Magness told Malone and Leslie on a visit to Arizona, where he owned property, that the winters were equally balmy in Denver.

"I can't pay you very much," Magness told him one day, "but you've got a great future here if you can create it." Malone found the challenge irresistible.[1]

Magness's top executives were roughriders, not the MBA types that Malone knew back on the East Coast. Malone felt that they were men of conviction, especially Magness, whom he regarded as quiet, straightforward, and wickedly witty. Magness liked whiskey. Cigars, ever-present fixtures in his mouth, seemed to grow shorter, though they were never lit. Malone learned from Magness's friends that the TCI chairman ingested unlit cigars, taking tiny bites, sometimes even as he chewed on his favorite meal of filet mignon steak.

Malone believed in him and had staked everything on this job— and then some. Upon shaking hands, Magness had agreed to a salary of just $60,000. Malone also had seen fit to buy 7,500 shares of TCI stock, which he helped to pay for with a $60,000 personal loan from a local bank.[2]

On the plane to Denver that afternoon, fears of what might go wrong crept into the back of his mind, but Malone banished them, at least temporarily, especially in front of Leslie, who abhorred flying. They were high school sweethearts, and though they had been married for a decade, it sometimes seemed as if she was still waiting for him to come into her life. Too much travel and too many long workweeks had come between them. Malone promised her everything would be different in Denver. It was cleaner than the East, and the people were nicer. Leslie could raise horses. He would travel less and spend more time with their two children. They could finally have dinner together in the evenings, just like a real family. Malone vowed never to leave home for extended periods, as his own father had done. Sure, there would be risk, he told Leslie, but he could make their fortune with this ragtag band of cowboys. He would be running the show.

After the jet landed in Denver, the Malones took a cab to the party. It was after eight o'clock. They were several hours late. Malone walked into the room and started to apologize, but his new colleagues weren't put off at all by the long wait. Some revelers hardly noticed the guests of honor had even appeared. Most of the TCI executives were already happily, rip-roaring drunk.

♘♘♘

Bob Magness had made it sound like he was doing John Malone a big favor by hiring him to run TCI, but in fact Magness had turned to the brilliant youngster in desperate need. Magness was exhausted, plain and simple. For two decades he had relentlessly driven himself and his wife, Betsy. They had started out with a single cable system in Memphis, Texas, that they had built themselves, and they had ultimately assembled a company with more than 200 cable systems in the top 100 markets.[3] Magness had done it by constantly doubling up on his bets and accumulating a mountain of debt, always gambling that Americans' hunger for this new thing called television would permit his company to grow fast enough to stay ahead of the bill collectors. For most of the previous two decades, this upstart approach had worked—but now Magness was in trouble. Debt threatened to cripple, or worse, destroy the company. It was 1972, and in just a year Magness had nearly doubled the size of TCI, which now had $19.2 million in annual revenue. Its debt load was at an obscene level for a borrower of its size: $132 million, or about six and a half times total revenue, when it should have been a fraction of that. In one year, TCI's stock had fallen more than 50 percent because of its ailing finances. If Magness didn't do something dramatic—like land John Malone to lead him out of this mess—he was in danger of losing TCI to a hostile takeover, or worse, to those bastards at the banks.

Magness had hated bankers almost from the moment he had gotten into the cable business. He had discovered the fledgling industry in a chance encounter on a summer afternoon in 1952, when he gave two strangers a ride after meeting them in a cotton gin outside Memphis, Texas. Magness was a 28-year-old cottonseed buyer at the time with blue eyes and a smile that revealed a wide gap between his two front teeth. On the rare occasion that he spoke, his voice was flat, slow, and deliberate. He was shy and shrewd, two traits that came in handy in the cotton business, in which buyers gave cotton-ginners a fixed price for seeds, then sold them to cottonseed oil mills. Among this coterie of seed brokers in West Texas, Magness enjoyed a reputation as one of the best. He made sure that his clients were always content, and the tools of his trade often included a fishing pole, golf clubs, and a jug of whiskey. Folks just called him Bob.

Magness had grown up during the Great Depression, an only child in a family of farmers and ranchers. He came from authentic

Sooner stock—his mother and her kinfolk arrived in Oklahoma in a covered wagon, and Bob was born there, in Clinton, on June 3, 1924. Fear of financial failure, which tore at a generation of children reared in the 1930s, tormented Magness throughout his adult life. Yet, despite this constant worry about money, or perhaps because of it, Magness was a risk taker, a trait nurtured by his grandfather, Tommy Cook. Part Cherokee, Cook was a bear of a man who rode a big white horse called Old Tony, stuffed a .45-caliber revolver in his waistband on trips into nearby Lawton, and raised cattle on fields in Comanche County, about 40 miles from the Magness home in Clinton. Magness spent summers with his grandfather, often with three cousins around his age. Between fishing trips, Cook took his young posse on rounds to go "doctor" cattle, which the young Magness particularly enjoyed. Of all the lessons Magness learned from Cook during those dusty summers at the ranch, the most valuable came from the poker table. Cook could be seen with one or more tykes studying a fan of cards behind a pile of matchsticks, verbalizing little and betting imaginary fortunes.[4]

Before Cook died, he passed on to Magness his old six-shooter. Magness tucked it in his belt after he was drafted into the army, three months shy of his 19th birthday, and was shipped off to France to battle Hitler's Third Reich. Magness fought in the armored infantry of General George S. Patton's Third Army, sometimes serving as a lead scout. In letters from the front to his mother in Oklahoma, Magness confided that he was "having a bad time with it," recounting stories of bullets that barely missed him and bombs that killed men with whom he had spoken moments earlier. He was sure of a few things already, he told her: He didn't like military life, and he didn't like to lead. "I don't want to be responsible for the lives of other men," he wrote in one of many letters he sent back home. "I came in this army a buckass private and I'll leave it a buckass private."[5]

Yet, in the army, Magness earned a reputation among his fellow GIs as a lethal gambler. He became a master at reading people at a poker table, and he liked horses, both to ride and bet on. One day on patrol, Magness "liberated" a German military horse branded with a swastika, standing in a field.[6] For two months near the end of the war, when the soldiers held horse races on the weekends, betting on a collection of captured and owned steeds, Magness was putting cash on his chestnut beauty—and winning. As Magness later discovered, the horse, a beautiful Arabian with apple cheeks and chiseled features, could consistently beat a big-boned thoroughbred in races over a mile, the smaller Arabian's stamina winning over speed. When he returned home, his pockets were bulging; he had made more money wagering than he had earned in army pay. But he never forgot the chestnut mare, which he was forced to leave behind; one day Magness would assemble the largest and finest herd of Arabian horses in the world, and he would own a world-champion stallion.

After the war, Magness pursued a college degree, determined to enjoy all the prosperity the postwar economy could offer. He worked in oil fields a couple of summers, then graduated from Southwestern State College in Wetherford, Oklahoma, in 1948, with a bachelor's degree in business. With his sights on a job in the cotton business, Magness proposed marriage to a girlfriend of three years who would become his lifelong partner, Betsy Preston, a strong-willed, straight-A student, just three months his junior who came from nearby Elk City, Oklahoma. Bob admired her pluck. It was Betsy who asked Bob out on their first date, to the annual Sadie Hawkins dance in Clinton. Betsy, whose family farmed cotton in Kentucky, was eager to start life with this quiet, gap-toothed war hero with a dry wit. Magness would gain more than a country girl in his wife—she would prove to be an astute business partner.

Magness launched his livelihood with Anderson Clayton Company, one of the largest cotton brokers and cottonseed oil producers in the world. He and Betsy raised cattle part-time, but cotton was his career. Magness learned to listen instead of talk, and within a short time he could read a customer like a poker player, anticipating what that person wanted from the deal moments into negotiation.

On that afternoon in 1952 when he unwittingly started on his cable career, Magness had walked into a cotton gin near Memphis, Texas, to do a little business. He knew most of the men there but couldn't place the two men talking to the ginner. He surmised from the conversation that their pickup truck had thrown a rod as they were driving back to Paducah, Texas, and that they were stranded at the gin. Magness offered the pair a ride. They visited for the next couple of hours, stopping to grab a burger, and the two men told him they had just built a big "community antenna system" that helped folks in tiny Paducah get broadcast TV signals from bigger markets far away. Community antenna television—they called it *CATV.* Magness thought his riders were intriguing, but once in Paducah, he dropped them off and thought nothing more of it.

Days later a business partner mentioned to Magness that "if you knew how to get into something called the CATV business, I understand that's a license to steal." To which Magness replied, "Hell, I know how to get in."[7] The next morning, Magness drove out and talked with the two men he had picked up, who introduced him to the owners of the Paducah cable system. They gladly showed Magness how the operation was financed and gave him key contacts. Magness drove away thinking two things: (1) Cable TV sounded like a bona fide business, and (2) West Texans must be the most hospitable people in the world.

ひひひ

Bob Magness had a plan: to build a new cable system in the isolated town of Memphis, Texas. It would have a tall antenna tower that would pull down the broadcast signals of three TV stations[8] in two nearby towns—Amarillo, about 80 miles away, and Lubbock, about 140 miles away. If he could raise the money to pull it off, Magness would be able to charge his neighbors a monthly fee for the television service—which he would get free of charge, basically pirating the programming from the TV stations themselves without paying them a cent. In cotton, business looked bleak because nylon and rayon were becoming the preferred material; cable TV looked like an industry with a future.

When Magness broached the idea with Betsy, she listened intently. She certainly didn't want to return to a life of ranch chores or, as Bob put it, "back to the cotton farm" that she grew up on. She told Bob she would do anything to support the idea.[9] So they decided to bet the ranch, literally, on cable. Magness sold his cattle, mortgaged the house, and borrowed $2,500 from his father. He directed the construction, climbing poles himself to string wire, while Betsy deciphered the finances and took service calls at the kitchen table. He invested everything he had, and still he had to go into debt. He needed help—in a hurry. So he brought on a partner, the superintendent of the cottonseed oil mill where he worked. Eventually, Magness paid $100,000 to a Forth Worth company to erect a tower more than 30 stories high, on a 60-foot rise near Memphis, and opened up for business.[10]

In a town of 4,500 people, word spread quickly. Magness's new community antenna service was trumpeted on the front page of the August 2, 1956, issue of the *Memphis Democrat:* "First Showing of Cable TV Slated for Friday Night." "The Master Antennae Service, as the organization is called, will hold open house from 7:30 [P.M.] until 11 [P.M.] at the American Legion Building. . . . Everyone is invited to view live network programs . . ." TV dealers furnished sets for the demonstration. "We will be able to begin hooking up sets at home in Memphis on Saturday," Magness told the paper. Subscribers paid a onetime hookup charge of $33, plus a $6.60 monthly fee. Bob and Betsy soon had their first 700 customers; the following year, they added another 3,000 in nearby Plainview.

At the time Magness was drawn into cable, most Americans, Bob and Betsy included, had rarely seen a TV set and certainly didn't own one. David Sarnoff, the chairman of RCA who crusaded for television's development, had unveiled the invention at the 1939 New York World's Fair. Two years later, commercial TV began its seduction of American viewers, and in short order 32 TV stations lit up around the country. As the economy boomed after the Second World War, America hungered for entertainment. Some 78 companies were selling nearly 200 different models by 1948, and nearly 600,000 TV sets flew off appliance store shelves. Each day, an estimated 1,000 new sets were being installed.[11] An avalanche of applications for broadcast licenses hit the Federal Communications Commission (FCC), which became so overwhelmed with technical and policy issues to create a national broadcast system, it simply stopped granting new licenses altogether. The freeze lasted for four years, and in the meantime, the 108 operating stations weren't plentiful enough to reach everyone. In the same period, however, the number of homes with TV sets increased to more than 15 million homes.

Viewers just outside the broadcast signal's range were trying to tune in from anywhere they could. Most viewers were doomed to hazy images and the dull roar of static over the speakers. So close, but too far for good reception. Just as with radio, hopeful viewers tried anything to catch a weak signal. The most common way was to build a really tall antenna and hope to catch a signal.

Many more far-flung locales couldn't get a picture at all. Hills and mountains blocked TV signals. This new business that Magness was sizing up was the bridge for a simple but critical gap. Like others in this CATV service, he would plant a large antenna on a mountain to catch the broadcast network signals from faraway local TV stations—gigantic rabbit ears, essentially—then string wire from pole to pole into the valleys, where folks had poor reception. The terrain of West Texas was just hilly enough to need the new business. And there were nooks, crannies, and bowl-shaped valleys all across America that couldn't pick up network TV signals. For a wave of cable pioneers, the opportunities were endless.

Folks erected massive homemade towers to catch a signal and would sit for hours watching—anything to see this marvelous, new big-city invention. Nothing in modern society compared with a TV, which in 1948 sold for $149 ($1,100 in today's dollars) in the Sears Roebuck catalog. The comedian Milton Berle, as host of *Texaco Star Theatre*, did more to sell TV sets in the late 1940s than any RCA salesperson, and by 1952, *I Love Lucy* drew 10 million of the nation's viewers. Little wonder that TV became the largest advertising medium in the world almost overnight. The mass embrace of the medium that RCA had so confidently promoted—despite a world war, technology snafus, and new regulations—was finally happening.

The fraternity that Magness had joined, cable TV, got its start in 1948 in response to the demanding wife of a man named Ed Parsons, who owned a radio station in Astoria, Oregon, a small town at the mouth of the Columbia River. At a radio convention in Chicago, Grace Parsons sat mesmerized at a demonstration of a new invention called a TV set, and she just had to have one. Parsons, a skilled engineer, located the clearest TV signal from atop the Astoria Hotel and ran a single wire across the street to his apartment. The 9-inch black-and-white set, which he initially called "wasting our money," suddenly sprang to life. People drove from more than 300 miles away to watch. "We literally lost our home," he later told an interviewer.[12] Parsons never made a business out of his antenna service, but he sold equipment to customers and gave answers to anyone who asked. Exhausted, he finally moved to Alaska and flew back to the Lower 48 only once—to dedicate a monument to his pioneering act. Despite other legitimate claims to be the first cable system, Parsons's discovery is forever etched in a plaque on Coxcomb Hill in Astoria, which reads: "Site of the First Community Antennae Television Installation in the United States. Completed February 1949."

An army of cable entrepreneurs tore out into the hinterlands to deliver TV to the masses, who, by all accounts, were starved for it. The grassroots creation and spread of the community antenna was inevitable, given the situation: a rural population dying to get what folks in the big city got, and a broadcast industry that was unwilling to invest the money needed to reach them. In high school gyms, parking lots, and appliance stores across small-town America, television started getting piped in from nearby cities by a CATV system, and the seeds of billion-dollar fortunes were sown. On January 8, 1951, the front-page headline of the *Wall Street Journal* said it all:

Stretching Television: New "Utilities" Deliver TV to Towns Outside Usual Reception Range

———

Firms Erect Big Community Aerials, Hook on Your Set for a Monthly Fee

———

The Appliance Dealers Grin

Every broadcaster in the West, it seemed, was trying to get in on cable. Entrepreneurs in the East began investing in cable around the same time. In Mahanoy City, Pennsylvania, in the cleavage created by the ridges of the Allegheny Mountains, John Walson, an appliance store owner, strung wire along treetops down the side of the mountain, and later, on poles rented from a utility where he worked, down to his store to display TVs with pictures from nearby Philadelphia.

In 1958, Magness moved to sell the original system he had built only two years earlier in Memphis, Texas, netting a handsome profit. Magness liked this new business, and he looked for a way to reinvest in it. Luckily, tax laws made it attractive. Cable operators could gradually write off the cost of their systems over a number of years, allowing them to reduce the leftover profits they reported as earnings and thereby sheltering a healthy flow of cash from taxation. And once they had written off most of the value of a cable system's assets, they could sell it to a new owner, who could begin the tax-eluding depreciation cycle all over again. Magness wanted some help in figuring out where to invest next, so he called the man whose name was known to every cable cowboy looking to strike it rich: Bill Daniels.

Daniels, too, had fallen under the spell of television; for him, it happened one night in 1952 when he stopped in at Murphy's Restaurant in Denver for a corned beef sandwich and a beer.[13] That's when he saw television for the first time. A Navy fighter pilot in World War II and again in Korea, Daniels started his first company in 1952 with the help of Gene Schneider and his brother, Dick, both of them engineers, who were at the time operating the Houston franchise of the country's first coffee dispenser, Quick Kafe. Over the next few years, Daniels built up a collection of cable systems in the West but quickly turned to a faster-growing business—acting as a broker of cable systems, matching buyers to sellers. So began the Daniels & Associates brokerage service, which would dominate the brokerage business for more than three decades. Asked later to describe technically how cable works, Daniels replied, "Beats hell outa me."[14] Daniels sold everyone within preaching distance on the promise of cable and, by 1956, served as the head of the newly minted National Cable Television Association.

When Magness called Daniels in 1958, the broker directed his attention to a system for sale in Bozeman, Montana. Magness, an avid fisherman, thought Bozeman could be a great place to raise his two boys, Gary and Kim. In September 1958, Magness made the move and quickly partnered up with Paul McAdams, who already owned cable systems in nearby Livingston, to import broadcast signals from Salt Lake City.[15]

Like Bill Daniels, Magness soon realized he might make as much money serving the new television industry as he could owning cable systems. Consequently, he and McAdams launched a signal transmission business, Western Microwave, Inc. It transported TV signals to commercial customers, typically broadcast companies, to Montana via common-carrier microwave. Microwave towers were used to bounce TV signals overland in short hops, from giant dish to giant dish. Magness's cable systems made money from individual subscribers in each town, while the microwave business made money relaying the signals of the Big Three networks to 21 broadcast stations, serving TCI's own cable systems at the same time. Traveling to some sites on horseback, Magness built a 130-mile microwave relay from Salt Lake City—unheard of in those days—making it possible for residents of the lonely outpost of Great Falls, Montana, to see their first live World Series game in 1961.[16]

"Bob would drive this new Mercury he had to the tops of mountains to select these microwave sights," recalled Larry Romrell, who joined TCI in 1960. "Paul McAdam drove a Cadillac with a boiler plate welded to the bottom to protect his oil pan. They would flash their headlights from one mountain to another to see if it was in the line of sight—that way they'd know if the microwave would work."[17]

When McAdam bowed out of the company after a heart attack, Magness partnered with John "Jack" Gallivan, president of the Kearns-Tribune, publisher of the *Salt Lake City Tribune,* and George Hatch, a regional broadcaster in Salt Lake City, who owned KUTV and other TV stations and some cable systems in Nevada. By 1965, the partnership had built six cable TV systems with a combined total of 12,550 customers. In 1968, Magness corralled the various cable and microwave assets and named the resulting company Tele-Communications, Inc.

Despite the company's larger success, Bozeman itself turned out to be an inhospitable home for TCI, and no one knew this better than the men Magness employed to hang wire. In the winter, the mercury often dropped to 20 degrees below zero. One TCI engineer sent to check on a remote sight on a mountaintop died in a helicopter crash. Another lost his toes in a snowmobile accident. Occasionally, the men would kill a deer and leave frozen venison hanging outside the shed that housed the transmitter at Monida Pass; it would feed anyone hemmed in by a snowstorm. All TCI engineers carried guns for hunting and for self-defense—it wasn't unusual to happen upon a mountain lion. New employees were asked: Can you walk 10 miles in 10-below-zero weather?[18] If a site was inaccessible on foot, as most were in winter, engineers made their way up the mountains with the help of a *weasel*, a surplus World War II cargo carrier that resembled a snowmobile. When the weasel was unreliable, TCI hired a biplane stunt pilot to deliver engineers and parts to remote sites; barrels of fuel for the generators were tied to the plane's wings with steel cables.

Back at the office, Magness never wrote a memo. More often than not, he poured a drink. In the early days of TCI, it was easier to find whiskey in the office than paper clips. Everyone took their cue from Magness, who tolerated no stars and no pomposity. Every evening a handful of TCI cowboys would sit around Bob's big desk, and he would open the bar and review the day's events.

The company's headquarters in Bozeman was spartan, which matched Magness's bare-bones management style. The wooden floor was so decrepit that the secretaries had to be careful about getting their heels caught in its many holes. When a new secretary was hired, she was given three cardboard packing boxes, and that was her desk.[19] TCI's earliest attempt at local programming was just as crude: a TV camera aimed at a news ticker service, another fixed on a thermometer and, occasionally, a camera trained on a goldfish bowl. Sometimes the goldfish died.

One day, standing alongside engineer Art Lee at a site where TCI was building a new system, Magness delivered a memorable lesson. Lee cut off a small scrap of coaxial cable and tossed it aside, prompting Magness to ask him for a quarter. When the engineer handed over the coin, Magness sent it sailing a hundred feet away. "Why'd you do that?" Lee asked Magness, and the boss answered: "Because that's what you did when you threw that scrap of cable away."

From Bozeman, where they lived for about a decade, Bob and Betsy started expanding, winning franchises in adjoining towns in Montana, Utah, Nevada, and California. Bozeman finally seemed too cold, too inaccessible to Magness's growing empire. Magness came under pressure to move to Salt Lake City where his partners were, but Besty didn't like the Mormon influence on the town. They compromised on Denver. It was one of the few communities out West with a direct flight back East, where the banks were. Convenient and clean, Denver would emerge soon as the capital of cable. Equipment suppliers made stops in Denver. Bill Daniels, the biggest broker in the business, was based there. So were other cable operators. Something about the Western city came to define the spirit of these pole climbers, in an era when individual men, not conglomerates, reigned sovereign over an industry. So in 1965, TCI moved to Denver to play with the big boys.

ひひひ

By the mid-1960s, Bob Magness had realized the potential of community antenna to fill a vast need; he likened cable to the oil rush days in his native Oklahoma and Texas. Though he was building his own wealth, building TCI had given Magness a thrill not unlike betting big in a poker game. He continued borrowing money and buying up systems. He had good reason to believe he held a strong hand. Few cable systems had ever failed up to this point, largely because the values of the systems that were trading hands kept rising. It was genius, really, to anyone who took the time to figure it out. Cable TV systems, to every new owner's delight, generated bundles of cash from installation charges, $100 to $300 a customer in the 1970s, and monthly services fees of $5 to $20. Most of the money was plowed back into the companies, with hardly anything going to pay dividends to shareholders. This high cash flow could service an immense amount of debt, which was used to buy more systems. So the actual value of the acquired systems was always growing. Moreover, the companies paid hardly any taxes because of the high depreciation on the equipment. The average cable system enjoyed a profit margin of 57 percent, far fatter than most businesses.[20]

But cash was in short supply, and Magness was always on the hunt for more. He quickly realized big banks hadn't a clue where the fly-speck towns he served were. Bankers had to ask for chamber of commerce brochures of the cities TCI wanted to wire, and they wanted to know details like exactly where on the map the city of Ogallala, Nebraska, could be found. TCI had started out buying or building systems in the West, wary of spreading itself too thin, but soon Magness realized that to tap the money markets back in New York, he needed to start operating cable systems back East; then the bankers would know what this new cable business was all about.

By 1968, TCI had tapped a healthy new vein of capital: insurance companies. In exchange for an initial loan of $10 million, Teachers Insurance and Annuity Association received a slice of TCI through warrants and convertibles. Like many cable TV operators at the time, Magness financed the construction of his systems through his equipment supplier, Jerrold, which had access to money when few cable companies did. Jerrold loaned customers like Magness what they needed, taking notes that essentially were promises to pay back the full amount.

The entire industry weathered a storm of capricious regulations throughout the 1960s and early 1970s by the FCC, which was unsure of what cable TV was and what it would become. The powerful lobby of the Big Three broadcast networks began to argue that free television was threatened by cable TV. The FCC was particularly concerned that cable operators threatened the newer, weaker broadcast stations in the UHF range (channels 14 to 83). Some broadcasters had invested early on in cable—in the early 1960s, nearly one-third of all cable systems were owned by such old-line media firms as Cox Broadcasting Company, CBS, Westinghouse, and Newhouse Broadcasting.[21] By the early 1970s, however, the broadcast lobby had won a set of FCC rules that effectively halted cable's growth. Citing the public interest and intent on protecting broadcast TV, the FCC by 1972 had imposed sweeping regulations. The rules prohibited cable operators from importing distant signals into the top 100 TV markets, limited the number and types of signals that cable could pull down from the skies, and required systems to carry signals from all three networks and to take them from the nearest network affiliate—no leapfrogging to bring a big-city affiliate into a small town. Moreover, technical standards were imposed for the first time, and larger systems were forced to make public-access channels available for citizens, governments, and schools.

Other rulings seemed outright bizarre. Pay services such as a movie channel, which charged viewers over and above their regular monthly fee, were limited to showing one feature film just one week each month, and it had to be more than 2 years old and less than 10 years old. Broadcasters continued to paint cable with the same broad brush: thieves pulling signals out of the sky, then charging John Q. Public. That the broadcasting industry had its way in Congress was no surprise. At least 30 U.S. senators and congresspeople owned interests in TV or radio stations, and even more had invested in companies that owned broadcast properties or in related industries.[22]

♘♘♘

As the 1970s began, TCI had gobbled up so many new cable systems that it was like the winner in a pie-eating contest—victorious, but a bit woozy from the pace of ingestion and a little anxious about keeping it all down.

TCI's bankers fretted over the torrid pace at which the company—and its yawning debt—had expanded. As their alarm rose, so did Bob Magness's blood pressure, a condition he blamed on the legion of bankers knocking at his door. Magness's diet was not exactly balanced, either—steak and potatoes, mainly, and plenty of whiskey. Magness drank almost daily, discreetly, at home and in the office, though few could tell unless they saw a bottle. Alcohol, however poisonous to his body, dulled the anxiety that gnawed at him. If economic conditions worsened, the weight of TCI's debt threatened to topple the empire that he and Betsy had worked so slavishly to build.

After nearly 20 years of struggling, the scrutiny was now unbearable for the white-haired cowboy. TCI and its subsidiaries were failing to meet critical financial benchmarks required by the terms of their loan agreements. Bankers wanted to know: Why hadn't TCI hit its cash flow projections? When did it expect to make the next payment? Why hadn't TCI foreseen all this trouble? Magness had simply run out of gas, and many of his executives were burned out, too. The complexities of running a public company and tracking the performance of more than 200 cable franchises in 21 states, all the while fighting regulators and lawyers, was becoming too much for the onetime cottonseed salesman. And so one day in the fall of 1972, after he had spent hours toting up TCI's financial position, Magness finally and fully grasped just how terribly precarious the whole situation had become. He skimmed the numbers, looked up at Betsy, and blurted out, "I'm gonna hire the smartest sonofabitch I can find."[23]

RUNNING THE SHOW

April Fool's Day, 1973—a fitting day, John Malone thought, for getting into the cable TV business. After the drunken welcoming party, it had taken him a few months to extricate himself from Jerrold in New York and move his family to Denver, and at first it all looked so damned promising. But in subsequent months, everything seemed to go wrong—for the cable industry and for his new employer, especially.

TCI, which now had 204 franchises in the top 100 markets, had an annual revenue of $19 million by 1972, but its debt had swelled to more than $130 million, and it couldn't stop the spending binge. To win new franchises from local governments in Memphis, Tennessee, and Vancouver, Washington, and elsewhere, TCI had promised to pour another $500 million into new construction, an ambitious sum it had no rational basis for embracing, and the mayors and city councils had no intention of letting TCI squirm out of the commitment. Malone knew that if just a few more things went wrong—a sudden spike in floating interest rates, a default on some old loans—TCI could become vulnerable to a takeover by corporate raiders or its own lenders, and Malone would fail utterly the first time he had a chance to run the show.

In the lag between accepting the new job and moving to Denver, Malone had willfully ignored an ominous sign: The Securities and Exchange Commission (SEC) had suspended trading of the stock of cable giant TelePrompTer on suspicion of accounting fraud, shattering investors' confidence in cable companies just when Malone needed their support. In 1971, the CEO of TelePrompTer, Irving Berlin Kahn, a nephew of the famous composer, had been convicted of perjury and bribery in connection with a $15,000 payment to city officials in Johnstown, Pennsylvania, to renew a license to operate there five years earlier. Prior to his conviction, Kahn had emerged as the industry's brightest luminary, predicting before anyone that two-way communications, such as phone calls and interactive TV, would be made someday over cable TV wires. Prescience notwithstanding, Kahn was sentenced to 5 years, and a U.S. marshal carted him away to Allenwood, a minimum-security prison in the Allegheny Mountains of Pennsylvania.[1] More damaging to the industry were the later SEC charges that TelePrompTer had booked phantom payments from customers and falsely hiked cash flow by improperly capitalizing its construction costs. The banishment of Kahn, cable's most notable and confident evangelist, cast a long shadow over the finances of the industry.

While TCI and other cable outfits tried to avoid the inevitable question of whether they were playing similar games in their own financial reports—and many were—the economy began to sputter. The brewing Watergate scandal sent confidence in the dollar spiraling downward around the world. The stock market began an epic decline, with the New York Stock Exchange index submerging to 1960s-era levels after rocketing to an all-time high of 1000 in 1972. Meanwhile, the oil-producing cartel known as OPEC had quadrupled prices, and consumer and producer prices began a scary and prolonged rise. Worse, interest rates shot up to around 11 percent, doubling borrowing costs. The dreaded and perplexing era of *stagflation*, marked by economic stagnation and high inflation, had dawned. Few industries were hit as hard as cable TV, for which debt was fuel. The cost of stringing wire from pole to pole had nearly doubled to $8,000 a mile by the early 1970s, thanks to new regulations and price increases from suppliers, and in big cities it now cost up to $50,000 a mile to bury the wire underground.[2]

All of this took a nasty toll on TCI's stock price, and by the fall of 1973 its shares had plunged to the $3 range and were bound to fall even lower. By the end of the year, Malone had the dubious pleasure of presiding over the first loss—$2.1 million—TCI had ever reported as a public company. "Should interest rates remain at these record-high levels, the company will have difficulty showing good near-term earnings performance," Magness wrote months later in the 1973 annual report to shareholders. The warning could have been much stronger, for TCI would hardly ever again report a profitable year; forever after it would reinvest prodigious cash flows to grow the business ever larger.

For Malone, all this was painful to his pride and a blow to his personal finances. It stunned him, how his radiant future had darkened so quickly. The value of his TCI stock options had sunk by more than half, and instead of reaping great riches, as he had envisioned, Malone was now cash-strapped and deeply in debt, at least on paper, for the sin of having invested in his own employer.

At home, Leslie was patient but clearly unhappy, and this made Malone all the more mindful of the promises he had made to her with such conviction, yet broken with such impudence. Les, the painfully shy love of his life, deserved so much more from him, but they were barely scrimping by; Malone had cut his own pay to help meet expenses at TCI.

They hardly ever ate out. No new furniture complemented their new home, and the couple had to go nine months without telephone service because they couldn't afford it. Worse yet, the pace and precariousness at TCI had shattered any hopes he harbored for a normal family life. He had vowed to spend more time at home, yet if he wasn't flying away to meet bankers, he was on the road, humbling himself before city councils and promising that TCI would spend money it didn't have to upgrade local cable systems.

Even before he had taken the TCI job, the pace was incessant. Back in Jerrold's Philadelphia headquarters a couple of years earlier, he had received an urgent message: His wife had gone into labor and she was headed to the hospital. Malone stopped short his meetings, gathered a few papers into his briefcase, then scrambled to the parking lot. The hospital was a three-and-a-half-hour drive away, and Malone broke every speeding law on the way. When he arrived at the hospital, he had missed the birth of his son, Evan, by an hour.

Malone employed dark humor to ease the guilt accumulating inside. Each day on his drive down Parker Road to the office in Denver, Malone passed a feedlot filled with cattle. And each day he saw the same steer, standing at the highest point in the yard, surveying all that was his. The hill happened to be a pile of dung, and the steer was keeping vigil over cows penned for slaughter. "That's me," Malone told himself. "On top of a pile of bullshit." He was a Connecticut Yankee who loved to sail, landlocked in the Rockies with a crew of cowboys who liked to drink. Back in his General Instrument job, he had managed to build Jerrold into a powerhouse, but at TCI he was struggling just to keep the rudder straight. In the few quiet moments he had to himself, a single question tugged at him: "Have I made the biggest mistake of my life?"[3]

ひひひ

John Charles Custer Malone was born on March 7, 1941, to a middle-class couple who gave him the middle name of Custer, after a wealthy grandfather whom his mother had hoped might include him in an inheritance. John was the second and last child of Daniel and Jule Malone, a complement to the baby girl who had arrived three years earlier. Malone's mother was a high school physical education teacher and had been an Olympic-caliber swimmer in New Jersey during high school. She had received a master's degree in education at Temple University but had sacrificed a career to raise young John and his older sister, Judy. His father, an engineer at General Electric (GE) for 30 years, was from German and Irish descent and grew up on a farm in Pennsylvania. Dan Malone was an "intellectual with white socks," as his son liked to describe him, a man who could change the oil in his car while liberally quoting Oliver Cromwell, a seventeenth-century English Puritan revolutionary who coined such phrases as, "He who stops being better stops being good."

After Dan and Jule married, he got a job at the GE plant in Bridgeport, Connecticut, and they moved in 1937 to Milford, a coastal town on Long Island Sound south of New Haven, where they settled in a two-story colonial house at 57 Gunn Street, a quiet middle-class neighborhood lined with elm and birch trees.

The Malones rarely argued, yet they possessed distinctly different personalities. Dan Malone was more reserved, while his wife was headstrong. For Dan, it was never cool enough in the house; for Jule, it was never warm enough. She shut windows that he had opened in the night. Though not a strict churchgoer, John Malone's father preached hard work and personal sacrifice. His hairshirted, Calvinist ethic was clear to everyone in the household: "If you didn't try your best, work the hardest, you're a failure. That's what people are put on earth to do," Dan Malone told his kids.

More than anyone, Dan Malone would shape his son's destiny. A stern but soft-spoken man, he often lapsed into the role of the professor he could have been, explaining how a two-stroke engine worked, or giving an impromptu lesson about the properties of electrical current. His father's rigid expectations and private tutorials seemed to inspire John, who would spend a lifetime struggling to prove his worth.

Dan was loquacious when instructing—but laconic in doling out anything approaching praise. No anger. No yelling. A nod of approval, a look on his face—these were the subtle signs John looked for from his father. He tried to impress his parents with feats of athletics and academics. Still, the bar was high: When John came home from school one afternoon with a report card of all A's and one B, he asked about the B. Over the years, Malone would internalize this model and become very demanding of himself.

Despite the strong connection, John rarely saw his father. Every Sunday night, Dan left the house on Gunn Street for a GE plant wherever he was needed—places like Schenectady, Syracuse, or Utica, New York—and would return on Saturday at the end of a long week. As part of Dan Malone's work in the electronics division, he tested and installed classified Navy radar systems.

From the time John was 7 until he was 12, his father kept the same rigid schedule, and the separation drove the boy to resent the time Dan Malone was away and to relish the little time he was home. When he was home, the son worked to tap his father's vast knowledge of how things worked. Before he was old enough to drive, Malone was underneath the chassis of his family's aging Fleetwood Cadillac, holding a light as his father operated on the car. The elder Malone, gifted with a mechanical expertise, gave his son lessons in self-sufficiency. If the windshield wipers went out on the Packard, Dan carefully removed the mechanism, took it apart and spread it out on the table, examined each tiny piece, rewound the armature, then put it back together. And it worked.

For young Malone, the big white barn that stood behind the family's house became a sanctuary. Benches inside strained under the weight of car engines, including an old Model A Ford motor, boat parts, and the carcasses of radios cannibalized for parts. Shelves spilled over with screws, springs, pipes, and parts assembled from decades of collecting. In the loft lay an entire case of government surplus weather balloons. And somewhere, up on a shelf, gathering as much dust as the paint cans, was one of the first television sets ever manufactured, a model of the one unveiled at the 1939 World's Fair.

It was in this barn that young John Malone would get his first look at television, well before most people in the world. On many evenings in this spot, Malone's father revealed, like a magician explaining a hat trick, the electronic mystery of it. The boy peered intently over his father's shoulder as Dan tinkered with tubes in the warm glow of a bare bulb. As GE moved into the business of making TV sets in the 1940s, Malone's father, an engineer in research, was called upon to help develop some of the first sets. Often, he was called to the homes of GE's top executives to repair the new contraptions. At the time, John could only marvel at the TV set as an end unto itself, a machine with a mass of wires, tubes, and circuits; he couldn't know this invention would eventually end up as the vessel for achieving his noblest ambitions.

Science and math also fascinated young John. In the seventh grade, he transferred from a public school in Milford to Hopkins Grammar School, a prep school in nearby New Haven, a place that liked to call itself "the fifth oldest educational institution in the United States." He attended on a partial scholarship he won for high test scores, and though he had a longer commute, Dan and

Jule liked that it wasn't as pretentious as so many of the Northeastern prep schools. Though shy like his father, John Malone developed into a fierce competitor at school. A chessboard was a favorite battlefield, but Malone also favored fencing, preferring the heavier épée to the flimsy foil. He lettered in three sports: soccer, fencing, and track.

On the track field, Malone discovered a trait in his budding personality: a quiet determination, free of the need for praise or encouragement, that seemed to give him the advantage over others. One day, Malone decided that he would try to break the record for the discus throw in high school. This struck a classmate, Steve McDonald, who later attended Yale with Malone, as curious: Nobody goes out to break a record, especially to the exclusion of serious drinking and chasing girls in college. But Malone was resolute. To build his physique, he drank a homemade high-protein concoction he called "tiger's milk," which he gulped out of a glass milk bottle. He pumped iron religiously until his upper body was V-shaped; he was nicknamed "The Bat" for his torso and his long arms, outstretched and twirling as he threw the discus. But his persistence paid off: He set a new school record for Hopkins—144 feet, 6 inches.

In his teens, Malone would find immense satisfaction in the same passions his father had inculcated in him, and he quickly learned he could make money if he exploited them. At the age of 15, he saved up $400 from a paper route and spent all of it to buy a red 1952 Jaguar XK-120 with jammed gears. Malone took apart the engine, as well as the trickier transmission, to find a broken gear. Using a welder, an electric grinder, and various hand tools in the barn, he accomplished what few mechanics have in a lifetime. "The son of a bitch works!" the 15-year-old cried as he drove it for the first time. He repainted the car, cruised Milford, and became a regular at Paul's Drive-In, whose large parking lot and greasy burgers made it a magnet for high school kids in the late 1950s. He raced the car along Main Street and soon started repairing neighbors' automobiles for money. Around the same time, ever the opportunist, he bid for, and won, a bin of radios for a dollar apiece from a GE small-appliance outlet in Bridgeport. His father had told him about the radios, which had been returned to GE for malfunctions. Using his father's test equipment out in the barn, Malone would repair and sell them for $3 each.

Just as mathematics held Malone's thoughts hostage, so too, did a fascination with the moon. His boyhood hero was Wernher von Braun, the former Nazi rocket scientist responsible for the successful launch of America's first artificial earth satellite in 1958 and the Saturn rocket for the Apollo 8 moon landing in 1969. Malone devoured von Braun's books, *Conquest of the Moon* and *Space Frontier.* There were other unlikely titles for a teenager who spent time under car hoods: *The Occident and the Orient,* and *The Decline and Fall of the Roman Empire.* Taking precalculus and calculus simultaneously, Malone had momentary visions of becoming a doctor or an engineer. He excelled even among particularly bright students; of the 52 graduates in Malone's class of 1959, one-third entered Harvard or Yale.

As he braced for college, Malone continued to seek counsel from his father, who one day gave his son puzzling advice about taking tests: "Guess at the answers," he said. John gave him a perplexed look. "Guess before you figure the problems out," Dan repeated. Uncertain at first, Malone quickly developed an intuition for engineering questions that called for empirical data. Malone was amazed at how quickly he could derive a number, how he could guess what waveforms would look like at the end of a circuit even before doing the underlying mathematics. This ability to make split-second calculations served him well throughout his school days, and it became the one weapon in his arsenal—to see the answers before others did—that gave him an edge over future rivals.

♘♘♘

On a bright summer day in 1958, at the age of 17, Malone met a girl who captivated him. Walking along Gulf Beach, a ribbon of sand along the Long Island Sound, Malone and George Hanlon, a buddy, stopped to talk to Malone's sister. When Malone fixed his stare on a curvaceous, auburn-haired beauty and asked his sister for a name, it would remain with him forever: Leslie Ann Evans. She had just turned 15, and within minutes, he and the girl were wandering down the beach together. Leslie talked while Malone threw rocks into the surf. He asked her to go see *South Pacific* at the movie theater. She accepted. She was shy yet opinionated, yet walking along the sand, Malone felt comfortable with her. Leslie, more than anyone, would come to embody the family life that Malone craved. That afternoon, with his buddy, Hanlon, Malone pulled a new silver dollar out of his pocket. "You see this, George? It's a bet. It's a bet I'll marry that girl." Smiling, Malone threw the coin in the air, and their eyes followed it into the surf.

John and Leslie soon began dating in earnest. While Leslie finished high school and worked as a secretary at the Milford Police Department, Malone attended Yale, 10 miles down the road. He gorged on mathematics and engineering, but he often argued over his scores with history and social sciences teachers, whom he loved to call "socialistic," because he believed they favored a society in which production of goods was controlled collectively or by the government. When he entered the engineering school, where the answers were either right or wrong, his grades rocketed. During his first year at Yale, Malone roomed with three other freshmen, Fred Issac, Fred Andreae, and Don Cook, on the third floor of Vanderbilt Hall.

Malone, six feet tall, with wide shoulders and bulging biceps, towered over his roomies. The quiet young man with thick black hair combed to his left, a dimpled smile, and a granite jaw kept to himself during school days and, on weekends, spent time with Leslie or back at his own home. His roommates found him aloof but not arrogant, and really brawny. Malone was the only guy Andreae had ever seen who could do a true one-arm pull-up.[4]

On occasion though, Malone played a tough guy, telling the boys in the room that he was going home to "settle a score" or "take care of business." While most Yalies wore their preppy best—khakis and oxford button-down shirts—Malone wore jeans and leather jackets à la Marlon Brando.

In 1963, Malone reached three important milestones in his life: (1) He graduated Phi Beta Kappa from Yale with a bachelor's in electrical engineering; (2) he married his steady girl; and (3) he accepted a job as a systems engineer at Bell Labs, the research arm of American Telephone & Telegraph (AT&T) and one of the few companies that promised to pay for his continuing education. AT&T would forever hold a place in Malone's heart for financing his advanced degrees: a master's in industrial management at Johns Hopkins University in Baltimore, which he received in 1964, a master's in electrical engineering from an NYU program at Bell Labs in 1965, and a doctorate in operations research, which he received from Johns Hopkins in 1967.

Malone drove a white Porsche Speedster, recalled former Bell colleague and roommate Gerald "Jerry" Bennington, who studied around the clock with Malone in a small rented white wooden house near school.[5] In their down time, the pair sped along the picturesque highways of the Shenandoah Mountains on weekends. "He was gregarious and self-assured," recalled Bennington. "He could get his mind around anything—I mean *anything*." They discussed politics, professors, and cars.

At Bell Labs in the late 1960s, when many his age were protesting the war in Vietnam or signing up to join it, Malone was focused on large-scale economic modeling. He penned such white papers as "The Impact of Regulation on a Monopoly Firm" and "Profit Maximization at a Regulated Firm," a plan that called for a radical change in financial strategy at AT&T. It was a massive mathematical model, but the end result was simple. After studying AT&T's balance sheet for months, Malone concluded that AT&T should be systematically shifting its debt-to-equity ratio to more debt; it should borrow more money and buy back its own stock from the market. It was a radical plan at the time, and an early sign of the shrewd knack for numbers that Malone would display over the next three decades. But on the day he presented it to the board of directors, Fred Kappel, chairman of AT&T at the time, walked a beaming Malone out of the room. "Son, that was great! Stimulating!" the chairman told him. Malone's grin widened. "But," the boss continued, "if in your whole career, you can do a single thing that changes the Ma Bell system in even the smallest way, you would be very successful."[6] Kappel's message: No way would the board buy Malone's plan.

"No shit," Malone said to himself, and he caught the next train home. Malone knew he had reached a turning point: He wasn't going to work for this company anymore. What could he achieve there? Whenever he complained about bureaucracy, Bell Labs supervisors quickly and pointedly reminded him that he was a rising star, one of the highest-paid executives for his age. In the labyrinthine Bell hierarchy, there was a natural order, a pay curve that covered all employees. And after applying hours of his math-modeling skills to it, Malone could come to only one conclusion: He knew exactly what he was going to make next year, and the year after that, and the year after that. It wasn't the fortune that Malone had begun to envision—not just the financial fortune, but his personal fortune. He was still haunted by a vague feeling of mediocrity, and he knew his calling was not at AT&T. Malone felt the same way he did when he passed long rows of tiny white crosses in military cemeteries or the driveways in big suburban neighborhoods. The sameness of them all—nothing individual about them—left him uneasy. A few weeks later, he quit.

ひ ひ ひ

In 1968, when he was 27, Malone joined the prestigious New York consulting firm of McKinsey & Co., which planned to start a special department for technology companies. The Malones moved from nearby New Jersey where he attended classes at Bell Labs to Weston, Connecticut, where Leslie anticipated that John would share in raising their daughter, Tracy, born a year earlier. Stung by memories of the void his own father left, Malone pledged to spend more time at home, but his first minutes on the job demonstrated to him the folly of that notion. When Malone walked into the office that first day, the receptionist directed him to his new desk, built for two employees. The other McKinsey executive, Louis V. Gerstner, Jr., who, 25 years later, would rescue IBM, was away, but on the desk was a note that read in part, "John, if you can't be in Montreal by 1:30 P.M. to have lunch with the chairman of Bell Canada, please call this number . . ." Attached was a plane ticket. Malone took a car to LaGuardia, flew to Montreal, and had lunch that day with his first CEO client. He ended up staying for six weeks, assessing the wisdom of Bell Canada's entry into microelectronics. At the first of many clients to follow, Malone interviewed everyone from the senior ranks to new hires. What works? What doesn't? How would you fix it? Over time, Malone found that if he interviewed 30 people or so and listened intently, themes would emerge. The best ideas were sometimes hidden, or they were lost on senior executives. By laying the patterns bare, studying in detail the disparate parts—not unlike disassembling a radio—he learned how big corporations *don't* work.

It was not rocket science, Malone quickly realized. You simply take the best ideas from anyone who has them, polish them, and serve them up to the chairperson. While at McKinsey, he consulted for Bell New Jersey, IBM, Traveler's Insurance, and GE, all sectors that would affect his own company years later. His mind was like a spread of glue—it held fast any concept or pattern it encountered. But Malone was getting bored fast in the intellectual and philosophical coliseum of consulting. Two years had been an eternity, and he had begun to grow weary of the interviews, the meetings, and especially the travel. Malone already had a little girl, and a son was on the way, duplicating the family of his childhood. He wanted to settle down. He wanted to keep his promise to Leslie.

One man would lead Malone out of the career he found exhausting and repetitive. His name was Moses "Monty" Shapiro, the head of General Instrument Corporation, a company that had come to McKinsey for help. Shapiro, an intense and loud labor lawyer, had built his company quickly by cobbling together miscellaneous assets—defense contractors (his most profitable, a betting-machine maker called American Totalizator Company), and an electronics business that had a de facto monopoly on UHF television tuners. Shapiro's most recent purchase was a company called Jerrold Electronics, which built and financed cable systems for potential owners. Jerrold was the weak link in General Instrument's chain of companies.

Working for McKinsey, Malone was looking for any way to cut Jerrold's costs, which had ballooned out of control. He quickly realized that the figures reported in the quarterly reports didn't add up. Someone at Jerrold, Malone surmised, had "pumped the turkey," or inflated the figures of its sales and profits before Shapiro bought the company. "You bought a real turkey here,"

Malone told Shapiro. "It's gonna take a lot of work to turn this around." After several weeks, Malone laid out a plan to Shapiro to fix Jerrold. But Shapiro surprised him with his reply: "I've got a better idea. If you're so smart, why don't you come and do it yourself?" Malone, then 29, accepted. Between Shapiro's frequent obscenity-laden tirades, which Malone secretly found amusing, Shapiro spoke as a mentor to Malone and plied him with bits of Talmudic wisdom. "Always ask the question, 'If not?' " he often said. "If the deal doesn't go as planned, what are you left with?"

In the process of studying Jerrold, Malone saw for the first time the potential of cable TV. At the time, Jerrold was a cable equipment maker that happened to be the third largest cable operator, with about 70,000 subscribers. Jerrold was also a world away from the theoretical life at McKinsey, where Malone hobnobbed with top-flight CEOs and pondered the future. Accepting Shapiro's offer, Malone descended into the trenches, taking responsibility for 3,000 employees and $80 million a year in revenue. Immediately, he fired executives in construction operations at Jerrold, which built cable systems and supplied financing and, not coincidentally, had the largest financial discrepancies in Jerrold's cooked books. He fired the entire purchasing department, too, en masse and brought in a clean guy. Then he set his sights on reducing manufacturing costs, moving assembly from Philadelphia to Mexico and turning to Asia for raw materials.

Slowly, efficiencies of scale stretched out before him. The bigger you are, the more parts you order. The more parts you order, the cheaper the parts. Before Malone arrived at Jerrold, the company paid 8 cents each for tiny connectors. Malone started buying them for 0.1 cent from a vendor in Asia. By having the guts to make volume commitments, buying components by the barrel, not by the piece, he saved the company a small fortune.

Given that so many of Jerrold's largest customers owed Jerrold money, Malone devised a strategy called *key account management,* in which he and two other executives personally visited far-flung cable companies to check on their clients. Malone took the five largest customers, often sleeping over at the homes of such pole climbers as Bob Magness and Gene Schneider on business trips. The visits were also crucial to embodying the main rule he learned at McKinsey:

Listen. He joined the budding National Cable Television Association and its board of directors, aiming to make friends in the industry. What he learned proved fruitful. He began hearing the same thing in these visits during the late 1960s: Cable was going two-way. The cable industry was lobbying the government, saying, in effect, if you will loosen restrictions, then the industry will offer new services to the American people, including interactive services. With a vision of TV viewers responding to polls and educational programming, the FCC required all cable operators to have two-way capability even though the upstream path would be rarely used for nearly two decades. Malone was ready with a new two-way amplifier at Jerrold, and the company's market share for cable equipment exploded, to about 80 percent from about 35 percent; profit margins soared by consequence.

Malone started piling up cash at Jerrold. One competitor petitioned the Federal Trade Commission (FTC) to investigate the company, charging that Jerrold tried to monopolize the industry by selling below cost. Lawyers for the FTC opened an investigation into the company's dominant market position, but they quickly closed it for lack of credible evidence. Jerrold lifted General Instrument's depressed stock price, and Malone became a rising star in Shapiro's company. Moreover, it occurred to Malone that Shapiro was going to have to retire soon. Flush with the power that success brings, Malone began to eye the top seat at General Instrument. All that stood in his way was a rival ahead of him in the line of succession: Frank Hickey, whom Shapiro had hired to oversee finances at General Instrument.

Malone did not like Hickey's abrasive style and knew he could not work for the man. One afternoon Hickey sent accountants to Jerrold's offices to audit Malone's books to ensure that Malone was following special instructions he had sent out earlier. Malone locked the auditors out, taking offense at the surprise visit and Hickey's failure to give him a courtesy call. Shapiro called Malone, yelling, to broker peace. Malone and Hickey continued to butt heads, but Malone knew what lay ahead for him. The board of directors, no matter how impressed with him, would not make him the chairman and CEO of General Instrument at the tender age of 30.

As Malone was learning yet another lesson in corporate politics (Hickey was made CEO), Jerrold was selling many of its cable systems to shave off debt, and focusing on its core mission as a cable equipment supplier. One bidder was Bob Magness of TCI, who Malone knew was accumulating massive debt. When Magness offered to buy Jerrold's cable systems, Malone quoted his boss, Shapiro, joking, "Look, Bob, we don't want any Portuguese escudos. We want cash—coin of the realm."[7] By the fall of 1972, the two men had become fast friends, albeit from different coasts and different eras. On one of Malone's visits to TCI in Denver, Magness asked the young man in his distinctive Texas drawl, "What do you think about coming out here to Denver and running our show?"[8]

CASH FLOW

By 1973, Bob Magness had finally placed one bet too many. His luck was catching up with him. Mounting a last-minute rescue plan to raise new money to pay off debt that was coming due, Magness had cajoled a consortium of banks into providing TCI with $78 million in bridge financing (i.e., a short-term loan with a higher floating interest rate) with the assumption that TCI would easily pay it back a short time later after raising $100 million by selling more shares on the stock market. Merrill Lynch had signed on to handle the financing, providing a big vote of confidence in TCI, and his new CEO, the 32-year-old John Malone would look after the rest.

But in a matter of months, interest rates continued to soar higher, and news of Kahn's conviction and financial chicanery at TelePrompTer put a damper on investors' appetites for cable. Then, at the worst possible moment, SEC regulators halted the secondary stock offering only days before it was to take place, which meant TCI couldn't pay back the big bridge loan.

Regulators were troubled by a TCI subsidiary called National Telefilm Associates (NTA), which was TCI's budding new programming arm based in Los Angeles. TCI owned 78 percent, and it was a vehicle for accumulating movies and old TV series that could provide programming for TCI cable systems. NTA already owned the rights to a trove of old films, including John Wayne's movies, classic cartoons, and the library of series that launched NBC, including *Bonanza, I Spy,* and *High Chaparral.*

NTA was run by Magness's partner and pal, George Hatch, who with his wife and family, owned broadcast TV stations, radio properties, and cable systems in Utah. Hatch was an early investor in TCI and still held a stake big enough that Magness needed his assent in any major corporate decision. And like Magness at TCI, Hatch had saddled NTA with piles of debt. Much to Magness's dismay, Hatch had obligated TCI as a guarantor of loans totalling $16 million.[1] NTA was a financial mess, and in the SEC's estimation, TCI was ultimately responsible, in which case the cable company must disclose that fact to any investors interested in buying more TCI stock. The SEC requested more documents, and that spelled delay, the one thing TCI could not afford.

While the SEC scoured NTA financials, conditions worsened for the new president. The five banks that had put up the bridge money, including Citibank, Chase, and First Security, put TCI on the critical list. NTA was bleeding money, $1 million in 1973 and $4 million in 1974, and if TCI, already creaking with its own debt, defaulted on the NTA loans, bankers could padlock the place. In a meeting with lenders in Los Angeles, a banker told Malone and Magness: "Boys, NTA is like a cancer on the tail of a beautiful dog. Nobody sees the beauty of the dog."

John Malone was furious. Many of NTA's problems were a direct result of poor choices George Hatch had made, and his ideas to save the company were no better. In one meeting Malone attended with bankers, Hatch had proposed purchasing a company that bought old black-and-white negatives from studios and salvaged the silver. Among the many strikes against the proposal was the fact that the company broke environmental laws. Another idea involved buying a shopping mall. Malone sat in a quiet rage, wondering what incredulous thoughts must be going through the mind of the Citibank official who had flown out to Denver from New York just to hear this gibberish. The whole thing was just insulting, Malone felt. Bankers scoffed at the short-term profit scheme. NTA executives, who flew first-class and spent lavishly, only annoyed Malone further.

One afternoon, Malone telephoned Magness back in Denver about another NTA screwup. "Bob, you're gonna have to find two new top executives," he said through clenched teeth, "'cause I'm gonna throw Don Havens [NTA president] out the fuckin' window, and then he'll be dead and I'll be in jail!" In the morning, all was forgiven.

By contrast, Malone and Magness showed tremendous respect for one another and never exchanged harsh words. Magness liked to be kept informed, but he never made overt decisions, instead indicating in subtle ways if he thought Malone was moving in the right direction. In rare moments when Magness wanted to push back against Malone's delegated authority, Magness never raised his voice or pounded on a table. A long pause or a skeptical question was all he needed to communicate to Malone that he was displeased; Malone read him like he had read his father.

Malone had repeatedly argued to Magness that TCI should repudiate the loan guarantee and sell NTA, later called Republic Pictures, at a loss, but Magness was loyal to Hatch. Magness was frustrated over NTA and the banks, too, and he often skewered his partner of more than a decade in face-to-face meetings, typically with dry wit. One night, Malone and Magness sat in a car outside of the office, a ritual of lingering before the last good-bye for the day. Malone could contain himself no longer. He blew up, yelling, "Shit, Bob, this is dragging us down!" Magness assuaged Malone's frustration by telling him loyalty to Hatch, an early believer in Bob and Betsy Magness, was more important than anything. "We've got to honor that commitment," he said. "We'll work it out."[2]

Whereas Magness had cultivated an intense hatred for bankers as a class long ago, now he began to hate them personally, individually. A framed cartoon in Magness's office captured the essence of his sentiment toward his lenders. Titled "Final Act of Defiance," it showed a scrawny field mouse standing fearlessly as a large eagle is about to swoop down and attack it. The mouse held one arm high, a middle finger extended. On the eagle, Magness had scrawled "BANKS." On the mouse, "TCI." The cartoon was one of few things that could tease a gap-toothed smile from him in those grim days.

Malone, by contrast, regarded banker meetings as a jousting contest, and he had developed a defensive strategy that could be boiled down into a series of survival tips: buy time, fend them off, give them confidence, keep them informed. It was in this arena that Malone's leadership skills were tested first and most often at TCI. Bank meetings raised Magness's blood pressure; they made Malone turn on the charm.

Malone dealt with seven banks for credit for TCI, and for NTA he contended with five banks. Malone also met regularly with two banks for a cable company that Magness had bought from Gulf + Western, Incorporated, called Athena, which had six cable systems, $11 million in debt, and no credit left.

In truth, most of the bankers with whom Malone and Magness dealt knew exactly what pressures TCI was under and felt fairly confident in the men's abilities to pull their company out of the trouble. Malone was fondest of Woody Oliver, who represented Mellon Bank and called after every meeting. "I think it went pretty well," Malone recalled him saying. "You guys are really working hard and we appreciate that." But 10 percent of the bankers, in Malone's view, were "absolute airhead assholes" who didn't understand the business and didn't want to understand. The bankers at Pennsylvania National Bank, a partner in the Athena loan, and Bank of America, which held part of the NTA loan, were especially tough on TCI. Often, when they broke for lunch in a daylong session, they left without inviting their clients at TCI.

Magness didn't like confrontation. He was always fearful of an awkward shareholder question at annual meetings, and he bristled in face-to-face meetings with bankers. If a bill collector showed up unexpectedly at TCI's door, secretaries would stall the visitor while Magness made a getaway through a glass door leading from his office to the parking lot. And there was the time two bankers from Bank of Boston flew to Denver to meet with TCI, and they had lunch with Magness and Malone at a restaurant in downtown Denver. Magness didn't speak when Malone introduced the bankers, nor did he shake any hands. Magness ordered a second martini by pointing at the empty first one and grunting, and he remained silent as he drank it. Malone talked, embarrassed and worried that soon, the bankers would start wondering what the hell was going on. Carefully choosing his answers, Malone gave them something to chew on, but he could see that Magness, on the other side of the tiny table, was growing restless. His second martini drained, Magness pushed his chair back from the table and without looking at anyone directly, said matter-of-factly, "Banks are whores, and bankers are pimps." The four men ate in silence.

Malone would liken these early years to the feelings men felt at Guadalcanal or Okinawa, sites of the most bitter fighting of World War II. Men forged a brotherhood fighting a common enemy, watching each other's back. Over a brief period of time, he would come to know his managers extremely well. Malone worked most closely with Donne Fisher, TCI's CFO, who first met Magness when he was a carpet layer in Bozeman, and one day had accidentally backed his truck into the gutter on Magness's house. Fisher had started out in 1960 as TCI's head accountant in Bozeman and had handled the banks until Malone joined the company. A feisty number cruncher who could recite TCI's various loans to the penny, Fisher helped Malone keep the lenders at bay, joining him in shuttle diplomacy to New York, where the two had to show up so often, hats in hand, that the company rented a tiny apartment in Midtown.

Malone would spend his first five years at TCI acting more like a treasurer than a president, fending off lenders, raising money, and sniffing out any angle that would give TCI breathing room. The demands from the seven banks financing TCI reached a crescendo three years after his 1973 arrival, when it was painfully clear to Malone that while TCI could still meet the minimum interest payments, he could not meet various financial covenants set by lenders, such as ratios of debt to cash flow.

When Malone had proposed some ways to ease the pressure further—mainly by having the banks grant extensions on the principle and waivers to the strict covenants—the seven banks financing TCI, acting as a consortium, sent representatives to TCI's flat brown home office to meet with the 35-year-old TCI president. Malone needed the approvals to get a clean audit, and tried to explain that part of the loans were leftover from NTA. After the meeting, the group of a dozen bankers sequestered themselves in TCI's paneled board room. Magness and Malone waited in his office until Magness, becoming unhinged with angst, left for home. Malone and Fisher stayed until the group broke.

"We've considered TCI's proposal," the lead lender finally told him, "but because of the deteriorated credit conditions, we think it appropriate to *raise* the interest rates of the company." Malone was stupefied. "*Raise* the interest rates?" he blurted, standing up. Did they know, he asked, how hard he had pressed his people in recent months? Malone fixed each man with an icy stare from his dark brown eyes. "If you can run the company better than I can, here's the keys," he declared, tossing them onto the table. "You may as well start running the company yourself. If you raise the interest rates it'll break the spirit of the company. We can't do it."

After a pause, the bankers walked out, murmuring. They left the keys on the table. Malone looked at Fisher. "We could be dead," he said. Malone didn't know whether the next day would bring bankruptcy; that night, he could barely sleep. The next morning, the bankers told him they would hold off raising the interest rates, and give TCI some breathing room. Malone's brinkmanship had worked, this time at least, but he couldn't shake the feeling that he was barely a step ahead of the bankers. "I'm the head of a little pipsqueak company in debt up to its ass, a couple million dollars in revenue, and not creditworthy to borrow from a bank—we're barely making it," he thought.[3]

While he could still see an upside in TCI, the bigger motivator that pulled Malone out of bed in the morning was the fear of failure. If TCI failed, Malone felt, he would lose much more than the company—he would lose the respect of his colleagues, the trust of his family, and perhaps the approval of his father.

Magness, in his enthusiasm for cable TV, had gotten carried away in TCI's acquisition program, and the way out was simple: Stop expanding so quickly. To meet budgets, Malone cut back office hours and salaries and took to personally signing any company expense over $500. TCI bought no more new vehicles. "If somebody wrecks one, they're going to have to ride with somebody else," Malone told his managers.

υυυ

Malone was fighting for TCI's life, and he intended neither to give up nor to take prisoners. Not long after he arrived, Malone had his first showdown with a city, and TCI's new president for the first time displayed how brutal his tactics could be in protecting his company. In Vail, Colorado, a ski town wedged in the Rockies about 100 miles west of Denver, the city council voted to end TCI's franchise to operate in the city. The council had declined TCI's offer to rewire the system, which it had only recently bought, and refused to renew TCI's contract.

Malone's response was silent but devastating. At 6:35 P.M. on November 1, 1973, the TV screen of every TCI customer in Vail went dark. TCI had pulled all programming, substituting it with the names and home phone numbers of top city officials, including the mayor. The blackout lasted through a Sunday Denver Broncos game against the St. Louis Cardinals, and the phone lines lit up. By Tuesday, the crisis was settled.[4] After setting new terms, Malone wanted to send a message to any city thinking of squeezing TCI at this delicate stage, and it set a precedent for the scores of franchise renewals it faced down in other cities.

With TCI's pending stock offering tangled up in the NTA mess, the company survived on short-term, bridge financing as Magness and Malone cajoled equipment suppliers to extend credit lines. TCI narrowly escaped financial collapse once more. TCI did stand by the NTA obligation. Finally, though, Malone unloaded NTA, the cancer on the tail of the dog. After writing off its equity investment and more than $8 million in debt, TCI eventually divested and distributed its ownership to TCI shareholders. That same year, Athena lost $4 million. With the stock of TCI at an all-time low, the secondary offering, which had been delayed, was pulled off the market entirely. "We're lower than whaleshit, John," Magness told his partner more than once. "I reckon I shoulda just kept what I had in Bozeman."[5]

When Malone had agreed to join, TCI's stock price was around $7. By the fall of his first year, it had fallen below the $1 mark, rendering Malone bankrupt—on paper, anyway. Thankfully, he had spoken with the loan officer at the Bank of Denver, as many TCI executives had, and there was a gentlemen's agreement not to call the loan taken to pay for shares in TCI. Throughout those early years, Malone displayed the steely resolve that had so immediately ingratiated him to the rugged cowboys at TCI. He had little choice: By the end of 1974, with the stock market fragile and falling, TCI's balance sheet showed a company hemorrhaging money. Debt was climbing toward $150 million, and interest payments had almost doubled in just 12 months to $12 million annually, consuming a large portion of yearly revenue, which had grown to $34 million.[6] "I have too much riding on this bet," Malone told himself; "I can't turn back now." He made a silent vow that if he could pull TCI out of the nosedive it was in, he would never let it again fall so close to failure.

The financial straits created strong bonds among the tiny crew running the company. Almost every evening, Magness, Malone, and Larry Romrell, a lanky engineer from Idaho, would gather at Magness's house to grill steaks and put away a little bourbon. One afternoon the talk turned to gardens, and the tipsy trio started to dig a vegetable plot in Magness's backyard. For years afterward they planted and weeded the plot, fertilizing it with manure from Magness's stables. Malone spent far more waking hours at TCI than at home, to the disapproval and dismay of his wife Leslie, and when he needed support, he found it in the band of old-timers at TCI. J. C. Sparkman, TCI's chief of operations, was Malone's lead dog in the struggle to pull TCI out of debt. A short man who spoke his mind freely in a deep, urgent voice, Sparkman ran his outfit like a Marine battalion, and his energy was infinite. He was as jovial as any man at TCI could be in the 1970s. He drank, shared jokes, and told stories with countless regional managers, but he was ruthless when he enforced a budget.

Under new plans outlined by Malone, Sparkman drove his various divisions with Teutonic efficiency. Within days of acquiring a company, Sparkman would descend with a squad and reorient the newly acquired managers and employees to the spartan ways of TCI. "You have one time to tell me that you didn't do it that way before," he told new managers in his signature brusque style. "The second time you tell me, 'That's not the way we did it before,' you're going to get the door hitting your ass on the way out."[7] Each time he cut overhead at a new property, he took possession of any company cars, reserving the best one for himself so that he could drive a series of progressively newer vehicles. Malone allowed Sparkman this little luxury; times were tough, and a new car meant a lot. It reminded him of pirates plundering the treasure of conquered rivals. "The only way somebody in this company is gonna get a new car," Malone once quipped to his lieutenants, "is to take it away from somebody else."

Sparkman didn't believe in spending money TCI didn't have on advertising it didn't need. Instead, he pushed TCI's door-to-door marketing, using teams of salespeople whom he would fly into small towns and pay on commission. In 1974, TCI added more than 80,000 subscribers to its base of 472,000 subscribers, largely through such house-by-house assaults. Malone and Sparkman began calculating precise formulas for predicting a cable system's performance, based on several factors, such as the number of installers needed per mile of cable, or office personnel required per subscriber. At annual budget meetings, where Malone and his chiefs scoured every facet of TCI's business, Sparkman sought out the leanest of TCI's systems, then grilled the managers of the rest of TCI's systems on why their businesses didn't measure up. Why did a TCI system in Oklahoma need one more secretary than the same-sized system in Wyoming? Malone set a budget, then turned his hatchetman loose to enforce it. Pretty soon, Sparkman had earned a reputation in the industry for himself and for TCI. There was a saying around the company in those days: "John shakes the trees and J.C. rakes the leaves."

ꙮꙮꙮ

The more he analyzed TCI's balance sheet and anemic stock price, the more fearful John Malone became that the company could be acquired by a hostile bidder. Bigger media companies had already begun sniffing around the industry. Gannett Company's chairman at the time, Paul Miller, visited TCI often. Warner Communications boss Steve Ross also made friendly passes at TCI in occasional calls to Malone, the promising young Jerrold chief who had slipped through his fingers a few years before. TCI was still undervalued, and it might be worth far more than the stock price if it were simply broken up and sold off as separate cable systems. "We are worth more dead than alive," Malone murmured more than once. "We're living on borrowed time." Malone knew, instinctively, that it was eat or be eaten. Once TCI had finished writing down the value of its assets to shelter cash flow from taxes, it would have to begin paying income taxes and keep on paying interest, and there would be nothing left to fund growth. It needed to keep expanding, no matter what, buying up new cable companies to start the write-off process anew and build cash flow.

Malone successfully used a handful of innovative financial techniques that would not only save the company from ruin, but also offer it some financial freedom. To fund TCI's expansion plans, he courted companies with capital to invest and an abiding interest in cable—but no expertise. After hosting a number of annual publishing seminars in the late 1970s, TCI formed a partnership with Knight-Ridder. Keeping control of TCI was crucial, but Malone and Magness still lacked any solid insurance that TCI couldn't be bought by an outsider. For starters, the stock was pretty spread out among the various partners. By 1975, Magness owned about 13 percent of the company. Hatch controlled around 13 percent, including his personal stake and the 10 percent held by his wife's family's company, the Standard Corporation. The conglomerate Gulf + Western owned about 9 percent; home builder Kaufman & Broad owned another 14 percent. Kearns-Tribune, the publisher of the *Salt Lake City Tribune,* was another big investor, and Myles Berkman, head of Rust Craft Broadcasting, owned a tiny slice.

More urgently, Kaufman & Broad wanted to unload its shares. The stock price lingered near $1 in 1974 and 1975, attractive to any raider. Malone and Magness couldn't buy any more shares, and bank covenants forbade the company from using borrowed money to buy and redeem shares back into the treasury. One idea was that TCI could loan money to an unrestricted, off–balance sheet subsidiary to buy the shares. But who was trustworthy? Banking covenants forbade family members from buying the stock.

Hunkered over Magness's kitchen counter, they began to tick off names. "John, who do you know you could absolutely trust your wife with?" Magness asked. Malone offered a couple of names with no conviction, and Magness couldn't think of anyone. The stock at stake was worth several million dollars. Magness took a pull from his Jack Daniel's whiskey while Malone nursed a scotch.

"God, isn't it terrible that in the whole world, all the people you know, and all the people I know, and there is nobody we can trust this with?" Magness asked.

After a slight pause, Magness realized the answer was sitting in the room with him and Magness. An old ranch dog, an overweight mixed beagle named Tiger, slept by the hearth. "Can we trust Tiger?" Magness asked. Malone grinned. "By God, I think we can trust Tiger!" he replied. It started as a joke, but the two men created a holding company called Tiger Incorporated, a company that would become one of TCI's largest shareholders over the next few years, owning at one point more than one-third of the company, including the stock of Gulf + Western and Kaufman & Broad. Magness and Malone never told a soul that TCI's largest block of stock was parked with a dog—avoiding a technical violation of the debt covenants. Tiger would evolve into two firms, including one known as TCI Investments Inc., 50 percent owned by an unrestricted subsidiary of TCI and 50 percent owned by Kaufman & Broad. To Malone and Magness, the idea of Tiger served a higher purpose, allowing TCI to keep shares out of hostile outsiders' hands, while giving TCI a chance to buy back its own shares from a subsidiary.

Months later, Magness and Malone moved the Tiger-held stock over to Jerry O'Brien, a friend, outside director, and the publisher of the *Salt Lake City Tribune*. Contractually, O'Brien controlled the stock, which was given to him, but TCI kept a foot on it through an option to buy it back for $1,000. Effectively, the men parked the stock in a shell company in O'Brien's friendly hands until they could figure out what to do with it sometime in the future. Later, TCI would exercise the option, redeem the shares, then split the stock simultaneously. The Tiger Inc. investment company, kept alive into the early 1980s, tickled Magness and Malone whenever they talked about it, particularly since it had let them get around bank rules. The two men rationalized the plan by telling themselves that they were protecting TCI shareholders. The Tiger Inc. ruse revealed, more than anything else, how far Magness and Malone would go to maintain control of TCI's destiny.

Which is why they began to regard the position held by George Hatch, the Utah broadcaster, as both a problem and an opportunity as the 1970s ended. Magness and Malone were concerned that if Hatch ever sold their block of stock, it could open the door for a hostile bidder. The Hatch family, who owned TV and radio properties, was interested in a collection of broadcast stations owned by Kansas State Network (KSN). But because the Hatches owned cable systems in the same markets through TCI, Hatch would have to sell his cable stock under the FCC's ownership limits at the time. If Hatch sold, "there goes control of the company," Malone thought. Malone and Magness had worked too hard to let that happen; they had to clinch their control over TCI or risk losing the company.

At the same time that Hatch was eyeing the TV stations of KSN, another cable company, Heritage Communications of Des Moines, was blocked in its own takeover attempt of KSN. Heritage had initially tried a friendly takeover, but the bid had turned hostile, with Heritage accumulating 25 percent of the Kansas broadcast company.

So they settled on a plan whereby all parties could walk away with what they sought—TCI would buy the 25 percent stake in KSN from Heritage, then sell the stake to Hatch, who would pay in TCI shares. Magness and Malone both knew Heritage Chairman Jim Hoak, and they flew to Des Moines to pitch him the deal. On the night before Magness and Malone were to meet Hoak, they rented a room together—times were that lean—at a dilapidated Holiday Inn in Des Moines, and then walked down to the bar. Sitting on stools beside each another, Malone and Magness started ticking off control issues clouding TCI's future. After a few drinks, Malone floated an idea that at first seemed audacious. But as they chewed on it, it became very real. "Two classes of stock," Malone began. "I've seen it done before." TCI could split the stock and issue a class B share for every share that existed. But the class B shares would have 10 votes per share, giving holders of that stock 10-to-1 voting power over regular class A shares; they just had to be careful to ensure somehow that they got most of the new supervoting shares.

Eventually, Malone worked what was the first in a career of intricately nuanced and complex deals. First, Malone and Magness floated the special offer of class B shares to all shareholders, with the intent to swap shares of TCI class A for the new B supervoting stock. Magness then swapped A shares for Hatch's B shares, and Hatch redeemed his TCI holdings with the company tax-free, thanks in part to a federal tax certificate granted because of federal media ownership rules at the time. In return, Hatch received the KSN stake he wanted, which TCI had purchased from Heritage. TCI had avoided taxes on the sale because of rules concerning stock-holder redemption. The stock of Heritage, some of which TCI bought at the time, shot up when it sold its KSN position. Most important, Magness and Malone had locked up hard control of the company, with nearly half of the vote now in safe hands.

♘♘♘

Until around 1976, TCI could afford to pay only the interest on its massive loans; it had no way to pay down the principal. Any cash TCI had left over after taxes and loan payments was plowed back into the company. As TCI began to digest Magness's binge of cable acquisitions and hit financial projections with some regularity, banks began to loosen the purse strings, albeit ever so gradually. Still, the company rarely produced earnings, the measure by which Wall Street values every stock. It was around this time that Malone started to espouse a concept little used by Wall Street analysts in corporate valuations—the true value of cash flow, defined as oper-ating earnings before interest, depreciation, and taxes. Through a combination of logic, jawboning, and sheer force of presence, Malone persuaded Wall Street to take a second look at the cable industry, long shunned because of its nonexistent earnings and heavy debt addiction. Malone argued, successfully, that after-tax earnings simply didn't count; what counted was cable's prodigious cash flow, funding TCI's continual expansion. Buying cable was like buying real estate. As the value of TCI's franchises rose, so would the value of its stock. Net income was an invention of accountants, he declared.

Think about it, he'd tell a young analyst: Because TCI had high interest payments and big write-offs on cable equipment, it pro-duced losses, and because it produced losses it paid hardly any taxes to the government. As long as cable operators collected pre-dictable, monopoly rent from customers, met interest payments, and grew from acquisitions, why worry? Malone liked the mathe-matics of it: Tax-sheltered cash flow could be leveraged to land more loans to create more tax-sheltered cash flow. A standing joke around TCI was that if TCI ever did report a large profit, Malone would fire the accountants.

Malone's theory of value was anathema to many investors, but it was the result of months of turning the issue over in his mind, and it dovetailed with Magness's ambition for the company and his hatred of taxes. He concluded that TCI would never be an earnings and taxes company, and he began to proselytize that right up front with shareholders; it evolved into a philosophy. "There is a big difference between creating wealth and reporting income," Malone liked to say, and the investors who held a long view rather than focusing on quarterly earnings would be rewarded handsomely. Even so, the rest of Wall Street didn't get it. Cash flow was controversial, and it would remain so for decades. When a young analyst for E.F. Hutton named Paul Kagan submitted a report on cable in 1968, the firm refused to publish it, telling Kagan, "We don't publish reports on companies or industries that don't show any profit."[8] Kagan went on to build a business analyzing cable financial data for his own clients.

Yet Malone seemed to draw energy from skeptics. He became ever bolder at annual meetings. "If you're going to ask about quarterly earnings, you're at the wrong meeting, and you probably own the wrong stock," he told one group of TCI investors. "What we care about is value. We want to create value for our shareholders. And I think the best way to create value is to have a very long view, so that's what we do. So when we have the opportunity to expand into an area we think is going to have long-term value, we do it. We don't have to worry about the impact on earnings. So it makes a different kind of organization."[9] Malone wanted to change how investors defined profit—and he would, opening doors to capital for cellular telephone business and, later, hundreds of dot-com companies.

〜〜〜

Slowly, imperceptibly at first, TCI started to turn around. The first big break came through a group of insurance companies. In the mid-1970s, as banks drew their purse strings tighter, Malone had agreed to operate a handful of cable systems that had been repossessed by three insurance companies: John Hancock, Connecticut

General, and Phoenix Mutual. After a few months, the cable systems started showing positive cash flow, and the properties started faring so well that they were able to pay back principal on the original loans. TCI was paid a management fee, and Malone hoped the insurance companies would remember the favor.

By 1977, they did remember, forming a consortium of seven insurers in refinancing TCI's towering debt, which carried high floating-interest rates. Teachers, Traveler's, Equitable, and the others agreed to lend TCI the unheard-of sum of $77.5 million, one of the largest loans to the cable industry at the time by insurance companies, at fixed rates and cheaper and more flexible than the banks. It was without a doubt the happiest day of Malone's career with TCI.

He celebrated the triumph with Donne Fisher, Steve Brett, and John Draper, a lawyer at TCI, at a lunch and cocktails thrown by the bank at Windows on the World, a restaurant at the top of the 108-story World Trade Center building that once stood in the heart of the financial district in Manhattan. They started drinking in the afternoon, and Malone drank more booze by the end of the night than ever before in his life. Later, Fisher could recall little except for standing on the corner of 56th and Lexington at 4:00 A.M. He never went to bed that night because his flight to Denver left at 6:30 A.M.

Back in Denver, Malone and Magness quickly called a meeting of TCI's biggest lenders at the Marriott Hotel on Hamden Avenue, relishing the chance to tell them they were no longer needed. The bankers filed into a large conference room and sat down, some half-expecting another shot of bad news from TCI. Malone stepped to the lectern. "Thank you all for coming. From time to time, various lenders to the company have expressed an interest in reducing their exposure to the company. I'm happy to announce we have arranged for alternate financing. It's going to be possible for any bank that wants to reduce their exposure to do so in a timely basis. In other words, if you want out, you can get out. Now." He savored the blank faces on the hushed audience fanned out before him. Incredibly, TCI could pay them off, up to the last red cent. Then, as if delivering the second half of a one-two punch, Malone let the bankers know that TCI had found cheaper money. "From this day forward, the company is a prime-rate borrower," he said, putting all banks on notice that the interest rate was coming down. Two of the banks were paid off in full. Five banks wanted to stay in, and rewrote their covenants to allow TCI more flexibility through unrestricted subsidiaries. A year later, institutional investors discovered the company's stock, and started to take the price up. TCI was finally able to go to the equity markets to raise capital. From that point forward, Malone never looked back.

One day in the fall of 1978, Donne Fisher's secretary received a phone call from a woman at Gulf + Western who wanted to know: Did TCI plan to sell its Resorts International stock? "It must be a mistake," Fisher told the secretary. TCI didn't own any Resorts International stock. But the woman insisted that TCI did own the stock through a company called Athena. Amused, Fisher asked for a copy of the document to prove it. Five years earlier, when TCI had paid $4 million in 1973 to Gulf + Western for control of Athena, among the hodgepodge of holdings that G + W sold to TCI were warrants to buy 463,000 shares of Resorts International at $39 a share. Until 1978, the warrants were practically worthless. Indeed, TCI's Athena was losing money and was $40 million in debt. But in 1978, when Resorts International opened the first casino in Atlantic City, the stock shot to as high as $96 a share. After converting the warrants and selling shares at a high, TCI made $31 million—a fortune for a company whose market value was only about $100 million at the time.

Lady Luck was beginning to smile on TCI.

THRILLA IN MANILA

hile John Malone struggled to put TCI on solid footing, he was aided not only by blind luck, but by the creativity of scores of cable entrepreneurs who were intent on improving the business model in their favor. Cable was bound for the big time, destined to transform itself from a mere antenna extension into an electronic medium in its own right, one that would rival the power and riches of the Big Three broadcast networks. The first and most dramatic signal of that storied destiny occurred on the night of September 30, 1975, 10,000 miles from the Rocky Mountains, in the Philippines. There, Muhammad Ali and Joe Frazier fought in a rematch for boxing's world heavyweight championship, in one of the most anticipated events in sports history—the Thrilla in Manila. The future of cable as a truly national force was on display in a guilded ballroom of the Holiday Inn in Vero Beach, Florida, where a crowd had gathered to watch the fight live on a large screen. Members of Congress, the press, and cable operators from every corner of the country filled the audience.

Their host was Time Inc.'s new pay-TV channel, Home Box Office (HBO). The HBO brass cared little about whether Muhammad Ali could beat Frazier, who had lost his title to Ali in 1974.

What mattered to HBO was that the boxing match could be viewed on pay TV in the United States without the help of a national broadcast network. Partnered with an electronics firm and two cable operators, HBO had promised something considered undoable for an event happening on the other side of the planet: It had vowed to air the fight live to paying subscribers, using a satellite that hung, at that very moment, 22,300 miles in space above the chattering guests of HBO. HBO president Gerald Levin smiled as he mingled through the crowd, outwardly calm, inwardly a bundle of nerves. Levin knew this event would make or break HBO, and probably his career, both of which he had worked hard to keep alive in Time Inc.'s buttoned-down culture. What he didn't know was that this breakthrough event, aimed at saving his career, would lift the cable industry off the ground.

HBO was the inspired idea of the man Levin had succeeded, Charles "Chuck" Dolan, a crafty entrepreneur who had won the cable franchise to wire lower New York City five years earlier. Most viewers could get clean signals from the local broadcast stations, and Dolan figured that to get them to sign up for cable service, he had to offer something extra. So he conjured up an idea, sketching it out on a portable typewriter while vacationing on the *QE2:* a channel that would be a subscription service offering commercial-free movies and sports, including New York Knicks and Rangers games. Dolan persuaded Time Inc., an owner of cable systems that supplemented its fabled stable of magazines, to back the idea.

HBO had a rocky start. The big Hollywood studios were afraid to sell films to HBO or any other cable outlet, concerned about a backlash from movie theaters. "This isn't a business for you," an executive of Twentieth Century–Fox told Dolan one day.[1] The National Association of Theater Owners feared HBO's uncut, uncensored movies would give people less reason to leave their living rooms to catch movies on the big screen. In a massive campaign effort to whip up public support, movie theaters replaced movie titles on marquees with "Save Free TV!" Moviegoers were encouraged to sign anticable petitions. An animated trailer shown in theaters in New York and elsewhere showed a cable wire that metamorphosed into a fire-breathing dragon that ate a TV set.[2]

By far, though, HBO's biggest obstacle to growth was the simple fact that it couldn't transmit its content beyond the northeastern United States. HBO delivered movies by beaming a signal from its base in New York to a string of microwave towers that bounced the signal from one to another on hills 20 miles or so apart. Like batons in a relay race, microwave signals finally reached a cable operator's head end, and if one dish malfunctioned along the way, the whole thing went on the fritz. Sometimes HBO had to resort to distributing movies by sending videotapes to cable operators via messenger. Two years earlier, Levin had hit upon the idea of using a communications satellite to transmit TV signals to paying customers after he saw a demonstration at a cable industry trade show by TelePrompTer, the largest cable operator in the United States. During the years after the launch of Sputnik by the Soviet Union in 1957, the federal government had pursued an open-skies policy to encourage commercial development of satellites, and several companies had stepped up to launch them, including Comsat, Western Union, RCA, and AT&T. Satellites would enable HBO or any other new cable channel to efficiently distribute themselves far more broadly than before, shooting their signals into space, then beaming back down on every single local cable system across the country, without having to bounce the signal through all those mountaintop microwave towers.

Energized by the idea, Levin marched back to Time's board and won more money to lease time on the satellite. It was a hard sell: He needed to build an uplink and lease time on a satellite transponder to the tune of nearly $10 million. Several on the board considered it an unproven technology being deployed to save an unprofitable cable TV business. A company called Scientific Atlanta made a receiving dish for $100,000, and two cable operators, Bob Rosencrans and Monty Rifkin, agreed to install earth stations (giant dishlike antennae for receiving the signal) on selected systems in Florida, Georgia, and Mississippi. As the minutes ticked down toward the beginning of the fight that evening, Time Inc.'s chief executive, Andrew Heiskell, and Richard Wiley, chairman of the FCC, made speeches to the crowd pontificating on cable's new mantle in the communications revolution. HBO had already warmed up the audiences at home with two movies—*Alice Doesn't*

Live Here Anymore and *Brother of the Wind.*[3] When Ali and Frazier appeared on screen, Levin could hardly believe his eyes.

In a flash, the opening bell rang out halfway around the world and reached subscribers in Vero Beach, Florida, and Jackson, Mississippi. So clear were the pictures, said Bob Rosencrans, the cable operator hosting the event, "it looked like they were fighting in the next room."[4] Viewers at the Holiday Inn and at home marveled at the clarity of the signals and the thought of how far they had traveled—more than 93,000 miles, according to press accounts. After 14 grueling rounds, Frazier couldn't answer the 15th bell. Ali won the fight, but HBO won the crowd. By airing a live sporting event from the Philippines, HBO, a money-losing upstart that operated principally in the Northeast, was scooping the Big Three networks on one of the hottest tickets of the year. While HBO had just transmitted the entire fight live, the broadcast networks were waiting for an airplane to fly across the ocean with highlights.

The Ali-Frazier demonstration transformed the economics of cable TV and sparked a new era in telecommunications. Not leastly, it proved an elegant point to cable's competitors, the broadcast networks: You are no longer the only game in town. A single cable program could now theoretically reach a national audience, and by anyone's calculation, it could make a lot of money. Indeed, the geosynchronous satellite, a.k.a. the bird, would forever change the economics of cable TV. Almost immediately, cable giant TelePrompTer ordered 65 earth stations. And that was just the beginning. Cable operators couldn't sign up fast enough for HBO, which could boost a system's subscriber rolls by as much as 20 percent. HBO and cable TV became synonymous. With VCRs and movie rentals still a decade away, HBO had a corner on the market for recent hits. "I can remember when *Jaws* was released on HBO, the entire penetration of TCI went up by a full percentage point," John Malone told an interviewer much later. "People were signing up for cable to get *Jaws.*"[5]

When HBO went up on the bird, a charismatic and restless entrepreneur known as Ted Turner made a simple leap: Old-fashioned microwave towers had expanded his local Atlanta TV station, WTCG, into an outlet with region-wide reach—so why couldn't the new satellites now make his regional network into a national one?

To do that, he would need the help of cable operators—and to get their help, he would have to win over leading players first. So around the time of the HBO launch, Turner flew to Denver at Malone's invitation to make his pitch to a pack of cable operators. In a TCI conference room, Turner paced furiously, preaching, yelling, and gesticulating wildly as he told the cablemen that he and they were all on the same team, fighting a common enemy, the broadcasters. With their help, WTCG, later renamed WTBS, could become a "superstation that serves the nation," beaming old movies and sitcom reruns, plus the games of baseball's Atlanta Braves and basketball's Atlanta Hawks (teams that Turner later acquired) to every cable operator in the United States. Unlike HBO, which made money solely by charging cable systems a fee per subscriber each month, WTBS would survive on advertising—a direct strike at the lifeblood of the Big Three broadcasters. Turner played the underdog and found a kindred spirit in the cable operators, who likewise were fighting the far bigger and richer broadcast networks. When Malone's secretary popped in to ask if anyone needed more coffee, Malone quipped, "Does he look like he needs more coffee?"

Malone knew Turner from various cable industry functions and liked the man's buccaneering, if quirky, style. And Turner certainly knew Malone, who had begun to emerge as an industry leader after three years of running TCI. The company was by 1975 the second-largest cable operator in the country behind TelePrompTer, and it now served 651,690 customers in 149 cable systems in 32 states.[6] And through an $11 million expansion plan, TCI's common-carrier microwave business was second only to AT&T's. Turner was more famous as the sailor with movie-star looks: pale blue eyes, a dimpled chin, and a Clark Gable mustache. He would etch his image in the national conscience in 1977 as the sailor who crawled under a table, drunk, on national television at a press conference in Newport, Rhode Island, where he had just captained the racing yacht *Courageous* to victory in the America's Cup.

Turner owed his tenacious, competitive streak to a strict and demanding father, Ed, who ran a billboard business. He had packed his son off to military schools, where the young Turner discovered his heroes—Napoleon, Horatio, and Alexander the Great.

Later, at Brown University, Turner raised hell, violating campus rules by bringing women into his dorm room, and once torching his fraternity's homecoming float. Finally, though, he turned serious, opting to study the classics over business. For that choice, his father turned on him. Ed sent home a scorching 10-page letter that read in part, "I think you are rapidly becoming a jackass. . . ."[7] After a brief stint with the Coast Guard, Ted returned home to Atlanta to a shocking welcome. His father, a success by anyone's measure, had put a .38-caliber pistol in his mouth and committed suicide. He had sold off the company to pay debts. Ted Turner was 24, and in a manner characteristic of nearly every endeavor he made thereafter, he ignored the best advice and raised enough money to buy Turner Advertising back. Then he proceeded to turn the firm around.

Throughout his career, Turner continually played the role of the underdog. No matter who was the Goliath, he was always David. Five years before HBO launched its service on satellite, Turner bought Channel 17, an ailing independent UHF station, which was dead last among Atlanta's five stations. The station, dubbed Turner Communications Group's WTCG ("Watch This Channel Grow," Turner liked to say), lost $1 million a year. He worked feverishly to extend WTCG's reach in the region through the use of microwave towers in a daisy chain. Though expensive, it allowed Turner to broadcast WTCG beyond its 40-mile broadcast range, first to Georgia's rural hill country, then to nearby towns. Cable operators in the region agreed to carry Turner's station, especially for its Braves and Hawks games, because there were few independent broadcast stations in the Southern systems they were serving. To sell ads, Turner would literally drop to his knees and beg.

Malone doubted that Ted Turner would be able to turn his regional broadcast station into a national cable network. The FCC would never let the plan get off the ground, he told Turner. Among the morass of restrictions hobbling cable operators was the *antileapfrogging rule,* which placed limits on Turner's ability to bounce his Atlanta signal into distant towns that already had a clear local signal. Malone's assemblage of cable operators was skeptical that Turner could survive the thicket of regulations. Sweeping the room with his eyes, Turner paused. "Goddam it, I'll do it myself," he huffed.

Malone himself hated the government's rules restricting cable. More and more he was beginning to feel that the industry's real problem wasn't market demand or even technology—it was government. Turner was branded a broadcast pirate in legislative hearings, and Major League Baseball's commissioner, Bowie Kuhn, told Congress that Turner had devalued the national pastime by flooding the regional market with Braves games. The Motion Picture Association of America accused Turner of reselling movies to cable operators—sales that should go to the Hollywood studios that owned the copyrights. But Turner, as fiery and sanctimonious as an evangelical preacher, railed right back, telling a congressional subcommittee in the summer of 1976 that the Big Three networks had led a "sheltered life from competition. They have an absolute, a virtual stranglehold on what Americans see and think, and I think a lot of times they do not operate in the public good, showing overemphasis on murders and violence and so forth." His superstation punchline: "So if we do become super, it will be another voice." Turner played David to the hilt, castigating the Goliath networks at every opportunity. "Free choice! That scares the networks to death, let me tell you," Turner once told a reporter. "When we get that, ABC will shrink down to a puddle like the witch in *The Wizard of Oz*. They'll have to start serving the viewers again, and not just the people who sell soap."

Gradually, the government began loosening the restrictions that dogged cable. Turner's break came when the FCC, which had been studying whether to soften or rescind many of the cable rules under a deregulation push from President Gerald Ford's administration, ruled in cable's favor. The loathsome leapfrog rule was dropped, and other changes gave cable operators more latitude in choosing which channels to carry. Malone could hardly believe Turner's good fortune. From that day forward, Malone started to see in Turner an almost mystical destiny borne of sheer willpower. "Here is a guy who is heading straight for the iceberg—and the iceberg disappears," Malone told himself. To a degree unmatched by anyone except perhaps Gerald Levin, Malone would cultivate a long and profitable relationship with Ted Turner. On December 17, 1976, with broad support from the cable TV industry, thanks to the clout lent by John Malone, Turner Broadcasting System (WTBS) put its service on RCA's Satcom I satellite, alongside HBO.

WTBS took off slowly at first. More satellites rocketed up into space, and engineers devised ways to fit more channels on the cable wire. As 1977 began, more than 70 million people were watching TV, and more than 12 million of those were watching cable. The Big Three broadcasters began to sense a threat to their oligopoly. Cable was no longer merely an antenna extension extending their own reach; cable now loomed as a direct competitor to ABC, NBC, and CBS.

Cable operators, the broadcasters liked to say, were like leeches that lived free off the programming that was created, developed, and paid for by the broadcast networks and Hollywood studios. "If cable wants to develop, let it develop on its own with its own programming," Leonard Goldenson, chairman and CEO of ABC, declared at the time.[8] The broadcast networks, studios, theater owners, and sports franchises marshaled an army of lobbyists to work the power centers of Washington. The Big Three, which collectively provided a free national podium for senators and representatives, made sure Congress knew their business would be irreversibly harmed by the new interloper. Behind the scenes, they warehoused programming to keep anything from going to Turner or HBO, buying up exclusive rights to films from studios simply to keep them off the cable dial; they had no real intention of ever airing them. In essence, they were paying Hollywood to forgo supplying the new rivals.

Cable was ultimately held responsible for paying for the use of broadcast programming, but rather than having to pay program originators a substantial portion of the cost of production, the cable outlets had to pay only token copyright payments to a newly created Copyright Royalty Tribunal.

υυυ

As the satellite revolution rocketed cable into the future, Magness and Malone found it all a little bittersweet. Like other cable operators, they stood to profit enormously from the efficiencies and opportunities that satellites offered in the wake of HBO's successful demonstration. Magness had eyed setting up a satellite system four years earlier, only to drop the plans because TCI was in yet another financial bind. The cowboy was dreaming big dreams all right, but he had no money to fuel them. Nor could TCI initially afford the earth station to offer HBO service. TCI was overextended and its restrictive loan agreements forbade purchases related to pay TV. During this period of penny-pinching, Malone had become skilled at devising ingenious ways to stretch TCI's dollar and evade the restrictions of certain covenants. If the banks wouldn't allow TCI to shell out the $100,000 it cost to buy a satellite dish, Malone figured, why couldn't TCI employees separately own a cable system that could buy an earth station? Malone formed a partnership comprising a small group of TCI executives who would buy and run a system in Minot, North Dakota, with financing help from a local investor and Jerrold, Malone's old employer. Soon the cable system in Minot started pulling HBO down from the heavens and more customers signed up.

By 1977, Malone had won concessions from lenders, and TCI was ready to add HBO to its cable systems. Meanwhile, another pay-TV service, Showtime, was planning to launch, and Malone immediately played the two rivals off each other, extracting a sweeter offer from HBO: It would help finance the earth stations and give TCI a hand in marketing the new service to potential customers. TCI also sold HBO a small regional pay service it operated. As more cable systems ordered earth stations, the price plunged from its initial cost of $100,000 to around $30,000, allowing cable systems with as few as 2,500 subscribers to offer HBO to subscribers. The FCC even helped foster the expansion by halving the required size of satellite receiving dishes from 30 to 15 feet, cutting their cost further, and accelerating the licensing process. Orders poured into Scientific Atlanta, the major maker of dishes at the time, transforming the small electronics company in a flash into a billion-dollar business. By the end of 1978, more than 800 earth stations were up and running around the country; just two years later, the number had exploded to more than 2,500.[9]

After the launch of WTBS, Malone watched from the sidelines as others followed in Turner's wake. A man named Bill Rasmussen created the Entertainment and Sports Programming Network (ESPN for short) in 1978 by packaging, producing, and selling University of Connecticut sporting events to cable systems in the Northeast. Thanks to foresight, Rasmussen had reserved a slot on the same Satcom I satellite as HBO, one of the most prized seats in communications in the late 1970s. Suddenly, the NCAA, which had long been searching for a way to gain more exposure for its athletic programs, was interested in a TV pact with ESPN. Offers to buy the company rained on Rasmussen hours after ESPN was officially assigned the slot. On Valentine's Day in 1979, as Rasmussen was closing a deal for exclusive rights to NCAA events, he learned his tiny minnow of a network had attracted the interest of a whale: Getty Oil. The multi-billion-dollar petroleum empire offered a cool $10 million for 85 percent of ESPN, with Rasmussen retaining the rest. Cable TV was hitting the big time.

The programming floodgates opened. WGN in Chicago became the next satellite superstation. In 1978, Viacom completed its launch of Showtime, a competitor to HBO. In 1979, a former cable TV trade-press reporter named Brian Lamb started Cable-Satellite Public Affairs Network (C-Span), a nonprofit network to cover Congress that would be funded by the cable industry; that was the same year that Warner Amex started a satellite channel for children called Nickelodeon. And televangelist Pat Robertson turned a group of small broadcast stations into the Christian Broadcasting Network (CBN). Then, in 1980, just as WTBS started producing a profit, Ted Turner confounded the critics again by launching a 24-hour cable news network called CNN; the broadcast networks called it the "Chicken Noodle Network." When ABC launched a competitor to CNN soon after, Turner ran the imitator out of business, then bought the remains from the broadcaster. For the next two decades, Turner would prove over and over that he was a programming maestro and risk taker extraordinaire, and his home was the cable TV industry. For years, one of Turner's favorite lines, which he turned into an ad, was, "I was cable before cable was cool." Despite earlier protestations, the broadcast networks jumped into the game, too, in an effort to woo highbrow viewers. CBS started CBS Cable, an artsy, cultural network whose early offerings included a Joseph Papp production of *The Taming of the Shrew,* with Meryl Streep and Raul

Julia.[10] ABC launched the Arts, which was merged with the Entertainment Channel to become A&E.

Despite the explosion of new content, most operators of cable systems paid little attention to programming; it was merely a commodity that brought in new viewers, not a value chain all its own. But John Malone quickly saw a more important role for all the new channels popping up—they had a dual-revenue stream: from advertising and from payments made by cable systems based on how many subscribers each system had. Someday, this dual-revenue stream might dwarf the single stream of ad revenue on which the Big Three broadcast networks relied. The new content providers promised both opportunity and risk: Their growth depended in part on getting steadily rising fee increases from cable operators like TCI. Through difficult negotiations, TCI had forced new networks into long-term, cheap contracts. But once those contracts ran out, Malone knew it would be tough to resist the price demands of an established, popular brand. Turning it over in his mind, he suddenly realized the answer: Rather than just owning the cable that delivered the new programming fare, TCI needed to own a piece of the cable channels themselves, thereby sharing in a whole extra upside. A big operator like TCI could give a new network a big head start, and as valuable as its laid wires were, if the cable industry kept growing, the new networks now launching could be even more valuable. By buying into networks, Malone thought, TCI could own both the pipe and the water flowing through it. The cable wire and the cable programming, if owned under one roof, could be leveraged off of each other to create innumerable efficiencies. Vertical integration of companies would become an awesomely powerful and controversial tool for Malone to use in building TCI.

Malone arrived at a simple conclusion: He wanted to own as much of the programming as he did of the wire. TCI, which would eventually reach 20 percent of the households, would seek to own 20 percent of every programmer that came calling. "I want to be hedged all the way," Malone told himself. He started out small, in 1979, with a bet on a company called Black Entertainment Television (BET), a channel for African Americans started by Robert

Johnson, a black Washington lobbyist for the cable industry trade association. Johnson knew Malone from industry meetings, and he flew out to Denver one day to present his plans for a cable channel devoted to minority issues. "How much do you need?" Malone asked him. Johnson replied that he thought it would take $500,000 to get it started. Malone had already made his decision before Johnson walked through the door. Black viewers had tremendous buying power and no TV outlet to call their own. More important, such a network would bring in more paying customers for TCI. "I'll buy twenty percent of your company for one hundred eighty thousand dollars, and I'll loan you the rest," Malone offered.

Johnson said yes. Malone immediately called in TCI's lawyer, who had drawn up a one-page agreement. Moments later, the TCI treasurer handed Johnson a check for $500,000 dollars. The entire transaction took about 45 minutes. Other investors, including Taft Broadcasting, joined, too. It was TCI's first direct investment in a cable network, and it would prove to be one of its most lucrative.

A few years later, when John Hendricks walked into Malone's office, he was more than willing to sell Malone a part of his new science and documentary network. Although he had drawn blue-chip backers for the Discovery Channel, including Westinghouse and venture capitalist Allen & Company, Discovery was only days away from filing for bankruptcy. But Hendricks had come to the ideal investor. Malone loved to watch documentaries and nature shows when he had time to watch. Malone directed his lieutenants to put together a consortium of cable operators to back Discovery, a group that ultimately included cable veteran Gene Schneider, Cox Communications, and Newhouse Broadcasting. TCI would eventually own 49 percent of Discovery after adding to its initial stake of 10 percent for around $6 million. Along the way, Malone scooped up stakes in more networks, including 16 percent of Pat Robertson's International Family Entertainment (which owned the Family Channel), 50 percent of American Movie Classics, and varying stakes in a string of regional sports channels under the Prime Network name.

But as TCI grew in power and reach, the channel investment deals would eventually make Malone vulnerable to charges of extortion and anticompetitive behavior. After all, his TCI systems reached 2 million viewers by 1981, officially making TCI the biggest cable operator in the country and far outpacing the nearest competitors; getting TCI to carry a new channel almost guaranteed its success. So when John Malone came calling, did the new channels really have any choice but to hand over a piece of the action? If they didn't let him become a silent partner, he might not allow TCI's cable systems to offer the new channel. Malone generally made the fledgling networks an offer they eagerly accepted, but also one they couldn't really refuse: For a small equity stake in the channel, usually well below a majority share, TCI would add the new service to its cable systems and give it a fast start in gaining critical mass. Now Malone was even deeper into America's homes—and their pocketbooks. After a decade, BET, the Discovery Channel, and the Family Channel all easily surpassed the requisite 20 million or so subscribers required to make a channel successful, though their reach was still tiny compared with broadcast networks. Malone envisioned owning an entire portfolio of networks to supply his growing cable TV empire. And this was just the beginning.

♘♘♘

Once upon a time, cable started out as a rural phenomenon. Now cities and urban areas, where cable operators weren't needed or weren't allowed before, were interested in cable TV. With HBO's reputation spreading from home to home, viewers literally chased cable trucks down the street asking when service was coming. Teens went wild for one of cable's earliest surefire hits, Music Television (MTV), which launched at midnight on August 1, 1981, with the Buggles playing "Video Killed the Radio Star." The network started out as a segment of short music videos, called *pop clips,* on a Warner system. Cable operators started a land rush to wire the cities in the early 1980s, and big media companies jumped in, too, placing multi-million-dollar bets on cable. Traditional cable operators rapidly found themselves outclassed in fierce competition with big, well-known companies such as Time Inc., GE, American Express, and Westinghouse for lucrative markets in Boston, Chicago, Milwaukee, and Pittsburgh. As more companies jumped into the bidding, the values of the franchises soared. Everyone, it seemed, was in the race.

A cable franchise was essentially a legal right to a local monopoly—operators had to answer to local government and win approval for rate increases; otherwise, they faced no competition in this booming business. Giants in the cable industry grew bigger by swallowing midsized companies whole. In October 1980, Westinghouse Electric, which already owned eight cable systems and Group W Broadcasting, spent a whopping $646 million and assumed about $300 million in debt to buy TelePrompTer, making Westinghouse the largest cable company in America overnight, with 1.3 million subscribers in 32 states. Cable companies walked away with entire cities as if they were prizes at a county fair: Cox Cable won New Orleans, Louisiana, and Omaha, Nebraska; The Times Mirror Company took Providence, Rhode Island; and Sammons Communications won Fort Worth, Texas. And the *New York Times,* one of many publishers to buy into cable, bought 55 New Jersey systems for $83 million from the infamous Irving Kahn, now out of prison and back in business as a cable operator. "Ten years ago, you could have had a cable franchise for the asking," one cable wag told *Business Week* in 1980. Not anymore.[11]

Everyone was in the race—everyone, that is, but John Malone. At such frenzied prices, there was little he could do but sit on the sidelines and watch the bidding. Malone knew the game was too expensive for cash-poor TCI—but he also knew to be patient. Many of the investors who had suddenly fallen in love with cable were paying way too much and were backed by way too little experience: One day they would be begging TCI to buy them out. So while he waited for the buying frenzy to collapse, he aimed to improve TCI's cash flow by building through much smaller bites. A typical purchase during those years at TCI was a $1 million cable system, in need of an upgrade, contiguous to another TCI system, whose sellers were the first and only owners. TCI would typically offer 20 percent in cash and a 10-year note. The assets of the company TCI had just bought secured the balance of the borrowed amount. In the process, TCI and other big cable operators made millionaires out of the cable industry's earliest entrepreneurs, a ritual that would repeat itself over and over throughout the country.

As he and his bare staff nursed TCI's balance sheet back to health, Malone kept a sharp eye on the boldest and most aggressive of these big-league competitors, Warner Communications, the colossal empire of film, music, and cable run by Steve Ross. Ross was so smitten with cable that his lieutenants often tried to restrain him in meetings with Wall Street analysts. Take ten minutes on cable, thirty minutes on the other operations, they'd insist—then come back to cable if you must. Ross would nod in agreement and spend 40 minutes on cable.[12] In 1979, American Express had invested $175 million for 50 percent of Warner's cable properties to create Warner Amex Cable. The new venture secured a massive loan of $800 million and galloped into city after city to bid on franchises. Warner and others promised to wire the cities of tomorrow, and investors and lenders began to warm to their vision.

Warner had a bigger warchest than TCI, and it also had a secret weapon that would help it win more cable franchises than any other operator in the early 1980s: QUBE, an experimental and interactive system hailed as a glimpse of the future. Warner had unveiled QUBE in its cable system in Columbus, Ohio, in 1977. Using hand-held consoles with 30 buttons, QUBE viewers selected from a dizzying array of services: interactive quiz shows, educational programs, or first-run movies. Polls? A favorite program was *Columbus Live,* a local talent show. If more than half of the audience voted electronically against an act, the performance was pulled.[13] But the promise of QUBE went further than talent shows. In city after city, Gus Hauser, who had assumed the top cable job at Warner after Malone had turned Ross down, promised city councils that QUBE set Warner apart from all other contenders. QUBE was the future.

This notion of cable TV as far more than an antenna service—but rather, as the electronic pipeline that would bind an entire nation together—arose almost from the moment cable first took root in rural America in the 1960s. The more puzzling thing was that it took the industry, a gaggle of undercapitalized and risk-addicted cowboys and timid corporate giants, three decades to begin delivering on the vision. In 1970, a clarion call for cable interactivity was delivered by one of the nascent industry's more vigorous prophets, Ralph Lee Smith, a political journalist who penned "Wired Nation," an article in the May 18, 1970, issue of *The Nation* magazine outlining cable

TV's potential.[14] Smith, who later turned the article into a best-selling book, painted a picture of a completely interconnected society. Calling cable wires an "electronic highway," he said that the existing wires one day would deliver "audio, video, and facsimile transmissions that can provide newspapers, mail service, banking and shopping facilities, data from libraries and other storage centers, school curricula, complete course offerings leading to college degrees, cultural programs, community-originated TV fare, and other forms of information too numerous to specify. In short, every home and office can contain a communications center of a breadth and flexibility to influence every aspect of private and community life." He added: "This is no dream. The cable could carry it all."

Warner's top cable executives vowed to make it so. Warner officials predicted radical changes and improvements in society because of the new technology as they presented their pitch to wire a city. QUBE polled local voters on questions affecting particular neighborhoods, and Warner shuttled politicians from far-flung cities to tour the 30-channel cable system of the future in Ohio. Warner's new QUBE seemed to be an instant hit, winning strings of big-city franchises in the 1980s, including Pittsburgh, Cincinnati, and Dallas. But QUBE was only one example of the lengths to which cable companies would go to win a franchise—and soon enough, Warner would pull the plug on its much-touted futuristic network; QUBE was cool, but it just wasn't good business.

As more competitors jumped in to compete for exclusive rights to wire America, they launched an era of what would become known in the industry as *franchise wars,* which lasted in varying intensity from the late 1970s to the mid-1980s. It was the only period in which cable companies would compete vigorously among themselves to win new licenses—a 15-year invitation for the profit glories of regulated monopoly service; thereafter, they rarely challenged the franchises of cable incumbents.

In wooing city officials, no promise was too big for a cable company to make. Operators promised gold-plated cable systems with channels for the local council and commission meetings, as well as public studios that were hardly ever used once built. Cities, in turn, enchanted with the idea of so many new services, demanded the most advanced systems that cable operators were capable of building, often imposing requirements that cable provide two-way cable or burglar- and fire-alarm services. And if an incumbent cable company didn't comply, city officials threatened to deny franchise renewals. Cable operators already faced a perplexing maze of state and local laws that dictated subscriber rates, system sizes, programming, and other issues as towns and cities sought greater oversight of the industry.

Cable companies battled head-to-head before city councils and aldermen, spending millions on lawyers, studies, and elaborate presentations to win them over. Full-page ads popped up in local newspapers where franchises were up for auction. In Dallas, considered a jewel because of its size (400,000 homes) and growth potential, six companies spent $500,000 each before the franchise was awarded. The Tribune Company won the Tampa, Florida, franchise by forking over $1.5 million for a trust fund for community projects—and $250,000 a year for the remainder of the franchise. Warner Amex, which promised 100 channels and city studios and ultimately won, helped the police apprehend a man trying to sell company executives information that would guarantee it the franchise.[15] In return for franchises, cities made ever more imperious demands. They demanded that a cable operator turn over a percentage of gross receipts, sometimes as high as 20 percent. Winning bidders paid for newly planted trees along city sidewalks and erected new municipal buildings. Continental Cablevision, which beat out seven other companies for Newton, Massachusetts, offered to build an annex to the town library for a media center. Of all the tactics used, though, the most popular and effective was *rent-a-citizen*. Cable operators offered local politicians lucrative investment opportunities in the cable franchise. In return, cable operators got favorable votes when the franchise issue came before the town council. In many cases, the bidding cable operators loaned the pols the initial investment money. When the cable company received approval, it either bought out the local partners or passed on the higher costs to customers.

As a result, politicians quickly discovered a quick way to get rich: extorting cable TV. Complaints of greed and corruption abounded. Many city fathers simply felt the way that New York City Mayor John Lindsay did when he said that cable franchises were like "urban oil wells beneath our city streets." Large cable operators routinely turned over anywhere from 5 to 25 percent of the stock in local subsidiaries when engaged in tough franchise competitions. In Milwaukee, a plum market of 250,000 homes, six different companies battled for the franchise. "There is no company that wouldn't pay $1 million for the piece of paper saying you have the franchise," said Franklyn Gimbel, a lawyer and investor in Cablevision, one of the applicants. "Spending $100,000 a vote would be a good deal."[16] How times had changed. Just a decade earlier, Irving Berlin Kahn had been thrown in jail for what was now a common and seemingly acceptable practice in certain locales.

When six cable companies came to Omaha looking to rent a citizen, one sent a letter to the owner of the local newspaper, the *Omaha Sun*. His name was Warren Buffett, better known in financial circles as the Oracle of Omaha. The letter wanted Buffett to get behind a particular cable bid because of "the ability of local investors to take the political temperature, make introductions and appointments on a timely basis, and lend their personal credibility to our formal business proposals . . ." Said Buffett: "I think it's a national scandal."[17]

He passed on the offer. Malone could not afford to compete, but neither was this a game he wanted to play. "Whether what's being done is illegal or not begs the issue," Malone said at the time.[18] "If you take your corporate jet and fly the entire city council to see one of your systems in California and you happen to stop in Las Vegas, I mean, is that bribery? I don't think it is; but on the other hand, I don't think it's proper, either."

Rather than coddling town officials to land a franchise, John Malone built an industry-wide reputation as a lethal force in franchise battles, willing to take on any foe and use almost any tactic to prevail. He was especially brutal when a local government threatened to refuse to renew a TCI license, which would have forced TCI to sell the cable system it had just built and bail out of that market. That threat was the only leverage local politicians had—yet it was so contradictory to everything John Malone stood for that it ensured he would fight it bitterly. He had invested TCI's money and built the infrastructure from scratch, and no one had the right to take it away. When Malone waged franchise battles, he seemed less intent on arguing the merits and more focused on making a show of fighting relentlessly and maiming the opposition. He wanted local pols and rival cable companies alike to get the message: Don't mess with TCI, or suffer the consequences.

This pugilistic approach came in spite of a basic truth: TCI simply didn't have enough money for basic upkeep of many of its cable systems, much less the capital to rebuild them into ever more advanced, state-of-the-art designs; sometimes service suffered as a result. Malone went to war with Boulder, Colorado, a small town about 20 miles northwest of the front door of TCI headquarters. The city began seeking competing cable TV bids to serve the city in 1973, and hostilities continued for nearly a decade. "For 13 years, TCI didn't add an inch of cable," claimed Richard Varnes, the city's director of media and programming.[19] Customers in certain sections of town waited years to get service, and calls for repairs were frequently, often indefinitely, put on hold. TCI's sins were repeated by nearly every cable operator in the country as the industry focused more on hanging wire than on customer service. Cable installers traipsed through tulip beds; repair personnel never showed. Complaints ended up on the steps of City Hall. More often than not, cable's image took a hit.

Eventually, a street fight broke out when the city of Boulder imposed a moratorium on the company's expansion, with an intent to open the franchise up to new bidders. Malone insisted on TCI's right to keep wiring the city and launched TCI trucks to claim the streets of Boulder, despite the city's order to stop. One afternoon, a city utility truck followed a few feet behind a TCI truck on a Boulder street. As the TCI pole climbers hung wire, Boulder public works employees pulled it down, coiling the wire neatly as they went. Ultimately, police arrested the construction crews.[20] After a few hours, TCI called its trucks back to the office. Then TCI sued the city on antitrust and First Amendment grounds. The legal fighting eventually wound up in the U.S. Supreme Court. By 1982, Boulder, fearing that a protracted legal battle would postpone cabling the city for years, settled out of court, letting TCI stay in place. Malone promised to wire the rest of the town within two years. After the clash, Malone's archnemesis in Boulder, Richard

Varnes, couldn't help but have respect for Malone's stand. "I understand they built the industry out of the dirt. They were real cowboys, and they were resentful of the government intrusion in their business," he later told an interviewer.

Malone also went to war in Jefferson City, the state capital of Missouri, named after the third president and nestled in a hilly region on the south bank of the Missouri River. There, Malone stepped into the longest and most costly battle in TCI's history. What the Alamo was to Sam Houston, Jefferson City was for Malone. It was one thing to lose out in the bidding for a new franchise—TCI had no "skin in the game," as Malone liked to say. It was far more devastating to lose a franchise renewal when the company had already spent millions of dollars hanging wire. TCI had taken control of the cable TV system in Jeff City, as the locals called it, back in 1973, but its lean operation allowed precious few improvements. City attorney Allen Garner rated TCI "somewhere below poor." Complaints of fuzzy reception and long waits for service were common, and TCI hardly seemed eager to improve the service.[21] In the three and a half years since it had taken over, the city said the price of a monthly connection had risen 186 percent, to $21.45 a month. Fed up with shoddy service and climbing rates, the city invited bids from rival cable companies in 1981. Only two companies responded: Central Telecommunications, a group of local investors, and Teltran, a cable company serving nearby Columbia.

Malone saw the loss of the Jefferson City franchise as a potential deathblow. If the city took the franchise away, TCI would be forced to sell the cable wires snaking throughout Jeff City for dimes on the dollar to the only logical buyers—the new operator. Indeed, Malone had already been approached about a possible sale. Local politicians were in a position to award a franchise to competitors for cheap, and to Malone it was extortion. "They are looters, trying to steal the business," Malone thought, "and we are simply fighting to keep our franchise."[22] TCI could not afford to lose the cash flow from Jeff City. TCI wasn't yet on solid financial footing, and if it lost Jeff City it would probably violate its loan agreements. "We could lose everything," Malone thought. He stopped TCI from entering the bidding on the grounds that TCI had a First Amendment right to continue providing cable TV service and that the city, as a result, had no right to award an exclusive franchise to another company. On March 1, 1981, TCI fired the first salvo, suing the city in federal court.

"I want to make one thing perfectly clear," a TCI lawyer told the city official responsible for the transfer of TCI's franchise. "And I am authorized to say this—nothing is for sale. We're not going to sell one bolt, nothing. We would rather have it rot on the pole." [23]

Each day, TCI created a new tactic to turn up the pressure. TCI started running ads in the local newspaper, saying that cable service would end unless TCI was allowed to serve the city. The company withheld franchise fees of more than $60,000. Then, in the summer of 1981, at the cable industry's big convention in Los Angles, Paul Alden, TCI's national director of franchising, spotted Elmer Smalling, the consultant to the city of Jefferson City. TCI's Alden walked over, according to Smalling, and said: "Go ahead and keep your seat. You are not going to like what I have to say, anyway."

The bully continued: "We are going to discredit you every chance we get. We had you checked out by a Dallas agency all the way back to CBS. We know where you live, where your office is, and who you owe money to. We are having your house watched and we are going to use this information to destroy you. You made a big mistake messing with TCI . . . We are the largest cable company around. We are going to see that you are ruined professionally." [24] Alden also threatened Teltran, the other company, with trouble in Columbia, Missouri, where it operated a cable system. Teltran dropped out of the contest for the Jefferson City franchise in the fall of 1981, citing the "distasteful environment" in the city. When word of Alden's threats got out, Malone fired him. TCI publicly stated that it had neither authorized nor condoned the man's behavior, and Malone labeled Alden a "loose cannon" and "amoral." "He could tell you a lie and believe it was true himself," Malone said later. Malone wouldn't admit the truth: Even if he hadn't personally authorized Alden's moblike tactics, they were in line with his own two-fisted, must-prevail ethos.

TCI kept up the pressure. In April 1982, after a series of secret meetings between the Jeff City mayor and various TCI officials,

TCI was awarded the franchise. Immediately, Central Telecommunications, which had been awarded the franchise, sued, alleging a conspiracy to unreasonably restrain trade, as well as tortuous interference with a business deal. TCI counterclaimed. For the trial, TCI turned to the same lawyer who had helped Malone in Boulder, Harold Farrow, an aggressive attorney who argued the case on First Amendment grounds. Unfortunately, what Malone really needed this time was an antitrust lawyer. For starters, his temperament was lacking—Richard Varnes, the Boulder cable official, described him as "mean as a snake," and a federal judge in Kansas City criticized Farrow for childish antics during the trial, noting specifically his muttering, rolling of eyes, and "hurling of pens and legal pads at the counsel table with great force."

In arguing that the cable system was like a newspaper, TCI was in uncharted territory. While the courts had agreed that cable operators had some First Amendment rights, jurists had not agreed on how far those rights stretched. Farrow was defending other cable companies against similar allegations elsewhere. Suits alleging antitrust violations against cities were brought in Tucson, Arizona; Palo Alto, California; and Los Angeles.

The battlefield was slowly moving to Congress, where the industry was pushing legislation that would limit the cities' power to impose restraints on cable TV. The federal government would change the laws concerning franchise renewals to allow a more orderly transition, but not soon enough to help TCI in Jeff City. In the 1970s, the role of government in the cable industry's short existence was marked more by confusion and reversals of policy than any straight course. TCI ultimately lost. In rendering a decision, a federal judge had called TCI's threats "nothing short of commercial blackmail." The appeals court had condemned TCI's excessive and intimidating conduct, and found in favor of Jefferson City. Essentially, the court found that the First Amendment did not offer immunity from antitrust liability to members of the communications industry. The Supreme Court turned down TCI's final appeal and, in 1987, ordered it to pay $48 million in damages, which it did. Fortunately for TCI, the original trial and appeals process wore on for nearly six years, by which time the company's finances had improved considerably—and its wires in Jefferson City had expanded their reach.

Stephen J. Long, a Denver lawyer who opposed TCI in Jefferson City, believed TCI executives had shown their true colors in the fight: that they felt they could do anything they wanted to do, and that local politicians were a bunch of buffoons. "So they run over them," he told a reporter.[25]

Malone cared little for anyone's opinion of him. But if ruthlessness was what it took to make this company succeed, he thought to himself, so be it. Malone saw it this way: Sure, TCI lost the court battle, and sure, it probably paid somewhere in the neighborhood of $500 per subscriber in damages—a one-time tax-deductible charge. But that was just a cost of doing business; in the long run, the local system was probably worth $3,000 a subscriber.

TCI gained even more notoriety in Morganton, a town of about 14,000 in the western foothills of North Carolina. In December 1985, after complaints over lack of upgrades, the city council voted against renewing TCI's franchise and began studying ways to build a city-owned system. The next week, TCI sued in federal court for $35 million in damages on several charges, among them that its First Amendment rights were being violated and that the city was unlawfully creating a monopoly.

"They didn't get us out of Jeff City," Malone told Magness, "and if we don't stand up now, what message do we send to every other town with another guy that wants our business? We have no choice." It was a classic libertarian battle against collectivism, against the looters, and TCI had to protect its property rights. Anybody who thought they could just steal TCI's assets was going to pay a price. And TCI had to figure out in each case what that price was.

TCI lost the first round of the Morganton case in federal court, but kept it alive through appeals that lasted nearly seven years, wending its way to the steps of the U.S. Supreme Court. Malone was determined not to lose Morganton. When the Supreme Court refused to review the case, TCI backed a group called Citizens Opposed to City-Owned Cable to defeat the mayor, Mel Cohen, an outspoken TCI critic who had called TCI service "atrocious," as well as another incumbent who was a councilman in the upcoming election. The incumbents spent $1,000. TCI shelled out nearly $150,000. Cohen and the councilman won anyway. In another campaign, TCI pushed the group to gather enough signatures to bring a referendum on cable ownership to a vote; included was a clause to renew TCI's franchise. TCI claimed that all Morganton taxpayers would have to subsidize the city-built system, which was over budget, and that higher rates would follow. One full-page newspaper ad pictured two buzzards sitting on an electric line and read: "Morganton politicians are sitting high on the perch." [26] Opponents of TCI paid for ads showing that TCI's rates had soared 137 percent from 1985 to 1991.

On March 10, 1992, Morganton voted by a 2-to-1 margin in the city's favor. Most observers saw TCI as a company that had totally misjudged the politics of a small town—which was partially true. And while the battle cost TCI an estimated $2 million in legal fees and more than $300,000 in campaign costs, Malone had, in some ways, bested the enemy. During the six years the case was in litigation, TCI's revenue in Morganton approached $2 million a year. [27] Meanwhile, Morganton was bloodied because of the fight, spending close to $1 million in legal fees. "We never thought we would lose the case in court," Morganton City Attorney Steve Settlemeyer told the *Rocky Mountain News.* "But the time and money almost forced the city to fold." That was precisely the message Malone had intended to send. In the end, Morganton remained one of the few cities in the United States to run its own cable system, representing one of TCI's rare defeats. "I've never enjoyed winning anything more in my ten years as mayor," Mel Cohen, the mayor whom TCI tried to oust, said later in an interview. [28]

ʊʊʊ

During the tumult of the franchising wars, cable operators began calling on Washington to intervene, and Congress increasingly became more interested in the business of cable TV. The dismantling of rules and regulations had begun piecemeal in the late 1970s and continued over time. In 1978, for example, after years of paying inflated fees to telephone companies to hang wire on their poles, Congress granted the FCC power to control utility pole attachment fees. The election of Ronald Reagan in 1980 and his 1981 appointment of Mark Fowler, a free-market believer, as chairman of the FCC were welcome news to cable operators. It was abundantly clear by that point that consumers were absolutely starving for cable. Cable was in 19 percent of American homes by 1978, after almost 30 years of building; penetration doubled to 40 percent in just 6 more years. In 1978, there were only 8 cable networks; by 1984, the dial had expanded to accommodate 47. This stunning growth had happened during one of the worst recessions since World War II, and the cable industry began billing itself as a viable competitor to the broadcast networks.[29] The industry lobby, the National Cable Television Association, pushed vigorously for new federal laws to abolish local controls or, at the very least, release cable firms from local regulations they considered onerous and unfair. At the same time, the political lobby for municipalities, the National League of Cities, was seeking to legitimize and formalize local control over cable. Key players on both sides met to forge a compromise. By early 1984, after much bickering between the two sides, schisms within cable's ranks, and many false starts, the industry and city government agreed on an outline for new legislation governing cable TV.

It would prove a huge victory for cable. Congress passed the Cable Communications Policy Act of 1984, the first national legislation establishing government authority over cable TV, and the landmark law ushered in a new era of growth, opening up financial markets, programming ideas, and billions of dollars in untapped revenue to cable. Though many rose to cable's defense, Representative Tim Wirth, a Colorado Democrat, was credited with propelling the bill through Congress. The Cable Act took effect in 1986, and while it formalized a city's right to grant franchises and require public-access channels and other concessions from cable operators, it essentially shifted oversight from states and cities to the federal government. Cable operators won on major points. The law capped at 5 percent of revenues the so-called *franchise fees* that a city could charge an operator for the pleasure of doing business in a town and using public rights-of-way. It also favored incumbent cable operators heavily in franchise renewals: Unless a cable company had failed dismally to meet basic service requirements, renewal of the 10-year franchise was almost automatic. The law also kept the giant phone companies at bay, forbidding them from owning cable systems in their service areas.

The new law's greatest impact, however, was on cable rates: It effectively prohibited the federal and local regulation of cable rates for the first time in industry history. Rate increases allowed cable companies to stoke their cash flow, and that gave cable operators a source of cash to invest in new cable networks and made the cable business look all the more alluring to investors on Wall Street. It was an astonishing concession to the rapidly expanding industry. Cities had granted the cable systems protected monopoly status in exchange for a presumption that elected officials would hold sway over whether the monopoly could raise its rates. Now the feds had let cable remain a monopoly—but had freed it to raise prices at will, which cable did with unabashed alacrity. The predominant thinking among those who supported the bill was that the budding cable industry would grow, and rates would be kept in check by competition from the broadcast networks as well as other new systems for delivering TV, such as videotape rentals, microwave TV systems, and satellite-dish TV. This would have been nice, but it didn't happen that way: Microwave went nowhere, and direct-satellite technology wouldn't pose a real threat to cable for another decade.

Small wonder, then, that James Mooney, president of the cable industry's lobby, kept a framed copy of the 1984 act hanging on his office wall. Freed at last from the whims of local pols and rate regulations, the cable industry brightened overnight. Cable operators started to pour millions of dollars into upgrading their systems, replacing parts of the main trunk of the systems' tree-and-branch architecture with fiber optics—the high-speed, high-signal-quality pipes that would help form the backbone of a new national data highway.

The cable industry was in the midst of a boom era. From 1976 to 1987, the number of networks a cable operator could pull down from satellites shot from 4 to 76, and the number of cable systems more than doubled to 7,900. Revenue expanded more to almost $12 billion from a paltry $900 million.[30]

OVERGROWN MONSTER

As media titans in the East tried frantically to outbid each other to wire the big urban markets, John Malone avoided the fray and waited for them to tire themselves out. TCI steadily expanded by buying suburban and rural systems at cheap prices, waiting until the mid-1980s to venture into urban areas. Then he moved in with a vengeance, scooping up some of the best bargains the industry had to offer—in some cases, buying from the same media firms that had rushed into the business only a few years before. Malone relished the role of bargain hunter amid the spoils of bad deals made by his competitors. By 1981, eight years after taking control of the company for Bob Magness, Malone had built TCI into the nation's largest cable operator, putting together dozens of acquisitions, system swaps, and other deals with a cunning—and nimble—ability to avoid almost all taxes on any of the transactions that his rivals had to admire. In the ensuing years, Malone would play a central role in some of the largest deals the industry had ever seen, corralling his fractious cable colleagues into formidable alliances that ended up serving, first and foremost, his own purposes.

He made TCI's first urban move in a fairly large market: Pittsburgh. Warner Amex, the joint venture of Warner Communications and American Express, owned the cable system and had already invested $100 million in it, but to win the franchise, the company had promised too many bells and whistles in its much-touted QUBE interactive service. It was bleeding cash. Since TCI already owned some cable systems nearby, Malone approached Drew Lewis, chairman of Warner Amex Cable Communications, Incorporated, and the former Secretary of Transportation in the Reagan Administration, who had been brought in to turn the company around. Warner Amex let the system go for $93.4 million in cash in 1984. Malone then quickly introduced the city to TCI's unadorned, and on-the-cheap service. Instead of the elaborate cable system of the future that Warner Amex had promised, Malone renegotiated the franchise to offer a plain-vanilla system that would let it cut costs, yet continue to charge essentially the same rates as Warner Amex had charged. The Pittsburgh system was, after all, a monopoly like thousands of others. To run it, Malone tapped the Chinese-born John Sie, who had quickly risen up the chain at Jerrold, the equipment maker, and Showtime pay service. Sie convinced Pittsburgh officials that Warner's system, as promised, could and would never make money. Instead, TCI promised a system with 44 channels instead of 63; it ripped out the QUBE system and the expensive equipment supporting it and sold the interactive boxes back to Warner for $30 each. Malone cut payrolls by nearly half, closed the elaborate studios promised to local officials, and moved the extravagant downtown headquarters to a tire warehouse.[1] Pittsburgh was a steal for TCI because within two years, TCI had lowered debt and improved finances enough to begin paying back banks using the system's own improved cash flow.

Malone was simply reaping the remains of a system someone else had already paid for and could not operate profitably. Many big companies, Warner included, had overplayed their hands in the urban building binge. Within years of winning a franchise—in some cases, months—cable operators unwittingly gave cities a rude awakening: The operators were unable to afford to build the futuristic systems they had so elaborately outlined to local governments. Only a few years earlier, city dwellers had seemed to be ideal customers because of their income, choice, and sophistication. But, as

Trygve Myrhen, CEO of ATC, the cable subsidiary of Time Inc., told reporters in 1983, "We looked at the crazy demands of the cities, the political opportunism, and the eagerness of cable operators to win at almost any price, and decided there was no way to make the risks pay off."[2] Winning bidders choked on the costs of new systems or tried to renegotiate. Many of the disputes ended in lawsuits. "The cities and the cable companies share the blame for the mess they're in now," Paul Bortz, a Denver cable consultant, told the *Wall Street Journal* in 1983. "For the companies, the strategy was 'Let's get the franchise now and worry about the costs later.' For the cities, it was a process forced by politicians trying to look good— pork-barrel politics on a local level."[3]

In Dallas, Warner Amex's actual construction costs exceeded projections by more than $100 million. "We promised more than we should have, and charged less than we should have, and the bottom line is that we have a serious problem," Lewis told the *Wall Street Journal* in 1984. Lewis spun off 34 percent of the programming side of Warner Amex, including the successful MTV unit, as a separate public company. By 1984, Warner Amex would abandon the QUBE idea as financially unfeasible.

Malone's strategy was simple: Get bigger. After more than a decade at TCI, Malone could tally a cable system's budget with precision and predict costs and returns with uncanny accuracy. Because of that insight and because of the company's sheer size, TCI could now buy a cable company and begin to improve the performance dramatically within a few months. TCI could buy programming and equipment on the cheap, and it could get cheaper financing rates. Malone focused on long-term growth, eschewed dividends, and handsomely rewarded management. He enjoyed an extensive network of industry contacts, but when trolling for information with investment bankers and colleagues, he often found that he knew more than they did. Before long, Malone won back credibility for TCI with banks and lenders. Toronto Dominion offered to put up 100 percent of the financing for new purchases under certain conditions. In effect, TCI wasn't required to put up any money. Typically, in less than a year, TCI was able to pay Toronto Dominion back and refinance the deal under normal terms.

Despite phenomenal growth, though, TCI was still a lean company. A dozen senior executives ran the whole shebang. When they flew to New York, they slept in the company's spartan two-bedroom apartment, doubling up two to a room. The headquarters of TCI was a square, flat, one-story brown building on the outskirts of Denver. Faux-wood paneling lined the offices, which were furnished with brown-plaid chairs and couches that looked as if they had been lifted from the lobby of a Motel 6. A lone receptionist greeted visitors in a carpeted area, and a door opened to a wide linoleum-tiled hallway that ran just inside the outer rim of offices. This way, the heads of engineering, operations, and accounting were mere steps from one another, and they were all close to Malone's office. It was from here that Malone commanded his fleet of cable systems. Like Magness before him, Malone did not believe in memos. No paper passed from his desk to underlings. No executive sought to curry favor or engage in the sort of Kremlinesque politics that causes ulcers in so many midlevel executives. Communication was direct, effective, and efficient. Every Monday morning, Malone sat with his closest executives at a broad round table, much as Magness had done, to figure a way to squeeze more out of TCI's growing cable kingdom.

They shared secretaries, and an automated service answered the phone. "We don't believe in staff. Staff are people who second-guess people," Malone told an interviewer.[4] At negotiations to buy a cable system, when a team of lawyers and bankers showed up to represent the seller, Malone brought only a lawyer or two. Malone refused the conventional thinking that TCI needed to have a brand name or a Madison Avenue image. The company had no human resources department, and it wouldn't hire its first public relations person until the end of the 1980s. Along the way, the men who ran TCI cultivated a Wild West image that set them apart from the many bankers, investors, and legislators whom they courted and contended with. In the eyes of John Malone, they were nothing like the effete East Coasters who ran bigger cable companies. The TCI men were cable cowboys. Though the term was repeated in derision by the bankers and politicians who coined it, the TCI team wore the nickname like a badge. Magness liked the ring of the name so much he gave it to one of his champion Arabian stallions. Over time, Malone adapted to the lifestyle of the West and embraced the freedom of the wide-open spaces he saw when he looked out on the Rockies on his drive into work.

With his dark hair parted on the right, Malone cut a dashing figure in dark suits and wing-tip shoes, but he gradually lost the suits and ties, except for banker meetings and, like the rest of the guys around TCI, wore slacks, open-collar shirts, and occasionally the requisite cowboy boots. On occasion, taking the cowboy existence to extremes, Malone helped castrate calves on the ranch of his lieutenant, Larry Romrell.

Malone saw to it that his executives were richly rewarded, sometimes through a nifty little bit of self-dealing that gave them sweetheart terms on cable systems they bought from TCI and sold back to the company in a series of complex transactions. Sometimes this approach helped the company sidestep rules restricting how many systems it could own in a particular market. When TCI was ready to rebuy the properties, it paid the executives in company stock, at a very nice premium. One deal went even further, raising charges that Malone had taken part in blatant self-dealing. In 1992, the *Wall Street Journal* ran a front-page article alleging that Malone and Magness had sold to TCI several cable TV franchises in Utah that the company already owned. Beginning in 1979, the *Journal* article stated, Magness and Malone bought personally several franchises in Utah through their own private company as part of TCI's strategy, dodging the cross-ownership ban, the federal regulations that barred a company from owning TV stations and cable systems in the same market. TCI was linked to the Utah broadcast properties indirectly through George Hatch, the TCI director and Magness partner. The article suggested that the properties TCI bought back were already owned by TCI, which the company denied.

The story caused Bob Thomson, TCI's legislative liason, to make an unaccustomed visit to New York to yell at top *Journal* editors. "It's an outrage!" Thomson bellowed, as one of TCI's first true full-time public relations executives, Lela Cocoros, looked on. It hadn't seemed to bother Malone nearly as much, who saw nothing wrong with such deals and defended them as perfectly legal. He explained later that he and Magness had cut several deals that allowed executives to own cable systems privately, then eventually turn them over to TCI. For Malone, it was a way not only to compensate his top employees as the values grew but, more important, teach them. "Guys will understand a cable system a hell of a lot better if they have skin in the game," he said often. If TCI, either for regulatory or for financial reasons, couldn't own the systems, Malone didn't want to lose them to someone else.

In one deal, Magness, Malone, and other TCI executives bought 21 percent of a cable company called Liberty Cable, in exchange for cable TV properties valued at about $4 million. Two years later, TCI bought their stock for nearly $15 million worth of TCI shares; by 1987, the shares were worth $40 million—a 900 percent profit on the original investment.

Critics may have judged the deal as enriching insiders, but Malone paid little attention. Malone's attitude was: You don't like the way we reward management? Don't buy the stock. Malone made no effort to conceal his compensation schemes: Every deal involving TCI executives was displayed prominently in SEC filings.

TCI also instituted an employee stock purchase plan, and it made even the secretarial staff rich. For employees and shareholders alike, 1,000 TCI shares bought for just $875 in 1976 were worth $450,000 by the end of the 1980s, thanks to two spin-offs, 12 stock splits, and an ever-rising stock price. TCI made millionaires of many middle managers, and even a few secretaries, and the payoff built loyalty among employees. In the first 16 years of the company, not one key executive had left for another job. TCI's outside shareholders benefited as well. One of them was Richard Reiss, who, after meeting Malone for the first time in 1978, declared, "He is the smartest executive I have ever met." Reiss continued to invest in TCI for the next 20 years. Among his investments in TCI, he bought $10,000 in TCI stock in 1978 for a trust he established for his three-year-old daughter's college tuition. By 1997, the trust was worth more than $800,000—a compounded annual return of 26 percent.[5]

All the while, TCI had consistently failed to report any earnings. As the stock continued to climb, Malone pointed out that it was the accumulation of valuable assets over time, not the flow of reported after-tax earnings, that was making TCI shareholders so wealthy. "Forget about earnings. That's a priesthood of the accounting profession," he would preach, unrelentingly. "What you're really after is appreciating assets. You want to own as much of that asset as you can; then you want to finance it as efficiently as possible."[6] And above all else, make sure that the deals you do avoid as much in taxes as is legally possible. And then some.

Soon, the scale of Malone deals was 10, 20, 30 times larger than the acquisitions he was putting together only a few years earlier. Bigger scale, higher risk. But risk was a function of skill and knowledge. If you know you can exert control on the outcome, Malone reasoned, the risk is far less than those who jump into a deal with no expertise or facts.

Malone kept TCI's enormous debt at bay by slicing it up and assigning it to various interlinked subsidiaries with an eye toward insulating the parent company. He liked to use naval metaphors, such as *bulkheads,* to describe the setup. Large ships are designed to withstand battle damage because they have watertight bulkheads, separate and self-contained compartments that can be sealed off to prevent an injured vessel from capsizing. "You can take a torpedo in any one part" and still stay afloat, Malone liked to say. With each new system he bought, the debt was secured by a TCI subsidiary, not by the parent company. So if the cable system defaulted on a loan, only one subsidiary would be threatened. Another way Malone eased risk was to spread it out among an ever-broadening array of partners, thereby protecting TCI and enhancing its influence in the industry at the same time. Aside from the cable systems that were wholly owned by TCI, the company was a minority partner in more than 35 cable companies, all of which got the same price breaks in programming that TCI got—which amounted to as much as a 30 percent discount.

Malone also grew big through alliances with other noncable businesses. Among publishers, whose political clout help blunt the broadcasters' pull in Congress, TCI struck deals with Knight-Ridder Inc., E. W. Scripps, and Taft Broadcasting, among others.

The bigger the target was, the broader the partnership that Malone constructed. In 1985, he put together a massive $1.7 billion bid for the cable assets of Group W Cable, Incorporated, having TCI provide $560 million for its share of Group W's 630,000 new subscribers, while four other cable partners—(1) Time Inc.'s American Television & Communications Corporation, (2) Comcast Corporation, (3) Daniels & Associates, Incorporated, and (4) Century Communications Corporation—covered the rest. The deal, the largest of its kind in the industry, was a bargain for Malone's crew, which paid an average of $900 a subscriber; two years later the systems would be worth $2,000 per subscriber or more. Group W bailed out in part because, like many other companies new to Malone's game, it had a hard time reconciling the earnings model that investors usually preferred with the cable business's mantra of cash flow. Group W had bought the cable systems in 1980 for $646 million from TelePrompTer and invested another $800 million into upgrading the systems, yet they had lost $50 million in the past three years. Shareholders wanted earnings. "I didn't think it would be easy" to cure TelePrompTer, Group W Chairman Dan Ritchie told *Business Week* at the time. "But I didn't realize it would be as difficult as it was." Group W bailed out, at a profit of $20 million.

Other big players began to rethink their strategies. In 1985, American Express, disenchanted with cable, sold its half-interest in Warner Amex back to Warner for about $400 million. Warner's Steve Ross turned around and reaped $510 million by selling to Viacom a two-thirds interest in MTV Networks and a 19 percent stake in his pay-TV channels (Showtime and The Movie Channel) for $510 million. The same year, Dow Jones, publisher of the *Wall Street Journal,* sold back much of its interest in Continental Cablevision.

Malone and TCI, meanwhile, continued expanding, doing deals that emerged out of years of patient courtship. In 1986, Malone struck one of the biggest acquisitions in TCI's history, buying United Artists Communications, Incorporated, which served about 700,000 subscribers in 15 states. The company, no relation to the fabled United Artists studio in Hollywood, was formed by the private and proficient Naify brothers, Robert and Marshal Naify, Lebanese-born entrepreneurs, and Malone had been wooing them, tirelessly, since the early 1980s. TCI agreed to purchase nearly all of the United Artists' stock owned by the two Naifys (around 51 percent of United Artists' outstanding shares) for $150 million in cash and $270 million in notes convertible into TCI stock starting in 1988. TCI announced that it would give other United Artists Communications shareholders a chance to exchange their stock for shares in TCI at the same rate paid to the Naify family. That would bring the value of the deal, including $530 million in debt, to about $1.3 billion.

For just $150 million down, Malone won what many would deem a bargain: control of the nation's largest theater chain operator, with 2,200 screens and, more important, a 750,000-subscriber cable system, one of the largest in the country. TCI would later sell United Artists' 1,100 movie theaters to a Merrill-Lynch-led investment group for $543 million in cash and assumed debt.

Then, Malone would merge United Artists Communications with another company in which TCI owned a controlling interest, United Cable Television Corporation, creating the country's third-largest cable company in a $2 billion stock swap. A few years later, TCI would gobble up that merged entity, called United Artists Entertainment.

Corporate raiders accelerated the turnover, realizing that cable stocks were priced lower than they should have been because of the antiquated emphasis on earnings. In 1986, their aggressiveness ended up presenting Malone with one of the biggest deals he had ever undertaken: a takeover of Heritage Communications, then the nation's 10th-largest cable company with about 1 million subscribers. Heritage was still run by James M. Hoak, Jr., the man who had played a key role in the 1972 deal that created two classes of stock for TCI and put control of the company squarely in Magness's hands. Hoak was a Yalie from Des Moines who had worked briefly as a legal assistant at the FCC in 1968, graduated from Stanford University's law school, and started a cable company at age 26. Heritage had built a strong operation of choice cable systems in Dallas; Philadelphia; San Jose, California; and elsewhere, relying on a loyal contingent of local investors and a heap of bank debt. Robert Bass, an oilman and corporate raider out of Fort Worth, Texas, had begun a *creeping tender offer,* quietly buying bite-size chunks of Heritage stock at market prices rather than swooping down and paying a premium for a single large, controlling stake. Before long, Bass had accumulated a 9 percent stake, and he vowed to buy more. A hostile takeover was imminent. In need of a white knight, Hoak called Malone, who flew immediately to meet Hoak in Des Moines. Malone made up his mind on the spot, and within an hour he shook hands with Hoak on a deal that would give Malone control of Hoak's company.

In January 1987, Malone agreed to pay $1.3 billion, or $32 a share, a $12 premium to the price of the stock at the time. Malone put up $400 million of equity, then borrowed the rest. Malone knew Hoak and his management team were the envy of other cable operators, and he structured the deal to give them a shot at the cable upside: In five years they would own an 18 percent stake in the operation of the cable systems they had sold. Hoak ended up making more money on his share in three and a half years than he had made over the first 17 years of building the company. Hoak appreciated the gesture so much that he later told associates: "Malone's the kind of guy you want to run through walls for."[7]

The rest of the industry bore witness to Malone as dealmaker, and his status as the cable business's godfather was secured. "Everybody owes something to John," J. Patrick "Rick" Michaels, founder of Communications Equity Associates in Tampa, Florida, put it later.[8] After less than two years of ownership of the Heritage systems, TCI was $80 million ahead on the deal.

By 1986, TCI was beginning to run the way Malone had wanted it to run—highly decentralized. He had cut the company into six separate operating divisions, each nearly autonomous, with its own accounting and engineering departments. "When you've got it running right, when you've got it decentralized, when you've got it structured properly, it's like flying the most powerful fighter jet in the world," he liked to say.[9] TCI wasn't as pure a cable company as Cox in Atlanta, Cablevision in New York, or Comcast in Philadelphia. Malone had dozens of different partnerships with other cable operators to own and operate systems, and TCI doubled as an investment vehicle, investing in an ever-expanding portfolio of cable channels. Malone viewed himself as an investor and shareholder in each of these enterprises. It was not unusual for TCI to make straight financial investments in operators he deemed shrewd. In 1987, a TCI spin-off, called Western TCI, merged with a cable operator called Marcus Communications, but Malone left the business alone under the able hands of its founder, Jeffery Marcus. Marcus would go away to build another cable empire of his own, but leaving the founder in charge would become a hallmark of Malone's management style. If you buy a property and find a manager motivated by ownership in the company, keep him or her in power and trust him or her implicitly.

From 1984 to 1987, Malone had spent nearly $3 billion for more than 150 cable companies, placing TCI wires into one out of nearly every five homes with cable in the country, a penetration that was twice that of its next-largest rival, Time Inc.'s American Television & Communications (ATC) Corporation. The following year, he set his sights on the country's fourth-largest cable company. In late 1988, TCI teamed up with Comcast Corporation to acquire Storer Communications and its 1.5 million cable subscribers from Kohlberg Kravis Roberts (KKR) for $1.5 billion, plus the assumption of $2.2 billion in debt. It was TCI's second attempt to buy Storer—Malone had been beaten out the first time by KKR, which pulled off a leveraged buyout of Storer in 1985. On one side of the table were Malone, TCI's longtime deal lawyer, Jerome Kern, and Comcast's Ralph Roberts and Julian Brodsky. On the other side were more than a dozen lawyers and advisers for Storer. And although Storer increased TCI's subscriber rolls by 20 percent, instantly, TCI didn't add a single person to the corporate headquarters staff. Almost overnight, the entire overhead structure of Storer, which was eating into its own revenue, disappeared.

As TCI and other cable companies wired more homes throughout the 1980s, Malone wanted to own more of the programming that would course down all those wires. He scoured the horizon for more cable networks in which to invest, and given the vast reach of his TCI cable systems, an offer from John Malone was difficult to refuse. He was by no means an impresario, but he knew the only way for cable to grow was to offer a broad and deep array of programming that could overcome the "hookers' lament" of American TV watchers—that people were reluctant to pay for television because they could get it free, from the ABC, NBC, and

CBS broadcast networks. Cable had to offer something more, and some new cable channels were coming into their own. Malone just had to own a piece of some of them; being left out of another way to create wealth ran counter to his being, and investing in them gave him another point of control.

Just three years after predictions of CNN's death, Ted Turner's all-news network was reaching 26 million cable homes. Disney debuted a pay channel for kids around the same time that the Playboy Channel launched one for adults. Lifetime, a channel for women, went on the air, followed by the Weather Channel and the Financial News Network. In 1986, C-Span II began live coverage of the U.S. Senate. In the eyes of Madison Avenue, cable was growing out of its amateur status. For the first time, cable snagged the rights to NFL games, when in 1987 ESPN landed a three-year, $150 million deal. CNN won cable's first Peabody Award in journalism the same year. And an HBO documentary, *Down and Out in America*, became the first cable program to win an Academy Award in 1987.

All of these new channels badly needed access to subscribers, and Malone controlled lines into an enticing 8 million homes, counting those that TCI owned through partners. In exchange for getting on TCI systems, TCI drove a tough bargain. He demanded that cable networks either allow TCI to invest in them directly, or they had to give TCI deep discounts on price since TCI bought in bulk. In return for most-favored-nation-status on price, TCI gave any programmer immediate access to nearly one-fifth of all U.S. subscribers in a single stroke. Those who dared to test TCI's resolve usually came around to Malone's way of thinking. Those who crossed him often came to regret it, for Malone retaliated swiftly.

ひひひ

As cable channels grew stronger, they began demanding a piece of cable systems' subscriber revenue by charging monthly fees of pennies per household for their programming, thus adding a second revenue stream to their first one, advertising. Malone acknowledged that programmers would have to be paid if cable expected to flourish as a business, but there was a limit to how much, and he could always shut them off from reaching nearly one-fifth of all cable viewers in America. One day in the summer of 1984, Malone received a letter from ESPN, alerting TCI that ESPN would start charging money for its service—25 cents per subscriber the first year, and 30 cents a subscriber the second year. Malone fumed. He knew what was going on—ESPN had just been acquired by ABC, which was putting the squeeze on cable operators as it searched for every return it could get to make the acquisition pay off. So Malone retaliated. ABC Chairman Fred Pierce was sitting in the stands at the 1984 Olympic Games when he received a message from Herb Granath, who oversaw ABC's cable business. Granath had received a letter from Malone, who had written that TCI would "shut off ABC's ESPN on every one of its systems at midnight" that night unless Malone heard from ABC "by the end of the day."[10] ABC called and bought some time, but later Malone sent ABC an ominous message: He announced a competing sports network called Sports Time, backed by one of the biggest names and some of the deepest pockets in sports advertising: Anheuser-Busch Company, which also owned the St. Louis Cardinals. ESPN, fearful of losing its hard grip on cable sports, backed down and signed a more favorable long-term contract with TCI; TCI and Anheuser-Busch abandoned the idea of a new channel.

When Malone looked back on it, he would argue the phantom Busch network wasn't just a bluff or a cudgel to strike back at ESPN, and he'd insist he dropped the effort simply because too few cable systems signed up to carry the new service. But his strategy with ESPN became a signature modus operandi: a firm conviction in his righteousness and a disarming—and alarming—lack of subtlety. "No one else stood up to them—I stood up to them," Malone told *Barron's* afterward. "Capital Cities had just bought ESPN and wanted us to pay for it. I thought I should warn people—you can't buy expensive properties and expect other people to pay for them."[11] And that is precisely the message he sent.

Malone never hesitated to use access to TCI's homes to extract the rates and conditions he wanted. In 1984, MTV informed cable operators that it would be raising the rates it charged for the network. "I Want My MTV" had become a mantra among teens, and the network was a bona fide hit for Viacom. Many systems took the hike, but Malone stood firm, politely pointing out that there were a lot of people who could spin records on TV for a lot less money. And so Malone was supportive when Ted Turner started talking about plans to start his own version of an MTV killer. Turner's new channel would not charge fees, unlike MTV, which charged around 15 cents per subscriber at the time. MTV backed off the rate increase and granted TCI a long-term discounted rate for carriage of MTV. The Turner channel folded within a month, but merely by launching it, Turner had created a stalking horse for cable operators to push back at MTV, and they could repay him with increased carriage of his other networks. It was not as if this was written down anywhere or even explicitly drawn out; it was just the way backscratching worked in the cable business.

And while Ted Turner clearly had been John Malone's ally in the MTV skirmish, Malone wasn't above putting the screws to Turner when it served TCI's purposes. In the fall of 1985, NBC was planning its own version of a 24-hour cable news network to compete with CNN, and top executives had flown to Denver to sign up TCI. Malone agreed to back the channel and offered to make an investment, and he notified Turner that he was looking at it to replace CNN on his hundreds of local cable systems; there was only so much room on the dial. "You put them in business and I'm gone," Ted Turner told Malone. Turner Broadcasting was already teetering on the brink of disaster because Turner had paid more than he could really afford—$1.5 billion in 1985—to acquire the MGM studio and its library of classic films. "You put them in business and I'm gone," he repeated. "I would have to sell out. I wouldn't just disappear; I would sell the company, because there's no way I can survive with MGM hanging over my head." Malone said he wanted to help, for a price; he agreed to withdraw his support from NBC—and thereby all but ensure the upstart venture's failure—once he had gotten Turner to agree to long-term agreements to carry CNN for lower rates than the rest of the industry had to pay.

By February 1986, NBC had folded its news channel. Later on, Malone maintained the matter was a straightforward act to strike a better price—which helped his customers and shareholders—and was not a manipulative plot to exploit Turner when he was vulnerable.

"Everyone accused us of using this to beat up on Ted, but that wasn't true," Malone argued later. The only reason he dropped the new NBC service, he said, was that "NBC wanted us to pay more than Turner." His critics were unconvinced, and Malone's reputation as a ruthless bully grew. When *Newsweek* asked him to explain himself in 1987, he put it this way: "Sure it's a threat" to flirt with a new channel at the expense of the incumbent, "but it's good business, too. If Firestone goes to GM with a 10% rise in price, GM calls Goodyear. I'd be indictable" to simply pay up when CNN or anyone else demanded a price increase.[12]

It was, of course, much more complicated than that; what drove John Malone, always, was getting the best deal, and part of his motivation in these disputes was power—which side had it, and how it was used. As he told a reporter years later: "We refuse to get raped by the programmers." His predilection for wielding his clout, visibly, created only more problems for TCI. In driving a hard bargain with Ted Turner over CNN, Malone also demanded that Turner make TNT, the new 24-hour network featuring classic movies, available exclusively to cable operators, not to newcomer rivals such as wireless and backyard satellite outfits. It seemed a small benefit, but it added ballast to the growing public debate over whether TCI was too powerful in its industry. The move made the nascent rivals seethe, and raised the eyebrows of legislators.

Malone tried to deflect the criticism with a common refrain of de facto monopolists, and it would be echoed years later by Bill Gates in the big Microsoft antitrust trial: Sure, we're big, but the industry is much, much bigger. Malone acknowledged that TCI could certainly give a new network a boost by investing in it, and, conversely, that not having TCI carry a network might reduce its chance of success. Yet he insisted that because the industry was so fragmented, "we are not big enough, nor will we ever be, to make or break" a new network.[13]

ᗺᗺᗺ

Inside the cable industry, the reality was that Malone could do that and more—and that he never hesitated to act when the opportune moment came. In his inner-world view, Malone was using this power for the good of the cable business; that TCI also benefited hand-somely was a consequent and happy corollary.

By the fall of 1986, Ted Turner was falling into trouble again. By most reckoning, he had paid $300 million too much for the MGM studio and its library of classic films such as *The Wizard of Oz* and *Citizen Kane,* and he was looking for cash to help set his balance sheet right. One night Turner called Malone at home and told him that Time Inc., a cable heavyweight given its ownership of HBO, had offered to buy 51 percent of CNN. "Ted, you can't do that," Malone told him. "That's the crown jewels." As he listened, Malone could hear the anguish and exhaustion in Turner's voice from fending off the wolves. Soon, Turner was in still deeper trouble, and in a pan-icked call to Malone, he quickly worked himself into a manic rant. Turner's stock had tanked, and if it dropped too low, the terms of his MGM deal (arranged by Mike Milken, the Drexel Burnham Lambert junk bond king) would require him to issue financier Kirk Kerkorian, who had sold him MGM, more shares to make up for their lower value. That would dangerously dilute Turner's control of his company. Another frantic call from Turner awoke Malone around 6 A.M. Malone, barely awake, could only listen as Turner yelled: "You've got to do something! You've got to do something! If you don't do something, it's going to be the KNN."

"What the hell's the KNN, Ted?"

"The Kerkorian News Network," Turner warned.[14]

Malone eased his anxious friend, but was worried himself about who might make a grab for Ted's portfolio of cable jewels. If any of the broadcast networks took over CNN, it would become an arm of cable's mortal enemy, and the balance of power would tip in the broadcasters' favor. Malone was even more concerned that Rupert Murdoch, the crafty Australian tycoon who was starting a fourth national broadcasting network, might come in and scoop up Turner's baby. The assets were critical: There was nothing like CNN or the TBS cable networks—no alternatives, no viable competitors. Turner's company looked wobbly. Malone decided to structure a rescue.

He started by signing up Viacom to jointly fund a restructuring of Turner's debt. However, in the middle of negotiations Viacom came under the control of a new owner, a Massachusetts theater owner named Sumner Redstone. Malone instantly liked the self-made billionaire, even after Redstone decided to back out of the Turner rescue completely. So Malone turned to his cable colleagues, calling a meeting in New York of a handful of the largest and most influential cable operators in the country, most of whom had started their own companies. He started in his trademark no-bullshit style: Given Turner's situation, it was imperative that they come together to preserve Turner as an independent programmer. "If anybody here is not on board, please leave now," Malone instructed. "We're not fucking around here. We've got to do this. If you're not seriously here to figure how you can put up real money, let's all go home."

No one left, and everyone put up real money: $560 million ponied up by 14 cable companies, including Daniels & Associates, Continental Cablevision, Warner, and Time Inc.'s ATC Corp., to buy one-third of Turner Broadcasting. The new cash not only valued Turner at $1.5 billion and wiped away any threat from Kerkorian, it also gave TNT enough money to bid on NFL football in 1988.[15] The meeting was a watershed event for Turner and the brash new cable company he had built from the billboard company he bought after his father's suicide. The deal made Turner a wealthy man and rescued him from certain catastrophe. When a reporter asked Turner a decade later about the intervention and how he viewed Malone, the volatile entrepreneur paused serenely in the middle of a signature rant, and said with rare sincerity: "I'd gladly give my life to save his."[16]

Not only had Malone saved Turner Broadcasting through the deal, he had accomplished something far greater. Ultimately drawing in 31 separate cable operators, Malone had strengthened the fragile bonds of a rogue bunch. Now, as in few other industries, they were joined at the hip and even more vertically integrated. They were a brotherhood and a family, and to each, Malone was the godfather.

Malone hadn't acted out of loyalty—he had acted out of self-interest, which turned out to be good for his shareholders, too. TCI would be handsomely rewarded for the Turner investment: nearly $6 billion in value at its peak 13 years later for an original investment of about $125 million.[17] By keeping Ted Turner in control, Malone ensured continuation of the long-term, on-the-cheap programming deals he had struck with Turner's company. And although the restructuring let Turner still hold 60 percent voting control, Malone and his cable compadres grabbed de facto operating control of Turner's company, imposing restrictions that severely limited how Turner could operate and what decisions he was allowed to make. For bailing out Turner, a truth that the swashbuckling entrepreneur came to resent—Malone demanded a big presence for the cable backers on the Turner board, who now had approval over any big expenses.

With Ted Turner propped up, Malone had gained influential input into one of the prized collections of cable channels at a time when the value of such channels was soaring. Once the domain of old network reruns and castoffs, cable channels were beginning to produce their own original programming. Lifetime, a network for women, would turn out 2,000 hours of original programming in 1988, compared with just 200 in 1983. Madison Avenue started to take note and give cable networks proper attention. The cable industry's ad revenues topped $1.1 billion in 1987, nearly triple just three years earlier. By then, Malone had made his first move into home shopping via television. In early 1986, out of nowhere he received a call from Irwin Jacobs, a corporate raider and financier who believed that the discount merchandiser he controlled, called COMB, had a future in TV. Malone knew nothing of Jacobs, except that he was a brash Wall Street dealmaker who had been accused of greenmail (i.e., looking for a payoff by threatening a takeover) more than once.

At the time, the dominant cable shopping channel was the Home Shopping Network, an independent company based in Florida and run by a man named Roy Speer. With an eye toward bringing competition to Speer—and lowering TCI's programming fees in the meantime—Malone promised Jacobs to launch COMB's new channel, CVN, on enough TCI systems to ensure a healthy head start. In return, he asked for a stake in the new network.

Malone took 14 percent and set out to buy even more, getting a seat on the board and naming one of his recent hires, Peter Barton, president of the company. Barton had joined TCI in 1982 after getting his master's degree in business administration from Harvard, which came after serving as a top aide to New York Governor Hugh Carey from 1977 to 1980. He was a piano-playing, professional freestyle skier who had once worked on an avalanche rescue team. Malone liked his intuitive intelligence and quick wit over his raw business knowledge. In 1986, the year he was assigned president of CVN, Barton made a bet with the CVN chairman Theodore Deikel for a new Rolls-Royce that he would sign up at least enough cable operators to give CVN a cable audience of 10 million subscribers by the following year—and he won.[18]

Malone continued to bulk up TCI's position in CVN, particularly after the October 19, 1987, stock market crash, and he eventually offered some of the biggest cable operators a cut in the deal. By 1988, in exchange for warrants, 32 cable operators owned half of the reorganized parent company, called CVN Companies, and the shopping channel was shown on 104 systems.

The more horses Malone bet on, the likelier his chances of winning. Though the Fashion Channel, a fashion shopping service in which TCI owned a small stake, would file for bankruptcy protection, others would win big. Around this time, Malone bought a slice of QVC Network, Incorporated, another home shopping network started by entrepreneur Joe Segel, an energetic entrepreneur whose first success was the Franklin Mint. Two years later, QVC, under Malone's watchful eye, bought control of CVN, also owned by TCI, and consolidated the second and third-largest TV shopping companies under the QVC name. Eventually, TCI would own 43 percent of QVC. In a few deft moves, Malone had maneuvered TCI into the electronic shopping business. But he wasn't the biggest—at least, not yet. The dominant service was Home Shopping Network, operated by Roy Speer, who would help spread Malone's reputation as a bully. Speer would tell a congressional subcommittee that TCI had directed its systems in many large cities to drop Home Shopping Network in favor of QVC, in which TCI owned a stake.

Speer had partnered with a man named Lowell "Bud" Paxson in 1978 to buy a troubled radio station in Clearwater, Florida. With the idea of blending two great American leisure pursuits—watching TV and shopping—the station started peddling electric can openers and other items left to it by an insolvent advertiser with a show called *Suncoast Bargaineers*. At first a hit on radio, it soon moved to local cable TV. As amateur as it seemed, the area's elderly retirees devoured it, and in 1985, it went national, beaming the Home Shopping Club to cable systems 24 hours a day. In May 1986, it went public, and the stock zoomed, making Speer, who claimed to be a descendant of a Key West pirate, a billionaire.

As TCI's financial might increased with its cash flow, Malone bought more programming and locked up more franchises. "We throw a harpoon at everything that goes by," Malone told *Newsweek* in mid-1987. By the end of the decade, Malone's exhaustive deal-making romp gave TCI a wide margin in its position as the largest cable TV operator in the country. Malone had boosted revenue 24-fold, increased subscribers to 8.5 million from 1.1 million, and given shareholders a 386 percent return for the 10-year period.[19] More than anyone else, John Malone was responsible for transforming TCI from a tiny firm that was teetering on bankruptcy into a media colossus, and he had done so not by focusing myopically on the next quarter's earnings and kowtowing to Wall Street; instead, he had done it by focusing on the long term and building asset value. TCI grew so big so fast that by 1988, the company generated $850 million in cash; though it had no earnings, it had more cash flow than ABC, CBS, and NBC combined.[20]

ᘔᘔᘔ

As cable TV spread its wire tendrils across America, shoddy service plagued the industry, and John Malone soon became Public Enemy Number One on this point. His critics painted him as a man obsessed over enriching his shareholders at the expense of serving his customers. But he hadn't mustered some of the most impressive profit margins in the business by coddling the subscriber base.

Rude installers, no-show repairmen, and busy signals were the norm for many cable companies, TCI included. It was like getting the Hell's Angels sent to your home. Malone spent as little money as possible upgrading his cable systems. The focus, he said to himself, should be kept on growing the company. But service soon became a problem even he could not ignore.

Horror stories filled the newspapers, and cable's infamous service record made great soundbite material for the politicians in Washington and in local markets. Suddenly, lawmakers furrowed their brows and began wondering whether the cable industry had grown too big, too powerful, too quickly. TCI no longer enjoyed the anonymity that enabled it to operate off the government's radar screen. Almost immediately after lightening up on cable with the 1984 Cable Act, politicians began mulling new ways to rein in the industry. Cable had been regulated, then it had been deregulated, and now the grandstanders in Washington were talking about reregulating.

Even before the 1984 Cable Act took effect, consumers and cities began howling that rate hikes had escalated. "They're rapidly becoming the newest generation of robber baron," Larry Munroe, president of Municon, Incorporated, a cable consultant to cities, charged in the press.[21] A report by the Commerce Department in July 1988 said that while the FCC had imposed limits on radio and television ownership, "cable by some measure has achieved co-equal status with television broadcasting. In some ways, however, it may wield greater power in the local market, with one firm typically controlling dozens of video channels and experiencing no direct competition.

The report warned that "ownership concentration within the cable industry has reached levels that warrant investigation and, perhaps, action from the FCC." Worse for Malone, the subtly scathing report zeroed in on TCI, whose market presence, the Commerce Department said, "had nearly doubled between 1986 and 1987." In 1986, TCI, as the largest cable operator, paid 90 cents a subscriber for HBO, the largest pay service, while a small cable operation paid $5 a subscriber per month.[22] The same was true throughout the industry, though. According to the department, CNN cost 2 cents a subscriber for cable operators with more than 3 million subscribers, and 29 cents per subscriber from firms with fewer than 500,000 subscribers.

To Malone, however, the government had it backward. TCI's size and market dominance was evidence that his strategy of mass-scale economics was working. The discounts he extracted from cable channels, which the government now found to be troublesome even though they yielded ultimately lower prices for consumers, were in fact a virtue. Moreover, the United States dominated this burgeoning market because of such size and efficiency.

ᙀᙀᙀ

For John Malone, building TCI's scale and market power was killing his family life, something he had sworn he wouldn't let happen. More than anything, he hated how TCI had pulled him so far so often from Leslie and the kids. Whether it was to bank meetings in New York or to cities where TCI was trying to win yet another franchise, he detested it. Leslie found his prominence in the industry insufferable. She quickly came to understand that people were interested in her only to get to her husband. Once while attending a function at the kids' school, a broker sidled up to her and began to pitch them on a commodity, and if it wasn't this stranger with a stock, it was another with insurance or real estate. "It was just this horrible feeling like you can't really relax and trust the people around you 'cause they want something," Malone recalled later. "You know, when are we going to hear the pitch? When is it going to come? It was all manipulative, uncomfortable . . . she developed a very thick skin, but a great deal of hostility, and I couldn't blame her." [23] Conversely, his growing wealth had also distanced him from the relationships he once held treasured; he found it impossibly awkward, for example, to offer money to a boyhood friend he knew was on hard times.

Malone flew overnight to the Northeast whenever he possibly could. This way he could say goodnight to the kids, sleep on the plane, and start the morning in the town where he had to do business. When TCI bought a cable system in lush Honolulu, Hawaii, all the TCI executives stayed the weekend for a rare break from the number crunching and the arid, rocky environs of Colorado. Except for Malone—he took the red-eye back. But even when he arrived at his house in Denver, Malone never quite came home. His mind was a million miles away in a TCI deal, forcing Leslie to ask him the same question twice. Unable to shake his insatiable need to fix and tinker and build the company, he would often awake from a momentary trance of calculating bank debt or finalizing details of a sale to hear, "John, are you listening to me?"

Even more frustrating, his promises to Leslie were often broken not by the workload at TCI but by the unpredictability of air travel. "I will definitely make it home and go to the school play," Malone promised her one night. The following afternoon, as the students were walking out onstage in Denver, Malone was stuck in John F. Kennedy airport in New York, his flight cancelled.

When Malone later saw the comedy, *Trains, Planes, and Automobiles,* about the misadventures of two loser businessmen (played by Steve Martin and John Candy), he failed to see the humor in it. "It hit too close to the truth," he told a reporter. "I've been there. I've been out there in the middle of that rental car lot and with the wrong keys. I've been in New York with a fifty-dollar bill trying to get a cab on a Friday when it's raining, to get me to the airport, and you get there and the plane's delayed and you're soaking wet with sweat and rain and you're as miserable as can be and even though you're a member of the Red Carpet Club it's packed and you can't get in. I've been through all of that." He found his first relief from a longtime cable partner named Jeff Marcus, who agreed to lease TCI a 15-year-old Aerocommander, a loud, propeller-driven airplane in 1983. Malone called it the noisiest sardine can he had ever flown in, but it beat driving. In winter, a flight from New York to Denver took nearly seven hours.

The prop plane made travel a little less taxing, but it did nothing to mollify resentment at home. Malone was on the road so much he did not even have enough time to finish a fight with his wife, Leslie. One day, just as he was leaving the house for a meeting of TCI regional managers in New York, he and Leslie were neck-deep in another quarrel. As he glanced at the clock, he told her he had to go. "I'm speaking at a meeting of 200 people," he said.

"They mean more to you than I do?" she countered.

No, they didn't, but Malone had to be there anyway. He objected, apologized quickly, and made his way out of the house. On the way to the airport, he quietly consoled himself by believing these were the sacrifices that an aggressive career entails, and no matter how you try to manage around it, at the end of the day, there are frequent and painful conflicts. In the end it would prove to be worth it; it had to come out that way. At the crescendo of their occasional fights on the subject, Leslie would say, "I should have married a plumber. At least he would be home more."

Though he was spending no more time at home than when he started, Malone could at least argue to Leslie that he was building one hell of a nestegg. Malone's net worth was now approaching $50 million. By this time, thanks to the rising value of TCI stock, and his cash compensation topped $350,000 a year. But Malone wanted more. He still didn't feel secure about his stake in TCI; Magness still owned the lion's share of the company that John Malone had taken into dominance. Malone was still, by definition, an employee. He had seen the stocks go up and down. His stock was restricted and not vested. True to the Calvinist ethic imbued in him by his father in childhood, Malone lived in the same small Denver ranch house until 1979, when he moved into a bigger house closer to town, with a pool, pond, and indoor riding rink. By 1986, with Denver becoming overly developed, he moved farther south to a 90-acre spread. Malone preferred to see these as investments, not consumptive purchases for his own pleasure or material pursuits. He bought a set of three of Gary Cooper's old Mercedes, not so much because they had belonged to the star, but more because they were a good deal at the price he got them. In 1982, he ordered a 59-foot-long Hinckley Sou'Wester sailboat, which he used as much for business as pleasure.

One day in 1984, while sailing with Leslie up the Maine coast in his Hinckley, the *Leslie Ann,* Malone unknowingly set in motion what would become one of the most extravagant personal acquisitions of his life. Malone had bought the craft back in 1982, and to help pay for it and soak up some business tax benefits, he had come up with a scheme of chartering the boat out to customers for light sailing in the Caribbean. Malone also used it for business meetings and as a perk for his lieutenants; J. C. Sparkman was a frequent beneficiary. This generosity, of course, let Malone offset the sailboat's operating expenses. True to his investment ethos, when the boat was sold 10 years later, Malone took in $100,000 more than what he paid for it.

Malone was sailing the Hinckley near Boothbay Harbor with his crew, a comfortable Maine couple in their 30s, and learned they had the same wedding anniversary as his own, just two days away; so he gave them a week off and set off puttering around the bay on his own, with Leslie in tow. The Hinckley, while a large yacht, was still navigable by a single helmsman, and Malone followed his crew's advice and ended up at one of the prettiest spots he had ever seen. It was a large cove with seals and eagles, surrounded by hills wooded with great pine and oak. Entranced by the silent show of nature, they anchored in the basin. Malone boiled lobsters on the boat and toasted their 21 years of marriage with champagne. In the morning, persuaded by a hangover, the Malones decided to spend another day in the harbor, and Malone's business acumen took over. There must be land for sale around here, he thought, and months later, in mid-1984, Malone bought a 1904 Stanford White house on 80 acres near Boothbay. The Malones renovated the structure, and eventually bought more than 200 acres around it. His Hinckley crew, the Lowell couple, took on the job of overseeing the restoration.

Leslie decorated the house to Malone's tastes—understated design and highly functional, with a 180-degree view of a lovely, pristine bay that had virgin salt marshes and little boat traffic. Malone liked to say he smiled more in Maine, where he could break away for a boat ride, to feed ducks, or to work in his beloved apple orchard. Leslie was inclined to ride her horses or paint in her studio. The Boothbay area was reasonably secluded enough to give the Malones the sense of isolation they so intensely desired, yet close enough to stores to satisfy Leslie's shopping urges. Around that time, the boatyard came up for sale and Malone bought that, too. The Malones always had been Easterners at heart, his embrace of the cable cowboy culture notwithstanding, and they began retreating to Maine. Despite their rising profile, Malone and Magness still shunned the Denver social scene. Both men detested cocktail parties and political gatherings. Instead of power lunches with media moguls, Malone set a practice early on at TCI to drive the eight miles home for lunch. He and Leslie warmed to the rural lifestyle.

Malone had told Leslie that life would get better in Denver, but it had only gotten worse. He vowed to redouble his efforts to be at home more, though the demands on his time were hardly social. Malone didn't cultivate friendships in the cable industry nor did he play favorites. Not even Malone's closest business associates were invited over for dinner at the Malone house.

♘ ♘ ♘

Bob Magness, meanwhile, had begun to truly enjoy his wealth, which *Forbes* magazine estimated at $170 million on the Forbes list of the 400 richest Americans by 1988. He had begun to give in to the twin passions he shared with wife Betsy: art and horses. Betsy's health was failing, and she had confided to Bob that she could go on only a year or two longer. Together they bought scores of paintings of Western art, which often hung in galleries, allowing Magness a generous tax deduction. Over the years, Magness had gradually built up a world-class collection of Arabian horses like the one he had "freed" on a battlefield in World War II. As professional owners and breeders, a favorte pastime for Bob and Betsy was to scout new sires and trade information. In September 1985, they had flown to an international Arabian horse sale in Eastern Europe, where she and Bob were scouting for breeding stock for the growing stable of Arabians. On the way back to the United States, in the airport in Frankfurt, Germany, Betsy suffered a fatal stroke. She was 61. Their son, Kim, filled her place on the TCI board.

Betsy's death nearly killed Magness. He started drinking more frequently and his face reflected the void he felt inside. Malone could see it in his old friend's watery blue eyes. "He looks like shit," Malone thought. "He's lost his motivation." [24]

A few years later, Bob Magness got it back: He began dating a younger woman. During the mid-1980s, a blonde woman 20 years younger than Bob named Sharon Costello ran into Bob at a horse auction. The two had met on one of the Magness's many trips before Betsy died. Costello, who helped run a horse farm in Phoenix, enjoyed the older man's dry wit. As the months passed, Magness saw her more frequently. By December of 1986, Magness asked Costello to move in with him. Magness's sons, Gary and Kim, were naturally suspicious of a new woman in their father's life. Magness had a prenuptial agreement drawn up while they were living together, and it noted that "Sharon recognizes that Bob Magness is one of the wealthiest men in America." [25]

Sharon Costello loved Magness, and after awhile, you could see some sparkle come back, Malone thought. During that time, Magness would slip his head inside the office doorway that connected their offices and give him a signature gap-tooth smile. "John," he would tease, "I'm sleeping with a younger woman." Magness allowed few into his inner circle besides Malone and Romrell. Magness kept his life as private as his poker hand, and he felt the same way about TCI business affairs. "Keep your cards to yourself," he would mutter to Malone. Whenever Malone shared a tactic with a fellow cable operator, Magness would admonish, "Hell, we got it figured out, what are we sharing with these other guys for?"

Malone did, indeed, have everything figured out, business-wise at least. Only a decade earlier, TCI was a tiny company with a rural base of subscribers, shackled with costly, floating-rate debt and a liquidity problem. Between 1973 and 1989, Malone closed 482 deals, an average of one every two weeks.[26] TCI had become a national titan and the biggest cable operator in the United States. From the low point that TCI stock had hit in late 1974, a year after Malone joined the company, up to the summer of 1989, TCI shares had posted a stunning rise of 55,000 percent. Hell, the payoff actually ran to 91,000 percent, from a low of $1 to $913, if investors held on to every stock that TCI had spun off, then tracked Malone's own buy-and-sell decisions.[27]

Malone was developing a formidable reputation in the industry, and that was fine with him. In June of 1989, *Channels* magazine summed up the growing feeling among Malone's critics: "They view Malone as an arrogant, opportunistic, no-nonsense, deal obsessed, hard-ass of a man with little interest in or passion for television, save what money he can make from it. In their view, chicken coops or tires could as easily be the product he was selling." All of which was pretty much on target.

The line beneath the cover photo echoed a question ringing throughout the communications world: "Is John Malone's TCI an overgrown monster or simply the best managed portfolio of assets in the country?"

CABLE COSA NOSTRA

As the fearsome reputation of John Malone grew, he became the perfect whipping post for politicians who were outraged by the cable industry's bully-boy behavior, its record of service horror stories, and its newfound propensity for raising rates with impunity. Malone all but invited this unpleasant public relations problem, for he was unrepentant and unabashed about cable's clout. And so it was that Malone, uneasy in his best dark business suit and a crimson paisley tie, found himself sitting before a congressional committee on November 16, 1989, trying to tame his temper as he answered testy questions from a panel of tendentious legislators. He believed they amounted to a lynch mob, and he knew all too well who was leading them: Senator Al Gore, a politically ambitious campaigner from Tennessee.

To Malone, the outcry over lousy customer relations and price increases was merely a by-product of good business: Charge as much as you can for a product or service, and spend as little as you can get away with in providing it. What pissed him off was that Al Gore had made this fight personal; he had made it about John Malone. Stumping on the issue back home, Gore had singled out Malone as the Darth Vader of the industry, the king of the Cable Cosa

Nostra. Malone rarely hid his contempt for the grandstanders in the nation's capital. "I'd rather cut off my leg than go to Washington. I have no respect for politicians, and I'm very poor at suppressing that," he once told the *New York Times*.[1] But he held his punches when it came to Gore's ad hominem campaign. As he later said, "You can't win a pissing contest with a skunk, so there's no point in getting involved in that kind of rhetoric."[2]

Gore had introduced a wide-ranging bill to reregulate the cable industry, one of a dozen newly filed bills aiming to rein in the runaway industry. When his turn came to speak, it was as if a bulldog had snapped its leash. He recounted a litany of cable rate increases in his home state in the past three years: up 71 percent in Memphis, 99 percent in Crossville, 113 percent in Nashville, 115 percent in Chattanooga, 116 percent in Knoxville. Malone breathed an inaudible sigh of relief—none of the systems were his. That didn't spare him the wrath of the senator from Tennessee. Gore looked out to the crowded hearing hall and turned up the volume. "Well, what's going on, Mr. Chairman, is that some people say, 'Well, that's just the marketplace at work; if they want to raise their rates 117 percent, that's just market economics,'" Gore said with a sanctimony that would become familiar to all of America a few years later. "Well, it's a monopoly! And the federal government has come in and told the local governments which grant the monopoly franchise, 'Hands off! Let them fleece the consumers as much as they possibly can.'"[3]

Then, in ominous tones, Gore touched on the cable industry's vertical integration, its ownership of both cable systems and programming, and how it had reached staggering proportions. He stared at Malone, whose TCI owned stakes in 33 different cable channels, and declared war. "TCI for one—we'll hear from its CEO today—is obviously hell-bent toward total domination of the market as it buys up not only more and more cable systems, but more and more major programming services, and even movie studios." Congress had fretted that the Super Bowl might one day be seen only on pay-per-view cable, but Gore suggested that his colleagues might have missed the point. "I think the real concern might be whether or not TCI will own the NFL outright!" The punchline, in the spirit of hyperbole, elicited chuckles from his colleagues.

Ever opportunistic, the congressmen had seized on shoddy service as an issue of dire importance—a populist problem in need of a government fix. It was, happily, a surefire platform for sound bites. By the time the politicians had framed the issue, cable TV seemed every bit as essential as in-house plumbing and electricity; it was a less momentous issue than, say, national security, but it certainly played well back home. In the eyes of Congress, cable TV had gone from a fledgling industry in the shadow of the Big Three broadcast networks to an arrogant gang of monopolistic robber barons determined to hike rates and skimp on service. All of this was especially galling to the elected servants, who only five years earlier had handed cable a gift, freeing the industry of burdensome local rate regulation in the Cable Communications Policy Act of 1984. Since the law took effect, basic cable rates had risen 43 percent, and complaints of rude, neglectful, and incompetent service had proliferated. In Denver, where TCI was a partner in the local cable monopoly, the rate for basic service had increased sevenfold by some estimates. "We can't close our ears to the shouts from our constituents," said Senator John Danforth a week before the big hearing. Danforth, a cosponsor with Gore on the leading bill to crack down on cable, was a Republican from Missouri, home of the infamous franchise fight that Malone had waged in Jefferson City.[4]

When Malone finally spoke, he clearly felt uneasy. His conversation was measured and his tone rarely changed pitch. "It's mornings like this that I wish I'd studied public speaking rather than thermodynamics in school," he began, trying out a thin grin. The line, clearly meant to get a laugh, earned him uncomfortable silence as the panel members shifted in their seats and stared at him with blank faces. Not even a polite titter. Malone's thick head of hair had gone almost completely gray now, a fitting tribute to his status in an industry built on worries. He had sacrificed much in the past 15 years to make TCI into the dominant power it now was. TCI reached 8 million subscribers nationwide, and looking at what he had created, he experienced profound satisfaction. All of his desires and dreams derived from, and were validated by, his precise and scrupulous logic. While others saw happiness in the freedom from struggle or effort, Malone seemed to relish the fight; he found comfort in a world of efficacy. He would never sacrifice his convictions to the whims of others, no matter what the price.

Malone attempted to explain his business philosophy. "We have been in business 20 years as a public company," he began. "We have never paid a cash dividend to our shareholders. We have invested every dollar that we've been able to scrape together through equity sales or borrowing back in the cable business. Our cumulative retained earnings in that time has been zero. We have plowed everything back into growth and renewing our technology. Cable companies are cash alligators, capital alligators. Our technology is evolving so rapidly we can't wait the 15-year franchise renewal cycle. We have to constantly reinvest, expand channel capacity. . . ."

Cable companies had raised rates at every turn after winning new freedom in the Cable Act of 1984, but the cash flow, rather than producing windfall profits, was indeed plowed back into the business, fueling reinvestment in cable systems and new programming.[5] Cable had morphed into something much bigger and more profound than its quaint origins as an antenna service.

From 1984 to year-end 1992, the industry would spend more than $15 billion wiring up America's homes, and billions more on program development. This was the largest private construction project since World War II. Sure, the industry had raised rates, but look at what that had yielded: The number of new national cable networks had grown from 28 in 1980 to 74 by 1989, with dozens more regional channels.

Somehow, as expensive as cable was becoming, more people kept signing up for it. By the end of the decade, nearly 53 million households subscribed to cable—57 percent of TV homes—from just 17.6 million in 1980. In the early 1980s, cable channels grabbed less than 10 percent of the TV sets in use during the prime-time hours of 8 P.M. to 11 P.M. against the mighty broadcast networks; by 1991, cable's share was 24 percent and climbing.

But these were points of business, not politics, and the senators sat unfazed. Finally, Gore lit into TCI and began directly questioning Malone, pausing only to upbraid the industry for its abuses. Malone put on his most obstinate game face and stared directly at Gore. The exchange turned testy:

GORE: Do you think that your size and power have made your company arrogant and heavy-handed?

MALONE: I don't beat my wife, either. No, I honestly do not believe so. I think that the actions that we have taken have been almost entirely, well, they have been entirely, really, trying to serve as honest purchasing agents.

GORE: Have you ever threatened a locality?

MALONE: Well, I don't know what constitutes a threat. I think we have indicated that if we don't get renewed, under federal law, we cannot continue to serve.

GORE: Well, let me read court testimony of what I think constitutes a threat. One of the top people in your franchise renewal department, according to court testimony, threatened a consultant hired by Jefferson City, Missouri, saying, "We know where you live, where your house is, and who you owe money to. We are having your house watched. We are going to use this information to destroy you. You made a big mistake messing with TCI. *We* are the largest cable company around. *We* are going to see that you are ruined professionally." Are you familiar with that case?

MALONE: I lost a lot of sleep on that one, Senator.

GORE: You were fined $25 million in punitive damages.

MALONE: That's correct.

GORE (with rhetorical flourish): Is that an aberration?

MALONE: That's an aberration.

Malone felt the life drain out of him. He believed strongly in his convictions and in what TCI had done to protect its franchises. He had gone to the hearing to defend the industry and TCI and to explain why rates had risen, but he had not agreed to appear so he could stand up for a loose cannon in his ranks. He resented the line of questioning, and he considered Gore an ignoble opportunist.

What galled Malone most, however, was that the lawmakers had criticized him for being big, as if bigness was bad. Malone's view of his job was "to work on behalf of the public investors within reasonable constraints to maximize their wealth, period." If investors wanted to have social motives, that was up to them individually—

but Malone saw his work as a directive to succeed. "In our society frequently that leads you in the direction of trying to become as monopolistic as you can."[6]

Malone had had the misfortune to first come into Gore's gunsights in 1985 when the senator was fighting for the rights of owners of rural satellite dishes. At the time, Malone had spoken out all too bluntly against piracy by private satellite-dish owners, who pulled cable programming from the skies without paying cable companies for it—in much the same way as cable itself had begun by essentially pulling down the big broadcast networks' signals. Every new dish owner was a customer Malone's cable systems couldn't sign up, and he wanted his channels to begin scrambling their signals to make it more difficult for the satellite customers to get hold of their shows. Malone warned programmers that they should start to think about forfeiting TCI's business otherwise. "If they aren't going to charge others, they aren't going to charge us," Malone declared at the time.[7] The brash remark only added to his reputation for lethal tactics. Gore became a hero to his backwater constituents by championing the Satellite Home Viewer Act in 1988, which allowed owners of big dishes to receive the broadcast networks (for free) in blind areas that could not otherwise receive them by regular antenna.

Gore's blood feud with the cable industry escalated not because of TCI, though, but rather because of a much smaller company back in his home state called Multivision, run by a former ABC executive named Marty Pompadur who, like many in the 1980s, had overpaid for the company when he bought it. Hoping to recoup costs, Multivision immediately increased rates by as much as 40 percent, sparking a firestorm of complaints that swept to the backyard of Gore. Squeezing the issue for all it was worth politically, Gore upbraided Multivision in the press, then set his sights on the man he considered a kingpin in a business he regarded as a racket: John Malone.

From the moment at the hearing when Gore and Malone stared each other down, the senator became the only man for whom Malone reserved unalloyed animosity. Gore's comments fueled the image of Malone as a rapacious monopolist. Malone had ignored the court of public opinion, but at his own peril. Malone and his family began to get threats. At first, they were intermittent, the same kind received by any big CEO with thousands of shareholders to satisfy. But later, they became more frequent—some written, some by phone, most of them from crazies and cranks. One person threatened to burn his house down and kill his kids.

It unnerved him; it was a lousy way to live. And in Malone's mind, much of it was Al Gore's fault. Malone installed electric gates at his family's home outside Denver, and hired security guards. What he, and Magness for that matter, feared most, was a kidnapping. Probably the biggest effect on Malone was seeing the psychological effect on his grown children, especially his daughter, Tracy. Fearful her own daughter might be kidnapped by some wacko who had read of Malone's infamy in the business press, she would later move out of Denver altogether and resettle on the East Coast. The intrusions into his privacy were deeper and more frequent, too. The local paper ran a map of homes of summer people, complete with details of the location of Malone's house in Maine.

Publicly, Malone brushed aside Gore's sniping, and he even chuckled when a few Darth Vader masks showed up at TCI's office. But he took the words very personally, even if Gore had not meant them that way. For Malone, there would be no forgive and forget with Al Gore. Years later, when Gore reached out to his old nemesis to say he was sorry for the tenor of his remarks, Malone refused to accept the apology. "That's one you don't forget," he said to himself. "That was beyond the pale." Malone never cared about public opinion, but he did care a lot about the safety of his family and anything that worked to intrude on them.

After Malone's uncomfortable appearance before Congress, bills to punish cable passed in the House and the Senate, but then stalled. Ultimately, the Reagan administration opposed federal controls over cable. Congress was busy with the federal budget process at the time and cable lobbyists, led by James Mooney, president of the National Cable Television Association, worked to thwart any new legislation. TCI and the cable industry escaped new strictures in 1989, but it was clear to Malone that this fight was not over. The government was going to take action, if not against the cable industry, then against TCI alone—against him personally—and that would be even worse.

As it was, regulators just wouldn't leave him alone. Everywhere he looked, Malone felt, TCI was bumping against antitrust regulation. And yet, it was the efficiency of his scale economics that had replaced so many tiny cable operators to create a world-class business. Malone may have been ruthless in the sense that he sought to dominate markets, but a determination to succeed wasn't dishonesty. If anything, Malone saw wealth creation beyond the realm of capitalism and more as a moral achievement. He railed on about it in frustration, bluntly telling a trade magazine in the summer of 1989: "I have a passion for this country. But I think this country is blowing it. I think we have an atrociously shortsighted political system that prevents us from dealing with our real long-term problems. And we are going to end up as a second-class country within my lifetime because of it."[8]

At the federal level, regulators had scrutinized his plans to buy 50 percent of Viacom's pay-TV services, Showtime and The Movie Channel, for so long that he eventually withdrew the offer, in mid-1990. As he later complained to an interviewer: "The frustration of running TCI was that you knew that if the politics broke right for you, that you could build a hell of a business, but you also knew that the guys who had the politics were not your friends. At least my perception always was that this is not a technological issue; it really isn't even a financial issue because if the rules went your way, you'd be able to raise the money. This was a political issue. And to me the question had become: Was the cable industry going to be allowed to develop, or was it going to be kept locked away like the *Prisoner of Zenda,* and fed a little bit of gruel by the Broadcasting Industry?"[9]

Malone got no more measure of respect at the local level. In Gillette, Wyoming, town officials criticized TCI for exorbitant rate increases that accompanied new channel packages and price changes, and set new lower rates, claiming authority under FCC rules. Gillette said its cable subscribers now paid a 30 percent rate increase, to $21.80, for the same level of service before the changes. "I've had more calls on this than the snow plowing or the power outage," Harvey Krauss, the assistant city administrator in Gillette, Wyoming, told the local paper.[10] TCI sued and lost. The town's right to regulate TCI was upheld in U.S. District Court, and TCI, concerned about a precedent, settled by freezing the rates, doubling the number of channels, and paying $500,000 in refunds to customers, which amounted to just under $100 per TCI customer.[11]

UUU

Despite defeats like Gillette, Wyoming, Malone ignored his critics and brazenly bought still more cable systems and invested in even more channels. Malone had achieved the overpowering market size he had sought for so long, and still he wanted more.

In July of 1991, Malone began tightening his grip on Number 3, United Artists Entertainment Company. TCI already owned a 54 percent stake and paid $1 billion in TCI stock and cash for the remaining 46 percent. The sale consolidated Malone's hold on important markets like Baltimore, Maryland; Hartford, Connecticut; Tulsa, Oklahoma; and some Denver suburbs. It also yielded immediate savings. Both firms were based in Denver, and Malone immediately whacked $20 million a year in duplicate overhead.

Later that year, Malone gave the press yet another opportunity to cast him as the Intimidator. The Financial News Network (FNN) was slipping into bankruptcy and put its 51 percent stake in the Learning Channel, aimed at kids, which was up for sale. A few bidders emerged, including the Public Broadcasting System, the Lifetime cable channel, which was jointly owned by ABC and Viacom, and the Discovery Channel, which was partly owned by TCI. Lifetime ultimately offered $38.9 million and Discovery offered $30 million. The same day that Lifetime made an agreement in principle to buy Learning Channel, TCI gave written notice that it would stop carrying the channel on almost all of its cable systems, citing a slip in quality, according to a lawsuit filed by FNN's successor company, Data Broadcasting Corporation.

In the programming business, the break-even mark was considered to be 20 million cable subscribers, and the Learning Channel reached 21 million households. Some 3 million of those received the program through TCI-owned systems. The TCI decision to drop the channel not only prompted Lifetime to drop its $38 million offer but also put a chill on the prospects of bids from other possible suitors.

After Lifetime withdrew, TCI's 49-percent-owned Discovery Channel successfully reemerged with a $30 million offer for the Learning Channel. On June 29, 1992, Data Broadcasting sued TCI in federal court in Manhattan, alleging TCI used monopolistic tactics to interfere with the sale of the cable channel, seeking $26.5 million.

TCI denied interfering with the Lifetime deal. Malone claimed that the quality of the Learning Channel was slipping, and he was worried that FNN's financial problems would hurt the quality of Learning Channel's programming, and it didn't want to have to put up with some new owner coming in and charging higher rates.

A federal judge dismissed the Data Broadcasting suit, saying that it fell on technical grounds, but the move also sent a loud and clear message to Lifetime: Drop the bid or TCI will drop the channel. Deals like these made many in the cable industry skeptical of Malone, and in March 1991, Congress called him on the carpet again, in a Senate hearing investigating the market power of cable. Senators heard from Roy M. Speer, the chairman and chief executive officer of Home Shopping Network (HSN), Incorporated. HSN was the only major independent home shopping programmer unaffiliated with any cable operator, and its largest competitor was QVC, the booming TV shopping network partly owned by TCI and a handful of other cable firms.

Speer told the senators that he had tried in vain to get carriage from TCI. The nation's largest cable operator "systematically refuses to carry" the HSN cable channel or its broadcast affiliates, Speer testified.[12] He rattled off a list of cities where TCI refused or dropped HSN in favor of QVC, including Scottsdale, Arizona, and Corpus Christi, Texas, and whenever TCI acquired a cable system that carried HSN, Speer testified, the system was ordered to carry QVC over HSN. His testimony was recorded for a bill making its way through the Senate, to reregulate cable TV. Though the senators couldn't rectify Speer's grievances, they got an earful and would use his testimony in the mounting trove of evidence against the big cable monopolists. And yet, the following year, Speer would agree to partner with Malone, selling him a controlling stake in HSN for $60 million in cash and nearly $100 million in shares of Liberty, the programming arm of TCI.

Malone's infamy grew, yet as the criticism of him increased, he seemed to go out of his way to invite more. In the summer of 1991, TCI launched Encore, a pay-movie channel, with a marketing gimmick that put a new spin on "The Godfather" and the offer that couldn't be refused. To attract as wide an audience as possible, TCI gave away the service free to its subscribers for the first month. If subscribers did not want to receive the service, the burden was on them to inform TCI; otherwise, they would be billed for it from then on. The tactic, pioneered by book and record clubs, came to be known as *negative-option* billing, and it put TCI in harsh public light yet again. By putting the onus on consumers to explicitly reject the new channel, TCI hoped to sign up as much as 80 percent of TCI households for Encore.[13] Customers screamed when they received their bills, and after 10 state attorney generals sued, TCI retreated and dropped the practice around the country.

ՍՍՍ

It was clear to John Malone that the politicians in Washington were going to get even with cable and that they might single out TCI, in particular, for punishment. Its web of ownership interests in cable's leading channels was drawing the stern eye of regulators. By 1990, TCI owned stakes in CNN, Discovery, BET, the Family Channel, and the two largest shopping channels, QVC and HSN, among others. Nothing in the regulations prevented this. "You tell us what the rules are," Malone liked to say, "and we'll tell you what we will look like and how we are going to operate."[14] But Malone knew he was vulnerable. "The whole package of investments we've accumulated has gotten increasingly controversial, and we're being sensitive to the criticism of our horizontal and vertical integration," he told the *Wall Street Journal* in 1990.[15]

Based on talks with his attorneys as well as his cable colleagues, Malone suspected that government regulators would try to force him to split TCI in two—a *distribution company*, owning all of TCI's cable systems, and a *content company*, owning interests in cable channels. So Malone decided to do it for them. In early 1991, he set up plans to form a new company, Liberty Media, and planned to stock it with more than $600 million worth of assets from TCI, roughly half the value in cable systems and the other half in programming stakes, mostly minority interests in a gaggle of small and large channels. Malone hoped this move would preempt regulatory intrusion and deflect government scrutiny and possible antitrust action. After 20 years of fighting the Justice Department, the FTC, local regulators, and politicians, Malone wanted a company free from the restraints that hemmed in TCI. But it had to be done in a way that ensured continued control for Bob Magness and John Malone. And Malone wanted to own a far bigger stake than the one he had built up in TCI.

With TCI, Malone carried a great burden, knowing that if he screwed up, Magness, a man whom he loved as a father, could lose everything. "It was much harder to take a risk, make a judgment for someone else than it was to make a judgment for myself," he told an interviewer much later. With Liberty, he figured, "If Liberty does great, that's wonderful and I really enjoy it, but if it makes a mistake and screws up, and I lose half of my net worth, it's not going to change my lifestyle. It's me losing the money based upon my own bad decisions. That's much easier. You don't toss and turn at night as much when it's your own thing, than when you're the trusted first lieutenant of somebody else's family fortune and control." [16]

Moreover, for more than 15 years of running TCI, what drove Malone was a determination to create the biggest and most cash-efficient cable operator in the country, and the challenge of turning it around. Yet, for all this, his equity investment in the company he built into the biggest cable operator was puny: a tiny fraction of 1 percent in 1991.

Oddly, it was Ted Turner who forced Malone to sit up and take notice that he was lagging behind his peers in personal wealth. One day, ribbing his friend, Turner told Malone, "Gee, John, I'm getting rich and Bob's getting rich. And the only one that's not getting rich is you." [17] Turner's words stung more than Malone cared to admit. Though he made a decent salary, Malone had no big stock options or equity in TCI—less than 1 percent as late as 1990—and he had never asked for any. As he looked around in the cable industry, a lot of his contemporaries were accumulating vast wealth and he wasn't. And in his mind, he was working harder, contributing more.

And if Ted and the rest of the group had made this their bench-mark of success, then Malone would show how quickly he could set new records, much as he had done with the discus back at Hopkins. "Up until then I had been more focused on TCI. I was going to have the biggest and best company," Malone said later. "And it was mak-ing Bob very rich. And Bob wasn't reciprocating. And that was just Bob. He would never do anything unless you pushed him into a decision. That's what created Liberty. It was a little schemey. Very tax-efficient. And it worked."

The terms, largely structured by Malone himself, defied under-standing by mere mortals. Indeed, the structure of the deal—out-lined in a 345-page prospectus—was so Byzantine, it seemed almost designed to obfuscate. Through something called an *exchange offer,* TCI shareholders would get a special rights offering—one right to buy one Liberty share for every 200 shares of TCI they owned. It was a privilege, not an obligation, and each of these rights, in turn, allowed an investor to swap in 16 shares of TCI stock for a single share of Liberty Media.

It seemed like such a lopsided offer: 16 shares of TCI for just 1 share of Liberty? That valued Liberty at about $300 a share, for a total market value of more than $600 million by Malone's reckon-ing. How could that be, analysts asked, given that Liberty posted a loss on revenue of a mere $52 million for the pro forma nine months? No one on Wall Street expected the stock to trade up to $300 anytime soon. Liberty issued $625 million in preferred stock to parent TCI; the preferred represented more than half of the capitalization of Liberty. "If you're a TCI shareholder, pass on the swap," advised a columnist in *Forbes.* "If you're considering buying Liberty now that it is trading on a when-issued basis o-t-c [over the counter], don't chase it."[18]

Doubters found the whole idea of Liberty a dubious proposition: TCI's shareholders were being asked to pay up to acquire ownership of a company whose sole assets they already owned, before TCI spun the properties into Liberty. Moreover, it wasn't as if Liberty was an operating company with a strong stream of revenue; its port-folio consisted mostly of passive minority stakes in cable channels controlled by other companies.

At first, not even Magness wanted to participate. "First, it's cats and dogs, and they'll never understand or value it," he told Malone one day.[19]

"So much the better for shareholders who do understand it," Malone replied, "because the assets are undervalued at the moment." He told Magness he should invest as much as possible in the Liberty offering. "You ought to do it because it's a life raft," he told Magness. When Magness questioned why it would be spun out, Malone told him, "You don't lash the life raft to the deck of the ship to try and float the ship. The whole idea of a life raft is you set it afloat, and at least you've got something if you hit an iceberg."[20] Moreover, Liberty did not have a high-risk profile, whereas if TCI hit the iceberg, it could be a serious collapse, given its high debt leverage.

Malone transferred to Liberty roughly 15 percent of TCI's market value in assets he considered speculative. TCI hung on to Turner Broadcasting System and Discovery Communications. After its spin-off from TCI, which had $3.8 billion in sales in 1991, Liberty would have interests in a sliver of TCI cable systems representing about 650,000 subscribers and would own stakes in 26 other entities, including TCI's 50 percent of American Movie Classics, 17 percent of BET, 30 percent of QVC, 16 percent of the Family Channel, and interests in 14 regional sports networks. Malone, president of TCI, would become chairman of Liberty.

Though Magness eventually bought in, he never believed that Liberty would amount to much. He was wrong: Liberty would build more wealth for both men, and build it far more rapidly than TCI had ever managed to deliver. Most TCI shareholders refused to participate; for them, the deal seemed a little lopsided, and the explanation for it was all too complicated. It was safer to just sit this one out. Their timidity was key to Malone's effort to build a much bigger Liberty stake for himself, for under the terms he devised, the fewer shareholders who participated in the Liberty deal, the more equity each of them would hold in the new company.

While fewer than half of TCI's shareholders took part in the Liberty spin-off, Malone bet as heavily as he possibly could and commanded a disproportionately larger share of the equity being handed out: 20 percent of all Liberty shares and 40 percent voting control. Yet to get it, he would reduce his TCI holdings by more than one-third. Malone got 8.7 percent of Liberty shares in return, three times more than he would have been able to claim had all shareholders participated.

Malone paid $25.6 million to exercise the options he was given in lieu of salary, but to the chagrin of critics, he had put up only $100,000 in cash, which he got by selling 6,250 QVC shares back to Liberty. Malone gave the company a $25.5 million note for the rest of the stock. He later paid off part of the debt to Liberty in TCI stock. By the end of the maneuvers, Malone owned 20 percent of Liberty's class B supervoting stock, giving him roughly 40 percent of the shareholder votes at Liberty. Over the next two years he did more financial engineering, splitting Liberty's stock multiple times—first, 20 for 1, then 4 for 1, and then 2 for 1. His aim: to increase the number of shares available for use as currency in acquisitions and to lower the stock price he had initially, intentionally kept high so more individual investors could afford to buy in.

During the preceding 15 years, Malone had enjoyed a reputation of being one of the lowest-paid, best-performing chief executives in corporate America. No one would ever again consider him underpaid. In 1991, TCI paid him just $300,000; Liberty, nothing. Estimated value of Malone's compensation in stock options that year: $26 million.

In crafting the Liberty spin-off, Malone had kicked on the financial machinery inside his razor-focused mind, and structured a highly complex, all but incomprehensible deal aimed at meeting his main goals: to mollify regulators, to ensure TCI's continued growth, and to feather his own nest.

♘♘♘

Liberty would, over time, become Malone's muse, his path to true wealth and de facto control of TCI's most prized assets. When the company finally went public in 1991, Malone liked to tell folks, "It took off like a Saturn Five." Content—programming—was hot on Wall Street, and Liberty's price took off. In less than a year of trading, the shares more than tripled to $770 a share. By the summer of 1993, shares that initially sold for $256 apiece were worth $3,700 unadjusted for splits, sending Malone's investment of $42.1 million, most of it borrowed from Liberty on a personal note, climbing to more than $600 million. For John Malone, the beautiful part was that he had realized these gains without paying enormous income taxes, since it came from stock swaps, which were not taxable. The few TCI shareholders who went along with Malone in the Liberty deal, including longtime investor Gordon Crawford, reaped fabulous rewards. After that, no institutional investors would ignore Malone again. In Liberty, Malone finally felt the singular satisfaction he had preached but so rarely experienced—he had grabbed a big stake in the ownership of the company he was running.

Malone put Peter Barton, a wily deal maker with a bag full of jokes, in charge at Liberty, but named as its CFO Robert "Dob" Bennett, a quick-witted executive from the Bank of New York, to rein in Barton's creative mind. "I'll make you CEO as long as you don't guess at the numbers," Malone joked with him. "Dob will do the figuring."

But the Liberty spin-off failed in its second major objective: to divert regulators from TCI's trail. They continued to see it as a mere appendage of its dominant parent. TCI argued that the Liberty spin-off would simplify the balance sheet, giving investors more of a choice in betting on which part of the TCI empire held more promise—distribution or content. Malone insisted that Liberty was an entirely separate, independent company. He just happened to be its chairman, and Liberty's six-member board of directors just happened to include four TCI executives.

On Capitol Hill, the campaign to rein in cable's robber barons grew louder. Competitors joined the chorus of politicians and consumer groups. Broadcasters revived a decades-old complaint, lobbying Congress to require cable to begin paying significant fees for network programming, rather than the cheap copyright fees Congress had signed off on years earlier. In late summer 1991, newspaper ads warned, "If cable wins, consumers lose," pointing out that cable rates had risen 56 percent in four years, "and now the cable monopoly is threatening to raise your rates again." Telephone companies got in on the act, too. Nynex, the Baby Bell of New York, lobbied the FCC to order rate cuts of 28 percent rather than the 10 percent rollback others proposed.[21] Bell Atlantic and GTE, both of which would ultimately merge with Nynex, made similar filings.

By early 1991, a bill had been filed, cosponsored by Gore, among others, seeking to restore regulations on cable. "Cable television customers are being gouged, and current law tells the cable companies it's OK to be a thief," Gore said at the time. The bill required the FCC to establish *reasonable* costs for basic service, converter boxes, and remote controls. It also required cable companies to make their programming available to competitors at a reasonable cost and gave local TV stations the power to charge cable companies for rebroadcasting their signals. All of this meant a huge defeat for John Malone and the cable industry.

Again, Gore went after Malone, citing more stories of Darth Vader's—and the cable industry's—anticompetitive behavior. In a front-page story in Congress' hometown paper, the *Washington Post,* on January 23, 1992, Gore charged that TCI initially kept NBC's Consumer and Business News Channel (CNBC) off the air until it extracted a promise from NBC that the new service wouldn't cover general news like CNN, which TCI and other cable operators owned. CNBC started out as Tempo, a fledgling cable network that TCI had sold to NBC in 1988. What cable considered shrewd negotiating to protect an investment and keep programming diversified, Gore called "a shakedown by TCI." "The cable marketplace is choked to death because would-be competitors are prevented from being in the game," Gore told the paper. Led by NBC President Robert Wright and his cable honcho Tom Rogers, CNBC would later take over bankrupt Financial News Network and grow into an enormous profit center for the broadcaster.

A new law began to take shape, and its passage seemed imminent. Cable operators, trying a last-minute campaign, stuffed monthly bills with fliers proclaiming that reregulation "could raise, not lower, your monthly cable rate." Giving phone numbers of senators and congresspeople, the stuffer ended in bold letters: "**Now is your last chance to stop the Cable TV bill.**"

Many of the top leaders in the cable industry refused to cooperate in crafting the proposed law's language. Cable executives, instead, were looking for a veto from President Bush, who had pronounced the bill harmful, not helpful, to consumers. For Congress, the upside was too good to resist. FCC Chairman Reed Hundt predicted that the rate rollback called for by the proposed legislation would affect 90 percent of all cable systems and would result in $3 billion in savings to customers. Hundt called it "one of the greatest consumer savings in the history of American business regulation." The Consumer Federation of America predicted $6 billion in savings, while the cable industry's study showed revenue loss of $2 billion.

℧℧℧

President George Bush vetoed the bill, but Congress, controlled by the Democrats, promptly overrode it. The override, by a vote of 74 to 25 in the U.S. Senate and 308 to 114 in the House, ended Bush's extraordinary run of 35 successful vetoes.

Congresspeople found it easy to get behind the Cable Consumer Protection and Competition Act of 1992. It was a pro-consumer issue, and it allowed them to pacify other large constituents, such as the broadcast industry, which wanted the new payments; the direct broadcast satellite (DBS) industry, which wanted—and received—access to new programming; and local political bosses, who could hold sway over new franchise fees. The new law restored the power to control rates to local governments, directed cities to stop awarding monopoly franchises, and allowed broadcasters to demand payment from cable operators for retransmitting their signals. It was ideal timing for Malone's old enemy, Al Gore, who was now the running mate of Bill Clinton in their first bid for the White House. He made a show of leaving the campaign trail to vote on the override. "Big cable companies, with President Bush's permission, have raised rates faster than inflation, shut out competition, and answered to no one but themselves since the cable industry was deregulated [in 1984]," Gore said.[22]

℧℧℧

The 1992 Act was like a broadsword to the knees of the cable industry. In the months that followed, the FCC would order the most sweeping price restraints on the cable industry in nearly a decade, promising a rollback in rates estimated to be at least $1 billion. The industry would be required to spend another $1 billion compensating broadcast networks for their programming under the new law.[23] The 1992 Cable Act also put ownership limits and rate restrictions on cable operators, dealing a blow to the underlying value of their stocks. The first day the new law took effect, TCI shares dropped almost 10 percent in value, to the $20 range, and other cable stocks fell similarly. Most cable operators felt Congress had swung an ax when a paring knife was needed.

One major goal of the new legislation had been fulfilled: Cable had been smacked down, hard. The broader goal of benefiting consumers would prove to be far more elusive—indeed, on that score, the new cable law would turn out to be an unmitigated disaster. Congress gave the FCC only six months to set up a framework to aid localities in regulating 11,000 cable systems, each offering a different number of channels to varying numbers of subscribers. Worse, this monumental task would be undertaken by an FCC staff that had 216 fewer people than when the cable industry was deregulated in 1984. "This was a nightmare of complexity," Robert Pepper, the FCC's head of plans and policy at the time, told an interviewer.[24]

For Malone, passage of the damning new legislation underscored what he hated most about the cable business: regulation. Congress had no place regulating a fast-growing, consumer-driven industry whose products were MTV, TBS, and HBO—hardly considered necessities of life along lines of other regulated industries, such as electric utilities. Cable had simply offered a more attractive product, Malone would argue; after all, viewers were glued to CNN during the Gulf War in 1991, not the broadcast networks.

Bureaucrats, with all their studies and reviews, rarely anticipated or accounted for new technology and future advances. While cable certainly had monopolistic characteristics, it would better be kept in check, Malone believed, by aggressive antitrust oversight and encouragement of competition from new players such as the regional telephone companies. What really went wrong? Some blamed industry behavior, others blamed politics, and some blamed a certain CEO in Denver. Said one resentful owner of a small Midwestern cable system: "John Malone is single-handedly responsible for the 1992 Cable Act."[25]

For the better part of two decades, Malone had been beholden to the regulators' wishes. He had always viewed TCI's fortunes as precarious because of its high leverage; it was as if TCI was always only a couple of regulatory decisions away from serious problems. Despite the company's healthy stock price, Malone didn't put much faith in it. He always believed that disaster and ruin hung over his head, dangling by a single hair like the sword of Damocles.

As he put it years later to an interviewer: "Any kind of regulatory decision that went against us could be enormously damaging to our economics. And it could be imposed on us by politicians who don't understand or who don't give a shit. I always felt like we never had the political power in our industry to protect ourselves, that we were always small fish in a big pond, and that our survival was always a function of our being dragged along behind other big fish."

Yet, even as the government put a spotlight on the cable industry's behavior, Malone did not shrink from creating wealth at TCI. Instead, the scrutiny made him act with a blunt urgency and a disregard for appearances. Even now, the question for Malone was no longer, "Will the government let me do this?" It was more like, "Who's going to stop me?"

FIVE HUNDRED CHANNELS

The new rate restrictions set by the Cable Consumer Protection and Competition Act of 1992 promised to cripple the industry's cash flow. "Prospects for new business were slim to none, and Slim had just left town," as Bob Magness liked to say. John Malone's darkest fear was of what loomed on the horizon, quite literally: competition coming from DBS services such as DirecTV. On the ground, the local phone monopolies, the seven Baby Bells, were preparing to offer TV services in cable markets. On Wall Street, the cable industry was beginning to look like a leaky boat headed for rough seas.

That was the unknown backdrop on December 2, 1992, when John Malone held a press conference and single-handedly launched the start of the interactive age with an idea that quickly became both myth and cliché: 500 channels. Malone hailed that futuristic vision—a world of instant movies on demand, interactive shopping, online communications, and sports channels by the dozens—in a much anticipated press conference at one of the cable industry's largest annual gatherings, the Western Show.

Malone created the vision of a 500-channel universe out of thin air. He wanted to divert attention from cable's many problems, and his dramatic speech to reporters would put Washington on notice as it prepared to impose new rules: Don't mess with the information superhighway. The Western Show was the ideal venue for Malone's purposes. Tens of thousands of the cable industry faithful gathered for the show at the coliseum in Anaheim, California, every December, staging a modern bazaar for programmers, operators, and equipment suppliers.

In a large room away from the cacaphonous din of the coliseum floor, a small crowd gathered for a press conference with the notoriously press-shy Malone. Cable engineers had figured out a way to squeeze 10 channels into the space that is typically required for one: "digital compression," Malone called it, and promised to deliver it to the first million subscribers within a year. So on an average TCI cable system with 50 channels, viewers could theoretically expect some 500 channels with the new technology. Voilà, a catchphrase was born.

Reporters scribbled, "500 channels!!!" and Malone hyped. "This is just the beginning," he told the rapt audience. "This first round of products is the first of an evolution. We want to deliver a broad range of services adapted to the individual needs of the consumer." The technology of compression, which other cable operators would be free to use, opened the gates to a panoply of new entertainment and information options for cable subscribers. There might even be a channel devoted to favorite shows, such as *60 Minutes,* in case viewers missed the initial telecast, Malone said. Subscribers would navigate through this sea of choices with an interactive programming guide operated through a remote control. The next day, the headlines took a phrase from Malone's lips and placed it forever into the public lexicon. "Need more TV? TCI may offer 500 channels," read the *Wall Street Journal.* The *New York Times* trumpeted it on the front page: "A Cable Vision (or Nightmare): 500 Channels."

Malone made interactive TV the new clarion call for media and telecommunications companies. From that point on, the entire focus of the media and entertainment industry shifted to Malone's vision, and the major players raced in pursuit of Malone's promise to provide interactive digital services. Like a sorcerer, Malone described a futuristic world that the cable companies were uniquely qualified to build. Deeply troubled over cable's future, he began trying to build a better one. He talked for hours at a time with John Sie, a loyal technology officer who had written extensively on high-definition TV and digital compression technology. Malone found a passionate advocate of digital TV in Sie, a wickedly sharp man who had fled with his family during the Communist takeover of mainland China in 1949, and who would later run TCI's Encore movie service. Malone began to question how the technology could revolutionize the cable business immediately. "It set off some lightbulbs in me," he told someone later. Technology would save cable, Malone decided, as it had done so many times before.

The promise harked back to the days of QUBE, the futuristic cable system that cost Warner a fortune before it pulled the plug. And as reporters fired questions at Malone, he made sure to point out that the new technology gave cable companies a decided edge over telephone companies. Undaunted by the 1992 Cable Act, effectively a ball and chain on the industry, he was promising a new kind of television. Even as FCC staffers were writing the rules to reregulate cable, Malone had fired the starter pistol for the interactive age—and he was already proclaiming that cable and TCI were in the lead.

But were they, really? TCI's engineers hadn't ever actually done much of this, they just knew it was doable, having tinkered with compression in the lab. Digital compression was just coming into use; various cable companies had used it for the first step of transmission (e.g., from an MTV studio to a satellite to a TCI transmitting station). But TCI's move marked the first time anyone tried to push compression technology directly into viewers' homes. Central to this was a digital cable set-top box, a gadget that would translate the signals into images with computer chips and other decoding hardware; it didn't even exist yet. But in theory it was terrific. Old analog technology tended to pick up shadows or snow during transmission. Compressed digital signals moved through the cable lines in a sharp, clear signal using a fraction of the bandwidth. Using digital technology, engineers could convert video, audio, or data signals into strings of ones and zeroes, which could be compressed and transmitted or stored for later retrieval.

Soon after painting his grand vision, Malone pledged to put big money behind it: He announced that TCI would spend $2 billion to upgrade its cable systems with 7,000 miles of fiber-optic lines, a much cleaner pipe that allowed signals to pass more freely to deliver expanded services.[1] For all cable operators, it made business sense to begin replacing the main trunks of their systems with fiber optics. Since signals transmitted by optical fiber can be carried for significantly longer distances, fewer amplifiers were required. This resulted in fewer points of failure, lower maintenance costs, and better signal quality. Moreover, TCI would spend another $100 million constructing the National Digital Television Center in Littleton, Colorado, just south of Denver, with a complex of giant satellite dishes capable of receiving and sending compressed digital signals to TCI and other cable operators.

His rivals were riveted, and for the next couple of years, the cable industry spun interactive dreams, visions of videos ordered at a whim, electronic shopping, instant-response advertising, and paying bills with the click of a button. Entire global strategies would be overhauled, and multi-billion-dollar mergers attempted to get a piece of this newfangled era of content and multimedia. Forecasters predicted a convergence of cable operators, networks, studios, computer makers, and telephone companies commingling to produce a new media revolution.

In the months following Malone's call to arms, cable companies launched a battery of new experiments using digital technology. Time Warner, the second largest cable operator in the United States, launched its Full Service Network—a two-way electronic superhighway into the home—into 4,000 homes in Orlando, Florida. It would be the "keystone of Time Warner's vision and strategy," proclaimed Gerald Levin, the old HBO chief who had ascended to CEO of Time Warner. "Our step today clearly establishes cable's technology as the primary pathway for information and entertainment." Later, Viacom Inc., another in the top-five cable operators at the time, started testing an interactive system in Castro Valley, California. Others followed.

The biggest battlefield—and intersection of common interests—was lying between cable operators and the local telephone companies, particularly the seven regional Baby Bells. It was shaping up to be one of the great business gunfights of the twentieth century, yet cable and the telcos needed each other. While cable had a fatter pipe, phone companies could offer cable firms badly needed capital and world-class expertise in switched, two-way communications. The first big move by a Bell came just two weeks after Malone made his 500-channel pledge. Bell Atlantic Corporation took its first shot across the cable industry's bow, trumpeting plans to offer interactive cable TV service to a small New Jersey town called Toms River by leasing its lines to a Pennsylvania firm.[2] The company, Future Vision of America Corporation, promised 60 TV channels to 38,000 homes already served by Adelphia Communications, run by long-time cable operator John Rigas and his sons. Bell Atlantic said the Toms River TV system would become a showcase of futuristic video and telecom services by 1995. By outfitting its existing phone network with computer technology and more fiber-optic lines, the company said it aimed to transmit hundreds of channels of TV, as well as videophone calls and other interactive services. The phone companies argued that if the video dial tone proposal was approved, they could begin transmitting cable TV, as well as movies on demand, by 1995. The cable companies, in 66 percent of homes, also hoped to get into the phone business using their coaxial cable wire.

It was the first time a cable operator would go head-to-head against a phone company delivering TV service. Both cable and telephone companies wanted to deploy similar technology, but over separate sets of wires: cable companies over their thick coaxial cable lines and phone companies over their twisted-pair copper network that linked virtually every home and business in America.

A coaxial cable wire is actually two wires—one copper wire sheathed by another tube of braided copper or aluminum, separated by a thick layer of foam and protected by an outer layer of plastic. Instead of signals moving in the wire itself, as they do in a twisted pair, the signal literally dances between the center axis and the inside of the metal sheath. This simple electronic phenomenon gave cable operators the physical ability to send more sound, video, and data by order of magnitude—far more than the high-speed lines of phone companies.

Sure, the cable companies had a bigger pipe, but what scared Malone was the phone companies' deep pockets: Bell Atlantic was three times the size of TCI, the cable industry's largest player.

And sure enough, on the theory of "If you can't beat 'em, join 'em," the telcos began buying into cable on a massive scale. The alliance was a natural outgrowth of common business sense. Already, the phone companies sold cable service in Europe in combination with U.S. companies. TCI teamed up with U S West, the Denver-based Bell, and the largest cable operator there, TeleWest International. By February 1993, Southwestern Bell, another Baby Bell, made history by becoming the first telephone company to buy a cable company in the United States—$650 million for the Washington, D.C., area cable systems owned by Gus Hauser, the former Amex executive who ran QUBE years before. Because the systems were located outside the service region of Southwestern Bell, they were therefore legal under cross-ownership laws.

In May, U S West, Incorporated, another of the Baby Bells, made the biggest splash to date by investing $2.5 billion for a 25 percent stake in Time Warner's cable systems, the Warner Bros. movie studio, and its HBO cable channel. About $1 billion of U S West's cash would be used for the nationwide rollout of Time Warner's ballyhooed Full Service Network. The Baby Bell also bought an Atlanta cable system serving 446,000 customers from Wometco Corporation and Georgia Cable TV for $1.2 billion.

It was as if no single company wanted to be left without a partner in this new and uncertain age. By the end of the year, there would be more. Cox, the third-largest cable operator, and Southwestern Bell agreed to marry in a record $4.9 billion merger, building on a joint cable-telephone business in the United Kingdom. And BCE, a telecommunications powerhouse and the largest publicly held company in Canada, agreed to pay $400 million for a 30 percent stake in Jones Intercable, Incorporated.

Telephone companies weren't the only reason cable operators had for alarm. Another technology that had the danger of growing quickly was satellite-dish TV. Malone took precautions like any good monopolist: He launched his own satellite-dish operator, later called Primestar, and invited fellow cable operators (TCI, Time

Warner, Continental, Comcast, Cox, Newhouse, and Viacom) to become owners. The new service offered a satellite service in cable markets using three-foot dishes to pull in signals.

〜〜〜

Amid the frenzy of newly forged alliances, the FCC was still trying to work out the mess of regulation embedded in the Cable Act of 1992. On April 1, 1993, the FCC took its first swipe, freezing the rates on all tiers of cable as of September 1992 and ordering rate rollbacks of up to 10 percent by September 1993. The FCC's *Report and Order,* the document explaining the new law, was 521 typewritten pages, single-spaced. One round of filings to the FCC—176 parties filed comments—weighed more than 40 pounds.[3] Figuring out what a fair cable rate would be, based on conditions where there was a competing service, was difficult, given that most all cable systems were monopolies. The FCC's new rate formula was vexingly obtuse, built on complex and cascading logarithms. Companies with rates above the FCC benchmark could be forced to reduce them by as much as 10 percent. The FCC also had to set new rate caps for popular channels such as Lifetime, MTV, CNN, and USA, imposing a rigid set of per-channel price limits based on the number of channels a local system carried and the total number of subscribers. There were even rules governing how quickly phones were to be answered.

Yet subscribers didn't get much of a break. Many systems created new packaging schemes to avoid regulation. Most had been charging higher rates than the FCC benchmarks would allow for the most popular, expanded tiers of service. But their prices were far below the FCC limits for basic cable packages. So, the cable operators reduced charges for the costlier packages and recouped the money by raising basic cable rates to the cap now set by law. That shift defied a major goal of the new law: to safeguard the affordability of basic TV service for low-income people. Other cable companies began slicing channels out of the basic lineup and offering them à la carte, for about $1 each. As a result, customers who wanted the same service as before regulation were now paying *more.*

In New York City, Paragon Cable used the new law to start charging $3.32 a month for converters and 20 cents for the remote.[4]

Sometimes, cable operators simply substituted cheaper programming for existing networks, creating new casualties of the law. C-Span, the public affairs network, was dropped in more than 4 million homes by mid-1994 as cable companies restructured rates and moved channels. Unlike other cable networks, C-Span was funded by the cable industry and was commercial-free, denying cable operators any share in the local ads that they traditionally shared with other networks. In the public affairs networks' place went home shopping channels, which were generally cheaper and paid local operators a percentage of sales commissions.

Years later, the true price benefits of the 1992 Cable Act were questionable at best. The government caps on cable rates may have cut prices, but only by retarding service quality, argued Thomas Hazlett, director of the telecommunications policy program at the University of California, Davis, and a chief economist of the FCC from 1991 to 1992. Hazlett argued that "the cable operator, not only a transporter of video signals but an editor and supplier of programming, cannot be effectively monitored by a First Amendment–constrained government." The government could set rates, "but the cable operator always has the next move . . ."[5] Hazlett argued the better test of a healthy market was consumer acceptance. His studies showed that while cable subscriber growth and viewing surged during the years of *deregulation,* the figures were flat or down during the period of *reregulation.*

Equally unintended results arose from another aspect of the cable law—the new negotiations between cable operators and the broadcast networks over how much cable should have to pay for the broadcasters' programming. The retransmission consent provision let TV stations, for the first time, demand payment from cable operators to retransmit their signals. Instead of demanding payment, the TV stations could insist on carriage, for no charge, a requirement known as *must carry.* Invoking their First Amendment rights, cable companies filed suit to throw out the provision, arguing they were forced to reserve as much as one-third of their channel space for broadcast rivals. Years later, the Supreme Court would rule to uphold the new law.

It was extraordinary testament to the political clout of the broadcasters. But the broadcast bunch didn't use this new muscle to extort extra big bucks from Malone and his cable brethren; rather, the broadcasters used the law to gain a new foothold of their own in cable. New agreements were being hashed out all over the country between thousands of cable systems and hundreds of broadcast stations. TCI, for one, refused to pay cash to any of the big networks, but it indicated it might be willing to make room on its systems for a new cable channel a broadcaster might like to start. One of TCI's first deals was with the Fox network, owned by Rupert Murdoch's News Corporation, Ltd. He was eager to forgo carriage fees for Fox's TV stations in exchange for a slot on the cable dial, where he could start a new Fox cable network that would receive a separate fee from TCI cable systems. Despite the vision of limitless channels, the reality was that cable operators were already operating at nearly full capacity, so the slots were precious until upgrades came. ESPN2 became a national sensation overnight through the shrewd negotiations of Capital Cities/ABC, Incorporated, and partner Hearst Corporation, who lined up carriage to more than 20 million homes with various cable operators—before the new network had so much as aired its first sky-surfing event. General Electric Company's NBC unit, likewise, signed agreements to carry a new channel called America's Talking, which later morphed into MSNBC.

The cable industry's reaction to the new law required the kind of bureaucratic pissing around that drove Malone crazy. He became increasingly bitter with the federal government. Sure, he conceded, cable operators were abusing rate deregulation and there ought to have been some way to rein in the bad guys, but, by his estimation, the Cable Act of 1992 had become a political football. The government, Malone believed, was trying to make millions of consumers happy by lowering the price of cable TV—at the expense of the shareholders whose investment capital paid for building these systems. If they can do this to us, Malone believed, they can do it to other businesses, anywhere. "It's about the most un-American thing I've ever experienced," he told a reporter at the time.

Malone's antipathy infected all of TCI and, occasionally, got the company in trouble. Despite its best efforts to the contrary, the company drew a glaring spotlight on a testy corporate attitude regarding the new law. In the fall of 1993, an internal TCI memo made its way to the press. Barry Marshall, chief operating officer, had written a memo to all TCI cable system managers, state managers, and division vice presidents, outlining a plan to deal with the onerous regulations. Dated August 20, 1993, the memo read, in part, that TCI should start charging full price for "upgrades, downgrades, customer-caused service calls, VCR hookups, etc." By itemizing all services that the FCC allowed cable operators to charge for under the 1992 Cable Act, "we can recover almost half of what we're losing from rate adjustments." [6]

Unfortunately for Marshall and TCI, the memo was leaked to the national press. The memo itself wasn't that offensive—until readers saw the kicker, which reeked of a company trying either to evade the law or even profit in spite of it. "We have to have discipline," Marshall wrote. ". . . We cannot be dissuaded from the charges simply because customers object. It will take a while, but they'll get used to it . . . The best news of all is, we can blame it on reregulation and the government now. Let's take advantage of it!"

The same day the memo was made public, Rep. Ed Markey, the bulldog Massachusetts Democrat who led the fight to pass the 1992 Cable Act, fired off a press release: "This is an unusual glimpse into the inner workings of the cable giant TCI," said Rep. Markey, urging the FCC to investigate. A red-faced TCI issued a statement the next day: "The tone of one portion of the memo was regrettable and TCI has extended its apologies to the FCC."

When the FCC demanded an explanation, Malone penned a three-page memo to Chairman James Quello, who was responsible for implementing cable rate regulation under intense scrutiny by Congress, the press, and not leastly, cable operators. In the letter, Malone listed each of the things the company was doing to comply with the strict code of the Cable Act. But he felt compelled, even in a letter of apology, to remind the FCC chairman the toll of the new law on his company. He noted the cost of compliance was more than $5 million in the third quarter alone, and that more than 40 people had been devoted at the corporate level, full-time, to completing rate regulation forms. Malone predicted that rate regulation overall would reduce TCI's revenue and cash flow by about $150 million a year. [7]

He couldn't resist one last jab. In closing, he wrote: "The substance of the Marshall memorandum is clearly defensible. Before regulation, cable companies typically recovered some installation costs and other extraordinary items over time by rolling them into our monthly rates for service. The 1992 Act and your regulations no longer allow us to do that. Thus, we must recover those costs by pricing these services incrementally in compliance with formulas established by the commission." The following day, the FCC's Quello sent a cordial note to Malone. Surprisingly, he declared that FCC data, "though incomplete, indicate that TCI is doing a much better job in lowering rates" than many cable operators.

Still, the industry grew livid at the government for constricting the flow of their lifeblood. Malone and others wondered aloud why the government had called on cable operators to build the information superhighway at the same time the FCC was financially hogtying companies, restricting investment in the new technologies.

ひ ひ ひ

Early on, the area promising instant payoffs was clearly electronic shopping, and outlets sprang up everywhere, including new channels from Macy's, Fingerhut Company, and Time Warner/Spiegel. Malone stepped up his investments almost immediately. Five days after he made the 500-channel announcement in Anaheim, he made headlines again in Denver with a brash $150 million cash-and-stock bid for a controlling interest in HSN, the chief rival to QVC, in which Liberty Media held a sizable stake. HSN was still run by its founder, Roy Speer—the same Roy Speer who, just months earlier, had said such nasty things about John Malone in the chambers of the U.S. Senate.

Peter Barton, Malone's Liberty chief, arranged a meeting between Malone and Speer at the Western Show in Anaheim, hoping for rapprochement. "They got their apologies and mea culpas out of the way, and I'd say within 20 minutes they were joking with each other," Barton said later. "John understood exactly why Speer did what he did. It wasn't personal. Two days later, the deal was done." They closed it over a weekend in December 1992. Malone, meanwhile, also had just succeeded in taking control of HSN's arch rival, QVC, persuading its board to hand control to Liberty and Comcast, which together owned a 53 percent stake in QVC.

The two deals would give Liberty a firm grip on the small but growing cable home shopping market, but they also sparked new criticism of Malone and TCI. The Justice Department approved Liberty's offer only after careful scrutiny of the voting control for possible antitrust violations. Then Home Shopping Network shareholders sued to block Liberty's offer, calling it "grossly unfair." Later, when Liberty made a $640 million offer to buy out the rest of HSN's public shareholders, Liberty dropped it briefly after a series of setbacks at the company. For a while in 1993, a grand jury investigated allegations at HSN that insiders profited from covert relationships with HSN's vendors. HSN's shares plunged to as low as $5, and shareholders sued HSN, charging that company executives intentionally covered up financial improprieties.

As the industry grew, Malone gazed beyond the wires to focus on the real value: content. He wanted badly to invest in a major Hollywood studio, and for years he had tried to land Martin Davis, the irascible head of Paramount Communications, parent of the storied Paramount Pictures. So Malone found a way in through another Liberty ally—former Paramount Pictures Corporation Chairman and CEO, Barry Diller, who by December 1992 had become chief of QVC Networks. He had built Rupert Murdoch's Fox Broadcasting Network from scratch in the mid-1980s, serving as chairman and CEO of Fox from 1984 to 1992. But Diller shocked his showbiz friends by quitting as chairman of Fox, Incorporated, in February 1992 and spending months roaming the country in search of his next big career move. Amid the many callers wooing him was Comcast President Brian Roberts.

The Robertses (elder Ralph, the founder and chairman, and son Brian, president) were early backers of QVC and the quiet, intense entrepreneur who had founded the company, a man named Joe Segel. He had launched QVC after selling another of his start-ups, the Franklin Mint, which sold collectible plates, coins, and porcelain dolls. Intrigued, Diller toured QVC's headquarters in West Chester, Pennsylvania, and was stunned at the sheer volume of product that moved through QVC's elaborate computerized processing center. After several conversations with Malone and Roberts, Diller agreed to leave Tinseltown behind to go run QVC. "My eyes first focused, lit up, on the selling floor of QVC," Diller told the *Wall Street Journal* after his first tour of the place. "I was immediately struck by how this form of interactive relationship between a television screen and a customer was one of the best promises for what was possible."[8]

All the while, Brian Roberts explained to him the enormous capacity for merchandise, as well as the technology behind a daily deluge of tens of thousands of calls per hour—from a telephone or a set-top cable box, all with instantaneous market feedback and inventory control. He was further impressed by what he saw one fall morning on QVC when his friend, designer Diane von Furstenberg (who later became his wife), bought time on QVC. She sold $1.2 million in dresses and silk separates in less than two hours, with Diller watching in disbelief. Sold, he joined QVC in December 1992, and by September of the following year, he began preparing a takeover bid for Paramount.

Malone, on the QVC board, excused himself from discussing the matter because he had an eye on Paramount, too. For several years up until that very summer, Malone's conversations with Paramount chief Martin Davis about a merger continued; many of the scenarios revolved around Paramount and TCI's partly owned Turner Broadcasting. But Malone made clear the implicit message: He couldn't stop Diller from going after Davis, and such a move would have benefits for Liberty and TCI, giving them access to a major studio and a huge flow of programming.

Before Diller could pull the trigger, Paramount's Davis, hearing footsteps, announced that the company had agreed to a friendly $8.2 billion merger with Viacom. Diller wanted to counteroffer, and Malone gave him the help he needed: QVC topped the Viacom bid with a $10.1 billion bid for Paramount, and TCI kicked in $500 million in cash to help Diller get the deal done. The move sparked an all-out firefight with a legendary warrior, Sumner Redstone, the aggressive and tenacious CEO who controlled more than 70 percent of Viacom's stock. A lawyer who once broke Japanese military codes in World War II for U.S. military intelligence, Redstone, 70 at the time of the battle, had survived a Boston hotel fire in 1979 when he was 56 by hanging from a scorching window ledge with his burned bare hands. After more than 30 hours of surgery, he was told he wouldn't be able to walk again; 20 years later, that bleak prognosis made his spirited play on the tennis court that much sweeter.

Malone's backing suddenly made the QVC bid for Paramount a real contender. Redstone retaliated in September 1993 by filing a federal lawsuit against TCI, its first public broadside from another cable company. It would sting the hardest not because of the financial damages it sought, or even what it would do to the proposed merger, but because of personal nature of the suit. For Redstone, it was a John Malone hatchet job, and the opening words of his lawsuit made that clear:

> In the American cable industry, one man has, over the last several years, seized monopoly power. Using bully-boy tactics and strong-arming of competitors, suppliers, and customers, that man has inflicted antitrust injury on plaintiff Viacom and virtually every American consumer of cable services and technologies. That man is John C. Malone.
>
> Malone seeks to exert monopoly power over key stages of the delivery of cable programming to the American consumer: control over the creation of programming in studios; control over cable programming services; control over the mechanics of transmitting programming by satellite; and control over delivery of programming to the home. At every stage in this process, the consumer has paid and will continue to pay—a monopoly tax to John Malone.

That same month, executives of Paramount and Viacom, including Redstone and Davis, visited Capitol Hill and the FTC, passing out the complaint. The suit chronicled a litany of misdeeds throughout Malone's 20-year history with the company. The main accusation: TCI was illegally trying to buy Paramount through QVC, and Malone was using TCI's clout as the nation's largest cable operator to sabotage Viacom yet again. More than anything, the legal attack put a magnifying glass on TCI's size in the cable industry, as if size itself was the lone criterion of what was fair.

Among other things, the suit claimed that Malone refused to renew agreements to carry Viacom's Showtime in an effort to force a merger between TCI-controlled Encore Media, or to eliminate Showtime as an Encore competitor. The suit also said that Malone hoped to monopolize even more cable programming through TCI's new compressed digital authorization center in Denver by refusing to carry networks not transmitted through the center, and by demanding overly expensive fees from programmers that TCI did not control. "Through cross-stock ownership and interlocking directorates," the suit said, "the acquisition of control of Paramount by Malone would be the latest step in a systematic and broad-ranging conspiracy to monopolize the American cable industry in violation of the federal antitrust laws."

In the suit, Viacom asked the court to enjoin Malone from making the QVC bid for Paramount and sought unspecified treble damages for alleged past injury. While not naming Malone as a defendant, Viacom named QVC, Liberty Media Corp., TCI, and several other concerns with ties to Malone. The suit would stand for almost three years, until Malone and Redstone would settle it in a business deal.

Meanwhile, the two sides built a leviathan of alliances. Viacom lined up $1.2 billion from a Baby Bell (Nynex) and agreed to an $8.4 billion merger with the Blockbuster Video chain to get it to join the fight. At QVC, Diller was backed by Liberty, Comcast, and Cox Enterprises, S. I. Newhouse's Advance Publications, and eventually the regional telephone company BellSouth.

In the end, Viacom ultimately won the crazy contest for Paramount, and the lawsuit against Malone was dropped. Then, only days after John Malone agreed to support the QVC bid for Paramount, he suddenly pulled out, leaving Diller momentarily in the lurch. Malone, as self-interested as ever, was moving on to something far bigger. He was working on the biggest deal of his life.

NICE TRY, MY FRIEND

In July 1993, John Malone took a rare moment to stop obsessing with business and evaluate his future. He was onboard TCI's Canadair Challenger jet headed for Sun Valley, Idaho, having just left a board meeting of the National Cable Television Association in Lenox, Massachusetts. He was on the way to an annual retreat of media moguls and deal makers hosted by New York financier Herbert Allen. Aloft in the clouds, Malone felt a familiar pang of uneasiness as he weighed life at 52: Here he was, leaving his family in Maine, hemorrhaging inside over the Draconian regulation of the cable industry under a new law, and not enjoying any of it. What he really liked was Liberty. "And what I really don't enjoy, what I really hate, increasingly, is this politically based, regulatory-afflicted cable business," he told himself. Maybe he should just take Liberty and go run it, arranging an exit from Bob Magness and TCI.

Malone began to dissect the issue, and soon a list was forming in his head. He pulled out a yellow legal pad.[1] At the top he wrote, "John and Leslie's goals and objectives." Under that heading he made a list:

- To reduce stress
- To have more fun

- To ensure a safe and liquid personal investment portfolio
- To generate predictable income to support our lifestyle
- To reduce government, media, and legal exposure by taking myself out of the public eye
- To honor commitments and moral obligations to family and business associates

He then started a second list, reciting actions to reach those goals. The first would, in many ways, be the easiest, and the other tasks would fall into place after it:

- Retire from TCI.
- Reduce outside public board memberships from 11 to 4.
- Remain chairman and controlling shareholder in Liberty and stay as chairman of CableLabs (a research and development arm of the industry).
- Stay on the Turner board, because it was a big TCI investment and because the old cable gang was in it with him.
- Get the government off TCI's back.
- Generate predictable income by deferring TCI compensation payments with stock dividends, which should produce sufficient cash to maintain our lifestyle.
- Say nothing publicly about the contemplated change until Bob Magness was comfortable.

It was the briefest of blueprints that Malone wanted for himself and Leslie, but one he wanted desperately to build on. His son, Evan, was 23 years old, and his daughter, Tracy, was 26, and he wanted more time with them and with Leslie. What was true the day he met her was even truer now: He could talk to her about anything, and there were a million things about himself that he wanted only her to know. He loved her now like before. He studied the list and knew the conclusion was inevitable, emerging before him like the tiny, sparse lights of Sun Valley as the TCI jet neared its destination. He must sell TCI.

All of the old cowboys who had built the empire—J. C. Sparkman, Larry Romrell, Donne Fisher, and so many more, were not getting any younger, Malone thought. They were all making plans for retirement. "Maybe I should, too," he told himself. When a search committee looking for a new CEO at IBM approached Malone about the job, he responded that he'd had his fill of running big corporations. A few months later, IBM would pick Malone's old office mate at McKinsey, Louis Gerstner. Malone had known something about himself all along, that he was a deal maker, a strategist, a fund manager—anything but an operator. He loathed simply running a company, and now TCI was under what he saw as occupation of the federal government, shackled by an inordinate amount of federal regulation. He could not handle the duress of running a regulated monopoly for years to come.

TCI, like the cable industry, had matured. The heyday of double-digit subscriber growth was long gone, and with interactive TV and telephone services on the horizon, TCI would have to reinvent itself to compete against an onslaught of nimble and well-financed competitors. Malone didn't have the energy. And TCI certainly didn't have the money. Competitors were closing in. The FCC would soon free the seven Baby Bells, AT&T, and other telcos to send video over their telephone wires. Moreover, the cable industry could ill afford to start offering telephone service over cable lines, a technically feasible, though enormously expensive, proposition. Malone was afraid the Bells might crush cable with their colossal revenues and balance sheets. Pick any two of them and their combined cash flow handily exceeded that of the entire cable industry.

Yet leaving TCI would be difficult and complicated. He had created Liberty from a "handful of cats and dogs," as he liked to call it, and forged it into a meaningful company with some of the most powerful brands in cable. Liberty now accounted for the lion's share of Malone's personal worth, and he and Peter Barton, whose witty repartee Malone liked as much as his deal-making skills, were having a blast running it. But Malone felt he couldn't simply jump to Liberty and bail out on TCI's shareholders. What about his promises to them, particularly the institutional investors with huge stakes in TCI? And what about Bob?

ʊʊʊ

Malone had told the TCI board a year earlier that the company faced some difficult choices ahead, and he had hinted heavily that TCI might have to partner up with a telecom titan before too long. Malone had met several times with executives at AT&T, where he had begun his career 30 years earlier, and he thought it could be an ideal strategic partner, but government approval would be hard won and the AT&T brass seemed too timid to give it a try. So Malone set out on a methodical quest to acquaint himself with all the regional phone companies. To all, he posed a version of the same question: "Would you be interested in a strategic joint venture, or even perhaps, in buying TCI? "I'll just wave my ass around," Malone thought. "See what interest there is." [2]

Around the same time across the country, Raymond Smith, the chief executive of Bell Atlantic, was sweating over his company's future for similar reasons. One night after work, in the basement of his suburban Maryland home, he discussed his concerns with a small group of Bell Atlantic executives. They knew the local phone monopoly would soon come under attack from waves of newcomers. A cable company, with its fat pipes able to carry far more data, video, and voice, would make the best bride. After much discussion, Smith realized he didn't want to buy just a piece of a company, he wanted the whole thing. And he didn't want just any cable company, he wanted the biggest—TCI. Soon after, Smith called TCI and set up a meeting with John Malone.

They had first met a few years earlier and had shared the stage at industry conferences, debating the future of telecommunications. Both men shared a strikingly similar vision of the new wired world, and each knew the time was coming when only the biggest players offering the most services would dominate. Malone genuinely liked Smith, 55, and Smith liked Malone, a man three years his junior who clearly abhorred the public spotlight, a place Smith felt most at home.

Ray Smith had bumped up against the bureaucracy of the old AT&T empire for the better part of three decades, emerging as the chief executive of Bell Atlantic in 1989, five years after the breakup of AT&T. Ambitious and impatient for change, Smith did just about whatever it took to push his ideas through: going around bosses, firing underlings, and running roughshod over any naysayers. Once, as a plant manager in the 1960s, when he couldn't get AT&T to repair potholes in a parking lot that were damaging the axles on his trucks, he hired a contractor to repave the lot, then sent the bill to a vice president.

Smith grew up in Pittsburgh in the 1940s as the only child of a working-class family and, for a while, worked alongside his father at a steel mill. He put himself through Carnegie Mellon and upon graduation joined Bell of Pennsylvania; to get his MBA, he slogged through night classes at the University of Pennsylvania for 10 years. Smith chafed at the "Bellhead" attitude of endless committee meetings and deliberating things to death. At one point in his tenure atop Bell Atlantic, he told an interviewer: "I've been into this five years, and I'm still running into brick walls."[3]

Despite the ingrained bureaucracy, Smith had forged Bell Atlantic in his own image: fleeter than the other Bells and the most aggressive telephone operating company in the United States. Bell Atlantic was the first to fight in federal court the right to provide video services over a telephone network, filing a lawsuit in 1990 to challenge the 1984 Cable Act, which barred telephone companies from owning the video services they delivered. He won the case in 1993. By that time, Smith had already poured $200 million into an interactive navigation system called StarGazer, planning to hook up 8 million homes in six states by the year 2000.

The two men met in TCI's headquarters on June 16, 1993. By that time, TCI had moved into a new white building with black windows in the Denver Technology Center office park. Many first-time visitors noted that the King of Cable had no TV in his office—he claimed he wouldn't get anything done if he had one there. Two vast windows and a stone terrace opened up to the snow-peaked Rocky Mountains, a view that seemed to allow Malone the space to think. On his desk, which was a cold gray slab of granite, a computer gave real-time updates of his key investments, with TCI's symbol at the top. No photographs of his family or Polaroids of him shaking hands with Bill Gates or the president. Visitors were typically drawn to the one thing in the room that represented art: a six-foot-high 1850s replica of an America's Cup schooner that rested majestically on a marble table behind the granite desk. Sailing was freedom.

Malone and Smith talked broadly about the shifting sands of the telephone and cable TV industries. Initially, they talked about a partnership, but the discussion quickly turned to a merger. It was brazen, given the nationwide hue and cry that such a move would unleash. It was as if the two biggest bullies in the schoolyard, rather than fight it out for number one, were talking about teaming up to terrorize everyone else. TCI was a monopoly, pure and simple, and so was Bell Atlantic; together they would be a fearsome juggernaut. It was all but unthinkable—and not necessarily even workable. The two companies' cultures couldn't be more incompatible. TCI was balls out, high cash flow, no earnings, and certainly no dividends for shareholders—they would get rich only if the stock went up in price. Bell Atlantic was elbows in, obsessed with producing earnings, and wary of ever messing with the quarterly dividend it paid on its common shares.

What made TCI so attractive to Smith was that TCI and Liberty controlled both pipes and programming. At first, Malone balked at selling Liberty, hoping just to bail out of TCI. "Not without you and Liberty. If you'll put Liberty in, then I think we can do the deal, but I'm not going to buy TCI, stripped of its programming assets, and I don't want you off competing with me," Smith told him flatly. Hesitantly, Malone finally relented. "Okay, we'll put Liberty back into TCI and we'll merge the whole thing," Malone said.[4]

For the next several weeks, security was paramount while the two sides haggled. Malone and Smith met secretly in Denver, Washington, and New York. Even in private talks, they referred to Bell Atlantic only by the code name Shamrock, and to TCI as Ireland. If the deal leaked, either company's stock could go up and derail an agreement, so neither side discussed the deal on wireless phones, which could be intercepted; notes and memos referring to the deal were shredded at the end of each day. TCI's longtime corporate counsel, Jerome Kern, did most of the negotiation. Only a handful of people at TCI knew what was going on.

At one point, Malone and Smith hammered out details during a long cruise on Malone's yacht, the 65-foot-long *Ragtime*. The two men volleyed back and forth over a mind-numbing list of scenarios for an equitable price for TCI, how much Bell Atlantic shareholders' stake would be diluted by joining up with the TCI side, and whether regulators would conceivably allow it. During the trip, the anchor got hung on an underwater power cable near Boothbay, nearly wiping out power for a nearby island and, more important for the men, blowing their cover if the media got wind of it. They decided to drop the line, and sent a diver back to retrieve it. The crisis was avoided.

Any deal would require Magness' blessing. Now 69 and ready to cash in his chips, Magness found Smith to be a likable fellow at a dinner held in New York in July. The talks between Smith and Malone continued in earnest throughout the summer of 1993. Malone was still trying to pull a better price out for the combined TCI-Liberty package, but Smith drew a line beyond which Bell Atlantic wouldn't pay. The two men agreed to meet alone, without a single advisor accompanying them, at the elegant Waldorf Astoria Hotel in New York. Summing all of his persuasive skills, Malone tried to explain why the combined TCI and Liberty were worth more than Smith had offered.

Smith countered by reminding his potential partner that TCI had a terrible customer service reputation and its wires in mainly small towns were in need of upgrades. Bell Atlantic, by contrast, had a superior network, adept customer service, and a billing system that could track every minute transaction between provider and customer. By marrying Bell Atlantic, TCI would win instant credibility in the race to wire the nation with pipes for interactivity.

After weeks of intense negotiations to arrive at a fair price, the two men were still negotiating late in the afternoon the day before they had planned to announce the deal. They shook hands again over the final document in the New York offices of the law firm Skadden, Arps. They agreed that Bell Atlantic would pay a premium for TCI and Liberty shares, and that TCI would first reclaim all Liberty shares, which had been distributed in the lopsided stock offering three years before. This deal would be the big payoff for Malone and Magness. Later, when Malone merged Liberty back into TCI to prep the whole thing for sale to Ray Smith and Bell Atlantic, Malone's stake in Liberty had grown immensely, and he exchanged it for 28 million shares, or nearly 5 percent, of TCI, valued at more than $800 million. If the planned merger was executed, Malone would receive Bell Atlantic stock valued at $1.1 billion, while Magness would receive about $1.5 billion. It would be one of the largest gains ever made in stock options history.

The announcement the next morning, on October 13, 1993, set the business world on its ear. On a stage at the Macklowe Hotel in Times Square, John Malone stood shoulder-to-shoulder with Raymond Smith as they unveiled plans to merge TCI, the largest cable operator in the United States, with Bell Atlantic in a deal valued at $33 billion, the biggest merger in U.S. corporate history to date. It was a titanic combination, a new empire created for a new era in telecommunications.

Standing up with Smith on the center stage of the telecom world, Malone believed he had finally hit upon the perfect dismount strategy for Magness. For himself, after running TCI from 1973 to 1993, Malone couldn't shake the feeling that this was the end of an era, too. Still, as vice chairman of the combined company, he was eager to strategize while backstopping Smith, who would remain CEO. It wasn't retirement, he'd be fully engaged, and best of all, he wouldn't be visible. "Ray was our kind of guy," Malone told an interviewer later. "He was ready to cut loose and think outside the box."[5]

The Bell Atlantic bid for TCI emerged as the single defining deal, setting off a gold rush by other Baby Bells, cable operators, computer companies, media companies, and Hollywood to realign, ally, and partner up. The new company would rank as the sixth largest in America. It would deliver voice, video, and data, and the ultimate in one-stop shopping. Bell Atlantic controlled 18 million phone lines in six mid-Atlantic states; TCI controlled 10 million cable households in 49 states and owned pieces of more than three dozen companies. The combined company predicted revenue of nearly $17 billion a year and cash flow of $7 billion, reaching 40 percent of all U.S. homes, a lead so great that the moment the deal was unveiled, it set off cries of a supermonopoly. "I view it with an arched eyebrow," Sen. Ed Markey said on Lou Dobbs's *Moneyline* program on CNN. "I think it's important for us to [e]nsure that competition is not replaced by corporate mergers."

♘♘♘

In December 1993, Malone was summoned to explain and defend the merger before a U.S. Senate antitrust subcommittee headed by Sen. Howard Metzenbaum. It was, regrettably, another uncomfort-able moment for Malone in an arena he was neither accustomed to nor prepared for. His old nemesis, Sumner Redstone of Viacom, had testified before him a month earlier, parroting the contents of his lawsuit against TCI. "He is the gatekeeper; he controls who and what runs over networks," Redstone said in fiery testimony. Malone hated this kind of grandstanding, he hated politicians, and he hated the notion that anyone had the right to stop him from build-ing wealth. He had set a target and moved toward it, as directly as the wires between poles that connected TCI to its customers. He had never asked for government subsidies, land grants, or special favors from legislators. He got money from anyone who had it— from the dark mahogany walls of banks in Manhattan to the rough pine doors of the loneliest subscriber in the smallest town TCI served. TCI wired dozens of schools for cable, but Malone never expounded about the public good. He had merely told people that he expected to create vast wealth with his investments in the cable TV industry.

By this time, the name John Malone was particularly notorious in media, political, and technologic circles. His name was invoked not in reverence but more often in resentful curiosity. Reporters, con-gressional staffers, and financial analysts snickered as they asked: If you have a gun with two bullets, and you have Abu Nidal, Idi Amin, and John Malone in a room, who do you shoot? Answer: John Ma-lone—twice, to make sure he's dead. If Malone had any admirers, they looked on him as if admiring a popular thief or successful pirate. Yet, there was scant evidence that Malone had obtained a penny of his wealth by fraud, trickery, or bodily force. Indeed, when pressed, his most vocal critics within the cable club could blame Malone for little beyond tough negotiating. Malone felt the feds had gone too far in their politically expedient war on cable, and he was sick of it. He felt he was guilty of nothing, except that he had built wealth on his own, and he hadn't forgotten it was his. Politicians unnerved him, and it especially rankled him that competitors used them against him.

At the Senate hearing, the normally laconic and poker-faced Malone lashed out at his critics with lusty directness. "I have become a target for a wide range of business competitors and consumer lobbyists who are dissatisfied at the pace of change in our industry, the first believing it to be too fast and the second believing it to be too slow. I regret that neither I nor my company can ever respond to this type of controversy in ways that Washington normally expects.

"For myself, I will continue to resist the notion that I need to sacrifice my privacy in order to respond to public misrepresentations about my motivations. Becoming a 'public figure' means unacceptable risks to the health, safety, and privacy of my family, and I will continue to refuse most of the hundreds of requests for press interviews to 'tell my side of the story.'"

Malone was especially harsh in attacking Sumner Redstone, saying Redstone's lawsuit against TCI during the Paramount takeover battle was designed "primarily to gain an advantage in the battle for corporate control of Paramount and secondarily to try to chill our competitive behavior." Redstone had complained that TCI's Encore movie channel had intentionally overpaid, in $1 billion in deals, to sew up exclusive rights to movies from several studios, depriving Viacom's own Showtime and Movie Channel of a flow of films. Malone returned serve accordingly. "These new contracts are for relatively limited terms, and all parties will be free to compete for future rights once the contract expires. Obviously, Mr. Redstone's complaints are nothing more than sour grapes from a losing bidder. And as far as the allegation that Liberty paid a 'predatorily' high price for the exclusive rights—a price that could be justified only by the anticipated harm to its competitors—this is a particularly silly complaint. If Liberty paid too high a price, the only party that will be injured is Liberty, because its cost of doing business will have increased compared to its competitors. This is a particularly good example of why competitor complaints are almost always about too much competition, not too little. If Mr. Redstone put as much energy into creating better products as he has historically put into litigating with his competitors, distributors, and suppliers, his customers and shareholders would be better served."

Malone added: "When Mr. Redstone complains about TCI or Liberty outbidding Viacom for film rights, what Mr. Redstone is really complaining about is competition. He doesn't like the fact he has to deal with a new and vigorous competitor." [6]

True to his Calvinist leanings, Malone also told senators that "with respect to TCI, we are not going to spend anywhere near the many millions spent by other companies on public relations, image advertising, or government affairs. Instead, we know our customers prefer we spend scarce resources on our cable systems and new programming." Malone argued that TCI and other cable operators were merely purchasing agents for cable viewers, buying services such as MTV, USA, and CNN wholesale, then selling these networks to viewers at retail prices. If wholesale prices went up, customers would pay more for cable service. And he noted that TCI's programming cost had escalated "several hundred percent" in five years.

TCI was large, but he insisted it wasn't a giant. Its revenue in 1992, including Liberty, was $3.7 billion; by comparison AT&T and IBM each had revenue over $65 billion, and each of the regional Bell operating companies dwarfed TCI's annual revenue. While TCI served 20 percent of U.S. cable subscribers, "AT&T still enjoys more than 69 [percent] of long distance revenues and Nintendo makes over 75 [percent] of video games systems sales," Malone pointedly noted for the senators. He took note to include as competitors video rental stores, wireless cable, broadcasters, SMATV operators, and backyard dish dealers—a $200 billion world. TCI took only a small slice of that giant pie.

As for charges of vertical integration, "the history of the cable industry has shown that cable operators, including TCI, often have been the investors or financiers of last resort for cable programmers," Malone told the subcommittee. He cited his early and critical financial support of BET and the Discovery Channel. Before cable TV came along, he said, consumers had a choice of three networks,

PBS, and a few independent stations. In Malone's view, TCI was an aggressive competitor in the best American tradition—started by entrepreneurs who wagered their own capital to build infrastructure, grace it with the latest technology, and buy or make programming. Instead of paying high salaries, Malone allowed employees to buy stock, which was far more effective as incentive for high performance. Malone openly carped that it was "frustrating to have our hard work and success denigrated by claims we have acted unfairly or anticompetitively and thus have not earned our success. We have earned every bit of it!"

While critics had charged TCI with controlling the lion's share of popular programming, Malone deftly argued that TCI's power was more in appearance than in practice. TCI didn't discriminate in terms of carriage of networks based on whether TCI owned them, Malone said, largely because it was prohibited by the 1992 Cable Act. Of the 15 most widely carried services on TCI systems, 10 (the Nashville Network, Nickelodeon, Lifetime, USA, ESPN, MTV, C-Span, the Weather Channel, A&E, and CNBC) were services in which TCI did *not* own a stake. But the best evidence that the market had not been "discouraged by all this sky-is-falling rhetoric about vertical integration" was that the number of cable networks had nearly doubled over the past 10 years.

"The problem, simply put, is that no one cable or telephone company has the financial resources or combination of skills to do the job. It will cost at least $60 billion to give existing cable and telephone networks the capacity of carrying broadband, two-way interactive video programming, and to equip subscribers to participate in these networks. Moreover, the task requires a thorough knowledge of national network operation, computer applications, and the video marketplace that few, if any, companies now have.[7]

"The notion that TCI 'controls' the lion's share of programming, as you heard Mr. Redstone loudly proclaim in your earlier hearing, is flat wrong, and he knew it was wrong when he said it." Malone had brushed back his critics for the moment, and the deal inched its way through the approval process.

Even as Malone endeavored to defend the Bell Atlantic deal in Washington, he prepared for an extended war on local phone companies across the nation. In December 1993, he led five of the country's largest cable TV companies (Tele-Communications, Time Warner, Continental Cablevision, Comcast, and Cox Cable Communications) into a joint venture that would organize local cable operators in large markets to attack one of the Bells' most lucrative offerings: service for businesses. Cable operators hoping to offer telephone services on their upgraded lines could be part of an umbrella organization called Teleport. The Teleport partnership proved to be a shrewd way around the telephone companies' broad, contiguous regional reach. For example, the Chicago market was served by only one regional telephone company, Ameritech, but 12 different cable operators. This way, local cable operators could share common marketing and advertising, research and development, regulatory advice, and branding of new offerings. "You don't want 12 different companies trying to position a business against one," Robert Thomson, a senior vice president of TCI, explained to anyone who wanted to know the rationale. "This is clearly a step that will enhance competition." AT&T would end up paying $11.3 billion to buy the company later, netting an average 10-fold gain for the top cable operators, including TCI, whose TCI Ventures received $2.9 billion for its 30 percent stake.[8]

By early 1994, cable operators were feeling the full brunt of the 1992 Cable Act, no one more than John Malone and TCI, whose stock had fallen nearly 40 percent to the $20 range five months after the Bell Atlantic merger was announced. As far as Wall Street was concerned, the government was kinking the cash flow hose, causing big problems for everyone. In Washington, regulators and congresspeople embarrassed by the first results, in which many consumers actually ended up paying more for cable service, were out for payback. And so in February, the FCC released an overhaul of cable rate rules—this one spanning several hundred more pages and complementing the original 500-page order that had gone awry. Replete with a newly fine-tuned formula for setting hundreds of rates, the new, improved model was a basis for arguing cable rates should come down 17 percent, not a mere 10 percent as originally planned.

The economic analysis struck Malone as somewhat convenient: The FCC all but admitted that the second round of rate cuts was necessary by dint of the simple fact that the first round of cuts hadn't brought prices down enough—never mind that, the first time around, regulators had spent 500 pages devising a 10 percent rollback. If they were right then, how could they be right now—and if they were wrong back then, why should anyone trust them to be right this time around? To Malone and other cable barons, it seemed damned unjust: It was changing the rules in the middle of the game. Back in the Arlington, Virginia, offices of Bell Atlantic, Ray Smith was no happier about it. He was glued to C-Span, watching the proceedings as the FCC announced the new and deeper rate cuts, when he got a call from John Malone. Malone began, "Ray this is a bigger hit than we thought." Smith replied: "Can you fly to New York?"[9]

The second round of cuts would pinch TCI's cash flow and hurt its stock price more than Smith, or anyone in the cable industry, had bargained for. TCI said it would suspend half of its $1.1 billion capital budget pending clarification of the FCC's rate rules, which sent the stock price of the industry's major equipment suppliers in a free fall.[10] Malone called the additional 7 percent "a club in the side of the head" and figured that the new round of cuts had shaved off $1.8 billion off the original price offered for TCI—yet he felt it was wrong to accept it.[11] "I won't sell my company at the bottom of the market," Malone told Smith, "and you'd be crazy to pay more than top dollar with this level of uncertainty."[12] From 1993 to 1995, the new federal regulations would cost TCI an estimated $300 million, not to mention the confidence of Wall Street.

♘♘♘

The Bell Atlantic merger was a merger of equals, but one key to making it work in Malone's mind was that he and Magness had won the right to name 6 of the 13 directors on the combined companies' board, and Ray Smith would be the seventh. This gave Malone the power to protect Smith if he made unpopular decisions on Wall Street, or forcefully persuade him to change strategy if he ran afoul of Malone's thinking.[13]

Even as a tot, **John Malone** (*top row, second from right, eyes closed*) could retreat to the silence of his thoughts for inspiration.

Though shy like his father, John Malone developed into a fierce competitor at school. A chessboard was a favorite battlefield, but **Malone** (*front, far left*) also enjoyed fencing, preferring the heavier épée to the flimsy foil. *(Hopkins School Chess Club, 1959. Photo courtesy of Hopkins School.)*

Malone (*left*) took a paycut, spurned a more lucrative career offer, and upruoted his family to help **Bob Magness** (*right*), a part-time cattle rancher, build TCI into the largest cable operator in the United States. *(Courtesy of the Cable Center.)*

Betsy Magness (*seated, right*) proved to be an astute business partner for her husband **Bob** (*seated, center*), but both had run out of gas by 1972. The early TCI management team was relieved when **Malone** (*seated, left*) joined the debt-racked company. *(Courtesy of the Cable Center.)*

Malone (*seated*) spent his first years at TCI fending off lenders, raising money, and sniffing out any angle that would give TCI breathing room, mostly with the aid of **Magness** (*standing, right*) and **Donne Fisher** (*standing, left*). The man wearing glasses (*standing, second from left*) is unidentified. *(Courtesy of the Cable Center.)*

By the mid 1980s, **John Malone's** hair had turned completely gray thanks to lenders, politicians, and the precarious nature of the cable TV business.

TCI owned cable wires—buried and strung—into one of every four homes at its peak. Under Malone's watch, TCI quickly grew into the nation's largest cable operator through building and buying.

Cable programmers complained that TCI was a bully in negotiations because of its size. Malone fought hardest with Disney, which would one day own one of cable's most expensive channels, ESPN. Here at Disney's launch on TCI systems in 1983 (*left to right*): **Malone, Betsy Magness, Bob Magness, J. C. Sparkman, and Mickey Mouse.** *(Courtesy of the Cable Center.)*

In the early 1980s, TCI moved into the big cities for the first time, bargain-hunting after many corporations couldn't make money with the elaborate systems they promised. In 1984, the same year the industry was deregulated, **John Malone** (*left*) and **Peter Barton** (*right*) present a check for TCI's franchise fees to **Harold Washington** (*center*), the mayor of Chicago.

Bob Magness met his second wife, **Sharon Magness**, through their mutual love of Arabian horses. Here they pose with **Thunder**, the mascot for the Denver Broncos. *(Courtesy of the Cable Center.)*

TCI's management team in the 1990s consisted of (*from left to right*) **Larry Romrell** (technology), **Fred Vierra** (international), **Peter Barton** (Liberty Media), and **Brendan Clouston** (cable). *(Courtesy of the Cable Center.)*

In 1993, a Senate subcommittee grills **Malone** before TCI's merger with Bell Atlantic. TCI was the frequent target of Senate antitrust hearings, Department of Justice investigations, and Federal Trade Commission reviews. "I'd rather cut off my leg than go to Washington," Malone once said.

Time Warner Chairman **Gerald Levin** (*right*) and **Ted Turner** (*left*) are all smiles as they announce Time Warner would buy Turner Broadcasting. Before giving his blessing to the deal, Malone won TCI favorable rates for carrying CNN, TBS, and the Cartoon Network, then converted his big stake in Turner into Time Warner. (*AP Worldwide Photo.*)

"Leo did us a hell of a job—and not just me and the TCI shareholders, but the whole cable industry," Malone said after his friend and CEO, **Leo Hindery**, helped turn TCI around. "I'll forever be in his debt for that." *(AP Worldwide Photo.)*

Microsoft Chairman **Bill Gates** (*center*) injected new life into the cable industry when he announced a $1 billion investment in 1997 in Comcast, run by
the president **Brian Roberts** (*right*) and his father, chairman **Ralph Roberts**
(*left*). *(AP Worldwide Photo.)*

John Malone (*right*) on stage
with **Michael Armstrong** (*left*)
minutes before they announce
the sale of TCI to AT&T for
$48 billion in stock and as-
sumed debt. Though Malone
would walk away with Liberty
Media after the deal closed, he
chafed on the sidelines as the
value of AT&T shares sank over
time. *(AP Worldwide Photo.)*

Fast friends and fierce competitors, News Corp.'s **Rupert Murdoch** (*right*) challenged **Malone** (*left*) and the cable industry with a satellite venture, but then backed down in the face of cable's threats. Malone would become one of News Corp.'s largest individual shareholders. *(Courtesy of the Cable Center.)*

John Malone (*second from right*) and **Robert "Dob" Bennett** (*far right*) are caught in a rare moment socializing, here at financier Herb Allen's Media Conference in Sun Valley, with old partner and Black Entertainment Television founder **Bob Johnson** (*far left*), and **David Geffen** (*second from left*), and **Jeffrey Katzenberg** (*center*), partners in the movie studio Dreamworks SKG.

Though he liked Ray Smith, the more he saw of Bell Atlantic, the more he recognized the atrophy and bureaucratic tendencies of the old Bell system. Malone had come to doubt Smith & Co. had what it takes to defy Wall Street's obsession for earnings and plow cash back into the business, even at the expense of paying shareholders dividends. More important, Malone wasn't sure Bell Atlantic shareholders would vote on the deal after seeing the new law's effect on TCI as both sides waited out the long months for regulatory clearance—and the breakup fee was negligible.

For months, he had been pressing Bell Atlantic to sweeten the terms. Malone was infamous for renegotiating long after final terms had been struck, and in this, the biggest deal he had ever contemplated, he was tinkering like a madman.

Bell Atlantic stock had soared to a high of almost $68 the day after the deal was announced, far higher than the $54 Smith had guaranteed TCI. But by year-end 1993, it had slid below $60, never to bounce back. Smith had planned to buy TCI with Bell Atlantic stock, keyed to how much cash TCI's cable systems generated. So when Bell Atlantic's stock price dropped more than 20 percent from a high of around $68 in October to around $54, Malone wanted more shares to offset the falling price. But Smith wanted to pay even fewer shares than he agreed because the FCC's new round of rate cuts would reduce TCI's cash flow, and the deal would value TCI at 11.75 times its cash flow in the months leading to the closing date—the lower the cash flow, the less Bell Atlantic would have to pay.[14] By the time they had met in the New York office of Skadden, Arps that day, the two sides had already renegotiated the deal a half dozen times.

Malone had begun lobbying for a higher price almost as soon as they had a deal. After reaching the initial agreement in October, Malone had drawn up a list of 23 questions outlining his biggest concerns for the merged company. Among them:

- Would Bell Atlantic be willing to cut its dividend and plow more money back into capital investment?
- Could management stick it out in a high-growth venture, willing to eat loses?

Smith, too, had a list of concerns. Malone argued that because the new shares that Bell Atlantic would issue wouldn't pay a dividend, they would trade lower than normal on the market, and therefore Bell Atlantic should pay out more than the 220 million shares it had pledged to pay for TCI. Bell Atlantic, on the other hand, wasn't ready to flood the market with even more shares; Smith was uncomfortable enough with the huge number of new shares he would have to issue, because the increase caused dilution—it reduced the earnings per share that Bell reported to Wall Street. And while TCI hadn't earned a dime in 20 years in business, Bell Atlantic's stock lived and died by how well it fared in meeting Wall Street's expectations for how much it would earn each quarter. Bell Atlantic already expected the TCI deal to reduce its earnings per share by 35 percent, and Smith was loath to do anything that would raise that figure.

Smith figured the value of TCI stock had dropped to around $20 a share, and he was still willing to pay somewhere around $25 a share. "But John still had it in his head that it was a $35 stock," Smith said later. "That's just too big a difference."[15] So Smith was demanding a reduction in how many shares Bell Atlantic had to pay to get hold of TCI and its coveted cable systems.

Malone balked. "If I take a reduced number of shares, I'll never get my major shareholders to accept it," Malone told him. "And there's no way you can give me the number of shares I need." Malone figured that Bell Atlantic would have to pay around 14 times cash flow.

"You're right," Smith said. In a final effort to see beyond the fog of the moment, Smith offered, "Let's take the price off the table." For the next 45 minutes, the two men hashed over the implications for programming and future cash flow growth. Then the talks veered unavoidably back to price. "It's no good," Malone said. "I can't cut another nickel." Smith agreed.[16]

In their final session, a two-hour encounter on a gloomy and wet winter day, Smith and Malone met, each flanked by a couple of their men. Together in a 44th-floor conference room of Bell Atlantic's legal advisers, Skadden, Arps, Slate, Meagher & Flom, overlooking Manhattan's Third Avenue, the two men haggled again over figures, but it was clear they couldn't reconcile the terms.

So on Wednesday, February 23, 1993, just one day after the FCC's new rate cuts were announced and five months after Bell Atlantic had agreed to buy TCI in the largest takeover in business history, John Malone and Ray Smith called the whole thing off. Despite their belief that they simply couldn't enter the multimedia future without each other's help, they went their separate ways. In the wake of the collapse, the rush to wire America lost two of the biggest builders of the new digital network connecting homes, businesses, and schools, which together were ready to spend upward of $20 billion over five years to serve up new interactive services.

In the fallout, the pace of talks and deal making paused. The much-touted collision, or convergence, of the cable and telephone industries suddenly sputtered, not so much because the players questioned the soundness of the strategy, but more because they no longer were driven by that most important motivation in business: fear. Two months after the Bell Atlantic deal collapsed, Southwestern Bell, the regional telephone company based in San Antonio, Texas, pulled out of its much-ballyhooed $4.9 billion merger with Cox Communications, the fifth-largest cable operator in the country. Like TCI and Bell Atlantic, the venture planned to pursue telephone and cable TV business in each other's markets, but after reviewing the rules issued by the FCC, the two sides decided that the cable company would be handcuffed. Another merger, between Jones Intercable and Bell Canada, was renegotiated to reflect the cable firm's lower value given the FCC crackdown.

The interactive future that Malone had so cockily predicted back in December 1992 was inching further from his reach. All around the country, cable giants grounded their interactive tests citing delays, high costs, and concerns about whether consumers would really pay more money for fancy new services. Time Warner quietly pulled the plug on its vaunted Full Service Network project in Orlando, where the 4,000 cable homes involved loved the online games, movies on demand, and ordering pizza by remote control, but where costs were astronomically high. The powerful new set-top boxes cost up to $7,000 apiece to produce, and fiber-optic lines and giant Silicon Graphics video servers added tens of millions of dollars to the bill. The logistics of creating such a system were overwhelming. The pizza-ordering application alone took programmers months of meticulous work and hundreds of thousands of dollars to create. The following year, Viacom announced it would close its interactive test beds in Castro Valley, California.

♇♇♇

In the place of interactive TV would come a far bigger next big thing: the Internet. At the time, however, Malone could feel only irritation and antipathy toward the government's approach to cable TV regulation. Months later, Malone would vent his frustration in the July 1994 issue of *Wired* magazine, which featured a computer-enhanced illustration of Malone on the cover as Infobahn Warrior, garbed in a leather jacket and brandishing a shotgun à la Mel Gibson in the postapocalyptic movie *The Road Warrior.*

During the Q and A, while explaining TCI's intent to build out the electronic superhighway, Malone irreverently made a vow: "I'll make a commitment to the [vice president], OK? Listen, Al, I know you haven't asked for it, but we'll make a commitment to complete the job by the end of '96. All we need is a little help . . . you know, shoot Reed Hundt! Don't let him do any more damage, know what I'm saying?" That ill-advised remark was quoted in magazines and newspapers around the United States.

Ray Smith would air his feelings about the big deal's flop in a *Wired* interview, too, though with somewhat more moderation. "Let me tell you what *is* true," Smith said. "There was a struggle in the shareholder base. We have a million shareholders and they are high-yield oriented. We froze the dividend and it frightened the life out of our shareholders. And our stock, which leaped for awhile on the promise of the merger, dropped as the yield-oriented shareholders peeled away." [17]

At one point when Malone was quoted as saying Bell Atlantic would have to cut the dividend, Smith said, "the stock dropped five points." "He thought that was what we had to do. John was just being honest. But to say that is like lighting a match in a gas-filled room. Not that you aren't going to tell shareholders the truth. You are. It's just that we were trying to find less onerous ways of making the deal work out financially . . . Why announce something like that before you know for sure? You see, John's approach to the issue was like his regulatory approach."[18]

Looking back, Smith could still recall the moment the whole thing unraveled. It was Malone who broached the uncomfortable ending in their final meeting. "Well," he had told the assembled executives, "we can't sit around here forever."

"Yeah," Smith responded dolefully, "let's look at the press release and get this over with." Malone had come prepared: He already had in hand a public statement announcing the deal's collapse and largely blaming regulators for it. Smith's lasting memory of the meeting that day was Malone's last words. As the two men shook hands, Malone patted Smith on the back and told him: "Nice try, my friend."[19]

CHASING TOO MANY RABBITS?

John Malone fell into a deep depression in the months after the collapse of the biggest deal of his career. It wasn't meant to be, the numbers didn't work, and in prior years that would have been the end of it. But this time, Malone couldn't shake an oppressive cloud of disappointment. Frustrated by the failure of his exit plan, Malone retreated. He did something he hadn't done in 20 years of running TCI: He took his eye off the ball.

He let his number two, Brendan Clouston, run things day to day and came to view TCI as an anchor around his neck. Malone didn't want to be exposed financially or personally, timewise, reputation-wise, to the operations side of the cable TV business. Had the company sold out to Bell Atlantic, Malone could have been done with running a government-regulated monopoly and could have focused on strategy and deals for the combined colossus. Ray Smith would have taken on the tasks Malone loathed: placating politicians, pressing flesh, and talking to the press. Now, Malone was stuck with all of it. In his mind he had already sold TCI, and when the deal unraveled, he seemed to avoid the responsibility of control. Malone dropped out of sight. He stopped coming to the office as much. Much later, some of his biggest investors said that he had checked out, had lost interest in the cable business. In an article entitled "High Noon for John Malone," *Fortune* magazine asked the question whispered in many circles on Wall Street, "Where has he been? After all, he never ceased being CEO in title or pay."[1]

Malone was cogitating on long-range plans, looking for ways to get TCI a toehold on the Internet. He had talked often with Steve Case, the founder of America Online, whose stock had soared on Internet hype. The two held serious talks about ways to team up, but Malone suddenly pulled back and turned to a much bigger partner: Microsoft. In December 1994, Malone agreed with Bill Gates to take a 20 percent stake in Microsoft's fledgling online project for $125 million. That partnership would give the online service a valuation of $625 million. Spurning Steve Case would prove to be regrettable. Two years later, TCI would end up pulling the entire investment in MSN to devote the cash to other Internet ventures; Case's AOL soared even more in value and ultimately acquired Time Warner, Incorporated.

Also, in the fall of 1994, Malone reached an accord with cable rivals Comcast and Cox Communications and long-distance telco Spring Corporation to offer wireless telephone service throughout the country under the Sprint name. Their joint venture agreed to pay more than $2 billion for federal licenses to offer a new generation of wireless phone service, called personal communications service, or PCS. But Malone and the rest of the cable partners would later scale back plans to roll out the wired portion because they didn't want to be locked into strict timetables to upgrade their networks. Still, the investment would pay off handsomely years later. At its peak, Spring PCS would hit a high of $65 per share in the spring of 2000, valuing TCI's position at about $12.9 billion—quite a gain for TCI's $1.4 billion total cash investment in PCS.[2]

And still TCI grew. In 1994, Malone agreed to pay $1.2 billion in stock and $250 million in debt to buy TeleCable, a private cable operator with systems in 15 states, expanding on cable holdings TCI had in the regions of Dallas, Texas; Kansas City, Missouri; and Lexington, Kentucky. By clustering systems together, Malone and other big cable operators began to turn contiguous properties into regional fiefdoms. TCI controlled wires into one in four cable homes in the United States.

By late 1994, TCI got one of its biggest boosts in subscriber rolls from an avowed enemy: Sumner Redstone's Viacom. After Viacom finally won Paramount at the end of a bloody takeover battle, Redstone and Malone finally broke bread together in Denver, and all was forgotten in the name of good business. Redstone announced that his "good friends" at TCI had purchased Viacom's cable TV operations in a $2.25 billion deal, which would ease the burden of Viacom's purchase of Paramount Communications Inc. and, later, Blockbuster Entertainment Corp.

After more than a year of delays caused by the repeal of a tax break the two men were hoping for, the deal finally closed. In a complicated two-step transaction, Viacom spun off its cable systems to shareholders, shifting $1.7 billion of debt to the new company. Then TCI purchased the new company for $350 million, giving it dominance in San Francisco, Seattle, and Nashville. Added to its immense reach, the deal gave TCI a total of nearly 14 million subscribers, nearly one-quarter of the nation's cable customers. Just as important for TCI, the deal became the foundation for settling Redstone's caustic antitrust lawsuit. Malone told the *Wall Street Journal* that he met with Redstone at a Sun Valley, Idaho, industry conference hosted by Herb Allen and talked "about how nice it is going to be not to be throwing rocks at each other."[3] Viacom's Sumner Redstone, whose motto had become "Content is king," gave up his cable systems in favor of acquiring more content—electronic programming in any form.

TCI still couldn't shake regulators. In December 1994, TCI was the target of investigators from both the Department of Justice and the Federal Trade Commission, who were inquiring about three pending deals: (1) TCI's $1.4 billion bid to buy TeleCable Corp.; (2) TCI's proposed $1.4 billion joint venture with Comcast Corp. to buy QVC; and (3) a trade of cable systems between TCI and Multimedia.[4]

ʊʊʊ

In the fall of 1994, in an effort to regroup after the Bell Atlantic implosion, TCI said it would go ahead with a sweeping plan to split the company into four separate businesses, each with its own class of stock: (1) cable, (2) programming, (3) technology ventures, and (4) international cable and programming. It wasn't the first time that Malone hoped Wall Street would assign a value to the sum of the parts that was larger than the whole.

As part of the plan for Liberty, TCI created a new class of stock, called a tracking stock, which would be distributed to TCI shareholders and give them an interest in Liberty's earnings. But again, Malone's reputation hurt him. All that Malone's critics seemed to recall is that Malone had made a hefty option-related profit the first time he spun off Liberty and then brought it back into TCI. "There have been too many transactions involving buying and selling Liberty, and they all seem to work in Malone's favor," said Rodney Linafelter, a portfolio manager wither Berger Associates, which had sold its entire million-share position in TCI in early 1995. Typical of many TCI transactions, the deal was extraordinarily complex. The idea of a tracking stock didn't appeal to many investors, no matter who was issuing the stock. That's because holders don't own the underlying assets, which belong to the parent company. A tracking stock, by definition, represents an interest in the earnings of the company.

To the naysayers, Malone said nothing. He let the numbers speak for themselves. Anyone who participated in the original Liberty deal, a Liberty share bought in 1991 for $256 had soared to $3,821 by August 1994, when TCI reacquired Liberty.

Still, Malone realized that much of the old TCI was fading. One by one, many of the original employees were leaving, and Malone felt a vacuum, a void that no amount of new hires could replenish. Malone felt himself getting older, too. He wanted to spend more time with Leslie, his two children, and his new granddaughter. He watched with a trace of unspoken envy as his friends at TCI left— Gary Bracken, Art Lee, Marion Novack, men who had helped string the first wires from town to town—to enjoy the wealth they had accumulated after decades at TCI. Now, when he walked through the glass doors of TCI's 11-story building, Malone recognized fewer faces, and he felt uncomfortable in elevators filled with people he did not know, especially the Harvard Business School types that

Clouston had recruited. It was no longer a group of the old guys. It was no longer fun.

Across the industry, a generation of cable pioneers who built large regional cable companies were selling out to bigger national players and cashing in, part of a consolidation craze that would continue until their numbers dwindled to a handful of national players. Alan Gerry, founder of Cablevision Industries, Incorporated, sold his systems to Time Warner for $2 billion. Amos Hostetter sold his privately held Continental Cablevision, the third largest in the country, to telephone giant U S West for $10.8 billion. And Glenn Jones went through with the sale of a 30 percent stake in his company, Jones Intercable, Incorporated, to Bell Canada. For the first time, Malone listened to the voice that told him to begin grooming a successor for the inevitable day when he would step down.

What kept Malone up at night was his unwritten oath to Bob Magness, and an unshakable sensation that retirement meant quitting. Anyone who bothered to watch the *NBC Evening News* on September 7, 1994, saw a rare and candid glimpse of Malone's state of mind at the time. The profile opened with a clip of Senator Howard Metzenbaum calling Malone a "big gorilla" who was "intent on squeezing the lifeblood out of the American people." In a one-on-one interview, anchor Tom Brokaw asked Malone:

> BROKAW: Did you always think that you privately had an edge on those that you competed against, and were you always driven to win?
> MALONE: You know I, ah, I think I'm primarily driven by insecurities. I think any . . .
> BROKAW: You? Insecurities?
> MALONE: Yes, me. Any psychiatrist would tell you that I—I suffer from the inability to please my now dead father.

Malone's reply was a stunning admission in spite of its unaffected delivery, and it underscored what Wall Street analysts had known all along: If you ask John Malone a direct question, he will tell exactly how he feels.

Long ago, Malone had made a promise to protect Magness's assets and grow his company, and he had done that. Now how to engineer a graceful exit, a way to dump TCI, and steal away with Liberty Media? Malone weighed it: "Is there an exit scenario for me, personally, after which everybody will say, 'He did a good job, he didn't leave us in the lurch'?" It was here, in the labyrinthine maze of these questions, that Malone resided during his absence from Denver.

♘♘♘

Malone did his best thinking in Maine. He loved rowing a boat out on open water, pulling the oars with sinewy arms and shoulders that could still make the craft move at a quick clip. He liked to garden and walk the property if Leslie was shopping or painting. Maine was a retreat from the world of business, government, and people.

"Escape is necessary," Malone later told one listener. "Getting away gives you a new perspective and makes you more human. When you're running a large corporation, you're not able to show your human side all that much. It's just not productive."[5]

Nourished by ocean breezes from so many summers on the Long Island Sound, Malone felt more at home on the sea than he did in Colorado. He loved everything about Maine, from the harbor where he and Leslie had anchored on the night of their anniversary a decade before and decided on the spot to buy a house, to the apple trees nearby that rewarded him faithfully with large, crisp fruit on cool fall mornings. More than anything, he appreciated the privacy afforded by the quiet and barren nature of the state. He had withdrawn there for much of 1995 and 1996, and as he and Leslie spent more time there, they set their sights on building a vessel for their trips off the Maine coast and along the Eastern seaboard.

Malone admired boats the way some men admire women, and some of his fondest memories he traced back to the summers of his youth racing boats and sailing along the New England coast. In addition to the Hinckley Southwester he owned, he had restored a handsome wooden 1928 Long Island commuter yacht, the *Ragtime*, to its former splendor. Malone loved the boat, built in

1928, but a harrowing storm in the Atlantic on a Maine-to-Florida trip in 1984 convinced Malone that it was a fragile antique that did not handle well in rough seas. In a Nor'easter off the Jersey Shore on the boat with Jeff Lowell years later, so fully did they expect the 10-foot swells to break the frame of the vessel that Malone, Lowell, and another passenger prepared to jump ship in a lifeboat.

In 1995, Malone indulged a dream he had harbored for years: He commissioned one of the oldest boatyards in Maine to begin work on a craft built to *his* specifications. Crafted by the fifth-generation Hogdon Yachts, the boat was modeled after a 1920s-style commuter craft, harking back to the days when wealthy men commuted to summer homes on the Eastern seaboard. The boat was Malone's pride and joy, a stunning, 80-foot motor yacht, built with graceful curves and lines, complex wood details, and high-tech carbon fiber. He christened it *Liberty*. A circular chrome logo, with *Liberty* spelled out in block letters, which became the emblem used for the company, was inlaid in the teak deck. "It was like the Sistine Chapel to him," Leo Hindery, a friend and fellow cable operator, told people later. If boats are the extended personalities of their owners, *Liberty* was no different. Malone set the performance criteria but Leslie chose the look. Glistening black and bedecked with the latest navigational gadgetry, the yacht turned heads in every port. It was built for speed as much as power, propelled by two 1,100-horsepower engines that could hit 32.5 knots flat out with a range of 900 miles. The wood was all varnished mahogany, except for the interior, which was warm quarter-sawn hard maple from Canada, pierced with silver knobs and hinges. *Liberty* was to be the reward after a lifetime at the wheel of the nation's largest cable company.

That summer, when Malone returned to Denver from a trip to Argentina, where TCI owned cable operations, he was "sick as a dog," with flulike symptoms. He and Leslie were scheduled to launch the new boat within days, an appointment that could not be easily rescheduled because it had been set with the tides in mind.

So Malone climbed aboard their customized RV, as big as a small bus, which they drove cross-country since Leslie didn't like to fly.

The last time the TCI pilot remembered Leslie flying in the TCI jet was when Malone's mother died, and she had soothed her nerves with a couple of stiff drinks during the flight. Instead, they drove the distance with a small herd of pugs, whose expressive eyes and wrinkled faces Malone found irresistibly cute. On the road they listened to books on tape; one of Malone's favorites was *Moby Dick*. At road stops, when curious visitors asked, Malone slyly replied that the big rig was a truck outfitted for country music singer Garth Brooks. His wife and brother-in-law drove the bus to Maine that summer "with me lying in the back like a recovering patient," he recalled much later. The launch date also happened to prevent Malone from attending the annual cable convention at the same time, and some people in the industry started to whisper that Malone was "deathly ill." The reality was that he was just up in Maine, still in contact with the office, he liked to point out. When the boat was finished in 1996, John and Leslie took it out sailing around his home port. In short pants and boat shoes, he looked "about as comfortable as a state trooper in uniform," quipped the local *Maine Times*.

Back at TCI, Brendan Clouston ran things and kept Malone apprised of the latest, but only in the most general way. Clouston was a banker and numbers expert, a Canadian who had helped run United Artists Entertainment's cable operations after TCI took over the company. A husky and energetic man, Clouston possessed a knack for numbers that made him a natural choice to run TCI's core cable operations. Clouston won Malone's confidence when he successfully integrated UA's cable operations into TCI through judicious changes in personnel and policy. In the end, the two disparate cultures melded, and for the first time, Malone had allowed a team of executives, including Clouston, to remain after buying a company.

Malone had ample confidence in Clouston long before the Bell Atlantic deal came and went, and he began to make his regard for the younger executive much clearer in the months after the deal flopped. Conspicuously, Clouston started to lead more meetings before TCI's largest institutional investors and the Wall Street analysts. Malone soon began to feel more comfortable that TCI was in good hands. "Brendan is basically the president of the company, though we just don't call him that yet," Malone told a reporter in February 1994.[6] Delegating more authority and declining to give direct orders "lets the organization grow up," Malone maintained. Clouston, who was technically COO, seemed to understand Malone's management style better than most. He once put it this way: "I've never had a direct instruction from him in 15 years. Instead, I have to try to understand his point of view, then make my decisions accordingly."[7]

Soon after taking control of operations at TCI, Clouston placed the company on a remarkably aggressive campaign to deliver three new digital services on top of plain old cable, all of which had never been delivered at once by a single company on the same wire: hundreds of digital cable channels, high-speed Internet access, and later, telephone service over cable lines. Clouston ramped up spending to plow millions into rebuilding TCI's creaky cable systems for high-speed, two-way communication, betting that customer demand would catch up to Malone's vision. He was an optimist, and when he stood before a roomful of investors as he did on April 17, 1996, his enthusiasm for TCI's future was genuine and palpable. He painted a rosy picture of TCI's prospects, similar to the vision the rest of the cable was projecting at the time. The objective was not only to launch new digital services (500 channels, telephone service, and high-speed Internet access), but to do so immediately.

But as Malone would come to learn, Brendan Clouston was not quite prepared to run the largest cable company in the country. His strategy sounded terrific, but it was expensive, and his hell-bent pursuit of the interactive, digital future caused costs to suddenly balloon out of control at notoriously lean TCI. Expecting titanic competition from telephone companies and DBS upstarts like DirecTV, Clouston launched a multifront war, pouring $600 million into new licenses for tiny wireless phones, $200 million into national TCI call centers, and vast sums into basic but necessary upgrades of TCI's aging cable systems. In some ways, TCI was in worse shape than other big cable operators at the time. In the 1980s, TCI bulked up the subscriber count by buying scores of smaller systems. Since then it had neglected to keep pace with the technological improvements other big operators had been making for years, and its systems needed hundreds of millions of dollars worth of improvements to reach all its subscribers. And TCI was already leveraged to the hilt, with $14.5 billion in long-term debt.

Clouston hired new managers and an army of consultants to help transform TCI, part of a marketing culture he had brought with him from the old United Artists. In 1996, the consultants billed TCI upward of $60 million, compared with just $3 million two years earlier. A lot of it was touchy-feely teamwork drivel that brought scorn in the ranks of TCI. Wags had a saying: If you want to be rich, be a TCI consultant. Clouston chose executives from outside the cable industry, such as former stars at Procter & Gamble and Martin Marietta who would promote the new digital services when they rolled out. Clouston launched a sophisticated billing system called SUMMITrak to replace TCI's antiquated billing methods. The new software was expensive, but it could keep track of several new products and services better than TCI.

On paper, the strategy looked sound, for cable was under attack for the first time in its history. DirecTV had suddenly emerged, and it was delivering hundreds of channels and up-to-the-moment movies like cable never could. This most visible threat came, oddly enough, from the largest maker of automobiles in the world, General Motors (GM). A division of GM, Hughes Electronics Corporation, sold the direct-broadcast satellite (DBS) minidish service called DirecTV, which also benefited from the new technology of compressing digital signals. Lest anyone question DirecTV's staying power, telephone colossus AT&T had paid $137 million for a 2.5 percent stake in DirecTV. At $500 or more a dish, the price was a bit steep for most consumers, even those who hated their cable service. But the cost was falling fast, and while DirecTV and its ilk reached only about 4 million homes to cable's 65 million in 1996, it threatened to inflict serious damage on cable's subscriber growth, which had slowed in the 1990s to less than 3 percent a year.

Elsewhere, cable was about to come under attack from the telcos. Congress was already breaking down barriers between the worlds of TV, telephones, and computers with passage of the 1996 Telecommunications Act, far-reaching legislation that phased out rate regulation for cable operators and invited new competitors of every size. The three industries that could inflict the heaviest damage on one another (cable companies, long-distance companies, and local telephone companies) were let loose and allowed to go into previously protected businesses. Cable companies could offer telephone service. Local phone companies could offer long distance. Phone companies could buy cable companies. The Silicon Valley firms would befriend them all. Long term, Malone knew that telephone companies posed the bigger threat because of their enormous wealth, but the new minidish competitors were far more dangerous at the moment.

Investors seemed to lose interest in cable altogether, avoiding TCI's stock more than any other. As a bull market raged, sending the Dow Jones Industrial Average soaring 50 percent in the previous two years, the unlucky investor who bought TCI must have felt gypped by the early summer of 1996: TCI stock had stagnated 24 percent during that period, hovering in the high teens. Malone, whose leadership many cable operators depended on and whose decisions at TCI certainly had never been second-guessed, suddenly seemed *vulnerable*. For the first time, his credibility was called into question, both privately and publicly. "Can TCI's Leader Walk His Talk at Last?" asked the *New York Times* in April 1996. "Stymied?" asked the May 1996 issue of *Forbes* about Malone's position. "They haven't met any targets," Larry Haverty of State Street Research declared to the *Wall Street Journal.* "It's like the emperor has no clothes."[8]

Clouston, then, had something to prove, and he was aggressive, even arrogant, in pushing his agenda for TCI. His attitude angered several in TCI's old guard—in particular, longtime TCI cable chief J. C. Sparkman. Sparkman's hair had long since turned snow white, yet his authoritative opinions on TCI systems, delivered in a raspy voice ragged from decades of smoking, had not changed a bit. He had joined Magness back in 1969, and his reputation was widely known in cable circles. Malone knew that Sparkman and Clouston clashed on several issues, particularly after Sparkman started questioning Clouston's judgment. "I don't think his plans are working," he told Malone one day. At first Malone dismissed J. C.'s comments as a natural jealousy. He felt loyal to Clouston, the closest thing he had to an heir apparent. J. C. was getting long in the tooth, in Malone's view; he had to bet on intellect, and the best guy he had, intellectually speaking, was Brendan Clouston. He had been to business school when Malone hadn't, and Clouston had hired the best outside consultants TCI's money could buy. For the time being, Malone found himself willing to give his number two the benefit of the doubt.

That inclination dissipated almost as soon as the phone rang in Malone's office in Maine, early one morning in the late summer of 1996. He had been savoring the end of a longer-than-usual vacation, sequestered in his white 12-room house on his rambling 200-acre estate, not far from picturesque Boothbay Harbor. He was pleased, at first, to hear the familiar voice of his old friend, Gordon Crawford, who also happened to be one of TCI's largest investors. Gordy, as he was affectionately called by those closest to him, was the unpretentious head of a Los Angeles–based money management firm called Capital Research that owned billions of dollars worth of media and entertainment assets. Crawford studied entertainment and media stocks and managed big positions in TCI, Time Warner, Disney, News Corp., and Viacom, among others. He knew their chiefs (Malone, Levin, Eisner, Murdoch, and Redstone, respectively), and he cultivated a familiarity beyond calling them by their first names. On the phone, Malone knew from the solemn tone of Crawford's voice that he was in no mood for chitchat. Within seconds, Crawford got to the point: He had a bad feeling about TCI's upcoming financial report for the third quarter ending September 30.

As Malone listened intently, Crawford laid out a dark scenario: Brendan Clouston had promised better days at TCI for months now. His strategy, which Malone had approved and supported, was to transform TCI from an old-style cable company that sold plain service into a true communications conglomerate, a one-stop shopping spot for any service a family could want. Besides hundreds of channels, the new TCI would offer high-speed Internet services and wired and wireless telephone service—all with the same reliability as the phone companies, with whom TCI would be competing. Clouston was spending millions of dollars to prepare TCI to sell these new services en masse, all the while assuring TCI investors that new products would translate into higher cash flow. TCI shareholders, stoked by Clouston's promises, were expecting a return to healthy growth in TCI's cash flow in the third quarter of 1996. But now Crawford had come to a troubling conclusion: TCI would fall short of Wall Street analysts' expectations for its third-quarter results, due in weeks. Cash flow, the mighty artery of life for TCI, would constrict when everyone was expecting it to open wider. On Wall Street, a downside surprise can kill a company's stock. Malone and others were originally expecting a slight surge in cash flow from subscriber rate increases earlier in the year. "It looks ugly," Crawford told Malone, adding that patience was wearing thin among TCI's big institutional investors, who kept expecting things to turn around. Malone hung up the phone, and Crawford's comments hung in the air like roiling clouds, as he wondered what was happening back in Denver.

When the third-quarter numbers were finally released, they were far worse than analysts, investors, or anyone else had expected. After a whopping 13 percent rate increase in June, TCI *lost* 70,000 basic subscribers and 308,000 pay-TV subscribers, mainly due to the price increases and, more alarming, to new satellite competitors selling minidishes. Cash flow had grown a measly 3 percent, factoring out the company's latest acquisitions, at a time when most analysts were expecting a healthy 10 percent growth rate. On October 25, 1996, when the preliminary numbers were released, investors bailed out of TCI. Its shares were the most active stock traded on the Nasdaq Stock Market, closing at a new 52-week low of $11.625.

To the press and to his investors, Clouston desperately explained that expenses had eaten up much of TCI's precious cash flow. He pointed out that TCI was launching critical new services, particularly the At Home high-speed Internet service, new telephone services, digital cable, and new billing software for the entire company. The quarterly numbers masked other problems. TCI's profit margin was thinning, and more worrisome for Malone was the towering debt of $15 billion—a new record for TCI. In retrospect, it was clear that Clouston's grand plans to transform TCI worked only on paper. TCI's strategy, while eloquent, could not be executed without piles of money that TCI could ill afford. Clouston was focusing on a point three or four years out in the future, while committing hundreds of millions of dollars near-term. In Clouston's world, a national TCI call center answered the phone 24 hours a day, seven days a week instead of local TCI offices picking up the phone only from 8 A.M. to 5 P.M. He wanted service trucks to respond within a two-hour time frame rather than "one day next week." He wanted better customer records and easier ways for TCI's far-flung offices to report information internally. He wanted to solve every problem, Malone thought, before he could solve any. If TCI had had enough money to do it and Wall Street had given it the time, Clouston's plan to overhaul TCI would have worked, but neither condition was true. Instead, TCI was faltering, and for someone—most likely for Brendan Clouston—there was hell to pay.

Malone boiled with rage. He jetted back to Denver, halted all spending at TCI, and threw himself into turning the company around. TCI stock had fallen 40 percent from its high in 1995, Standard & Poor's Corporation had just put TCI on credit watch, reviewing the rating on TCI debt for possible downgrade. So Malone acted urgently. He surprised Wall Street by abruptly suspending all orders for equipment from TCI's major suppliers, including General Instrument. When an October 13 letter to its suppliers asking them to suspend orders was read on CNBC, TCI stock dipped again. He cut executive salaries, including his own, some by as much as one-fifth, and froze others. He laid off 2,500 people, mostly in marketing, and he sold the four TCI jets. Malone personally reviewed all expenses not directly related to delivering the core cable service. "It was clear we had to do something. Had we not done something, it could have meant tens, if not hundreds of millions of dollars of losses to our bondholders," Malone said later. "And we didn't want that."

Malone inhabited an entire conference room, where he studied profit and loss statements and only then came to realize the extent of TCI's finances. He held all-day meetings with department heads and met with Clouston's direct reports—the financial teams, the marketing department, even the line construction managers. He cut off the consultants, froze the high-tech billing system, and threatened to collect TCI bills by hand if necessary. Stacks of reports covered his large marble-topped desk, and he pored over individual budgets. The more he dug, the more spending he uncovered, and the angrier he got.

"He was rip-shit mad," Liberty president Peter Barton would recall much later.

Malone was rip-shit mad because he wasn't asking enough of the right questions of Clouston and his staff, and they weren't pushing hard enough to keep him in the know. In November 1996, anyone within earshot of the 11th floor at 5619 DTC Parkway in Denver could hear a very rare thing: John Malone yelling. TCI's capital budgets, which covered the costs of upgrading the systems, had soared. Malone scoured thousands of horizontal lines in budget reports, reviewing every city where TCI was building to determine its budget, cost, and progress. Almost all were over budget and behind schedule. Malone tried to put on the brakes. "Stop, we're going to regroup," he would decree, trying to put on hold some of the overhaul.[9] But the momentum of spending at sprawling TCI continued, even though Malone had his hand steady on the brake lever. As Malone's lieutenant, Larry Romrell, would later recall it: "He'd say, 'Stop,' and the next meeting it didn't stop, it didn't even slow down. He would review the new numbers, and he was so frustrated. And he'd tell people, 'Your job is next! You're not going to have this job if I don't see this thing stopped!' It was pretty brutal. It takes a lot for John to blow his cork over something. But this was the maddest I've ever seen him over an extended period. It was months maybe before he started to level out."

Part of Malone's outrage arose from personal embarrassment over the delay. It was, after all, his call for 500 channels that had started TCI down this rutted road. By his public proclamation, TCI was supposed to be delivering the digital era over cable by now. Yet no cable operator had delivered a single new interactive service, and it seemed to be getting farther and farther out of reach. It had all promised to be so simple, and then nothing was. One big obstacle was a phantom box—black, about the size of a cereal carton, a powerful computer that could handle movies on demand, downloadable video games, home shopping, and hundreds of TV channels. It was the magic bullet the cable industry was betting on to transform the TV set, and it was extraordinarily complex and expensive to build. Promised in 1992, four years later it existed only as a picture in a General Instrument press kit. TCI had ordered a million new digital boxes from GI, John Malone's former employer, but GI had yet to deliver the first one. It hadn't helped, either, that Malone kept adding requests for new capabilities as the box was being built.

The delay was deadly to cable stocks, weighing them down and growing heavier with each passing day. Malone didn't hesitate to show his frustration with GI, whom he considered the real culprits, in private and public. Once, at a cable trade show in 1996, Malone was brought onstage before a large crowd by Dick Clark to introduce the evening's entertainment, Little Richard. While the band set up, Malone, in a rare role as a warm-up before the main act, launched into a version of his favorite joke: "A young lady goes to the psychiatrist," he began, "and says 'Doctor, you've got to help me; I've been married three times and I'm still a virgin.'" Her first husband was a salesman who was hit by a bus. The second was a poet who wrote about love but never made it, then died of a heart attack. Finally, the dumbfounded doctor asks about her current husband. "Oh," she said, "he's a GI salesman, and he just constantly tells me how good it's going to be when I get it," Malone bellowed to the crowd, eliciting guffaws.

As the months passed, Wall Street grew increasingly skeptical that consumers would want to pay extra to shop and interact via television. Polls showed most folks, at day's end, wanted to do only one thing with TV—watch it. The costs, everyone suddenly realized, would be enormous. Industry executives pegged the cost for a digital overhaul of the nation's cable systems to be around $100 billion.[10] Malone realized he had to change the perception of the company on Wall Street quickly. He chose a media conference hosted by Bear Stearns in Phoenix to tell the world he had taken back the reins at TCI, which at the time was trading at around $11, a four-year low. On October 24, Malone told a crowd of analysts: "Rumors that I have expired, or am terminally ill or have lost interest in the cable company are substantially inaccurate."

He and Clouston made presentations in the afternoon, and Malone took over the audience at dinner, proving that he could still hold a crowd spellbound by his edifying explanations of TCI's business. He spoke in metaphor like a prophet before a skeptical flock. "When we're free, like Gulliver and the Lilliputians, to use our muscle, we'll use our muscle," he said in a nod to the tortuous government restrictions. He told the crowd TCI would be rolling out a digital TV cable service of 200 channels for less than $20 a month. And before the end of the evening, he predicted TCI would have free cash flow of up to $1 billion by the end of 1997, a whopping increase that set analysts' pens scribbling. His easy manner of speaking, his strong grasp of the facts, and his judicious use of humor seemed to ease their fears, put TCI's problems into perspective, and keep the focus on next year's results. Malone seemed downright confident in the face of a company hemorrhaging cash and facing competition. He called the entrants in the satellite business—who had just stolen 70,000 subscribers from TCI—the "seven dwarfs."[11]

Malone also broke his usual silence to go public with his explanation. "We were just chasing too many rabbits at the same time, and the company had gotten a little overly ambitious in terms of how many things it could do simultaneously," he told the *Wall Street Journal* in late 1996. Conspicuously, Malone shouldered the blame and held nothing back. "My ambition was to be more of an investor and director and to be less of an operating guy," he said. "And every time I look back and see poor Brendan, I see I've created quite a monster of a company here, and I had better help out from time to time." In the extended interview, his first in months, Malone said his job was to "prick the bubble" of expectations. "If you read our annual report last year, you'd think we're one-third data, one-third telephone, and one-third video entertainment, instead of 100 percent video entertainment and two experiments." The hype, he conceded, "influenced our staffing and the market's perception of the business."[12] The mea culpa was so blunt that several shareholders filed lawsuits against TCI management for its role in the stock's bad slide. Back in the saddle, Malone also called a meeting with the company's top 10 institutional investors, and he brought Clouston along. Neither accusatory nor defensive, Malone opened the meeting with, "Tell us what we're doing wrong. How do you perceive it? I'm not here to propose anything, I'm here to listen." It was a bitch session.

TCI needed money. With anemic cash flow, TCI's negative credit rating meant that it had lost its ability to borrow money. Malone couldn't issue and sell TCI stock because it was at an all-time low. He couldn't bear to bring in a strategic investor, for fear of giving up control too cheaply. And he was concerned that if the stock stayed stagnant for a long time, the pressure to sell, or even liquidate the company, piece by piece, could become intense. If that happened, Malone would lose control of TCI's destiny and his own. The only thing TCI could do was fix the operations, which meant that even programs that he believed in had to be killed. Malone longed for the days of J. C. Sparkman and Marvin Jones, two men considered the backbone of TCI's growing operations in the 1970s and 1980s. Though a manager like Sparkman cared little for customer service, he had always delivered growth as head of TCI's operations. Typically, he managed his men through fear. "At the end of the day, if you didn't meet your cash flow growth, you were gone," recalled Sparkman. And that was precisely the type of Draconian remedy that TCI needed now.

Meanwhile, Malone turned his attention to programming costs. Malone saw TCI as a purchasing agent for its customers. TCI, like other cable operators, bought programming wholesale and sold it retail. That meant TCI had to be especially stingy about the rates it paid, and under Brendan Clouston the company had lost its backbone. Clouston gave in and agreed to price increases even for channels that were owned by TCI's Liberty Media. TCI had allowed cable programmers to squeeze ever more generous increases out of the company, forcing it to raise rates, which would, in turn, prompt more customers to drop TCI cable service. Malone was livid: A channel would walk in and demand a 100 percent rate increase, and Clouston would agree to a 50 percent hike—and think he had won the negotiation.

ESPN, with lucrative contracts for major-league baseball, the National Football League, and other big-ticket sports, perennially asked for and received double-digit rate increases. When ESPN wanted carriage of its sister channel, ESPN2, which aired extreme sports, the subtle threat during negotiations, as Malone saw it, was that parent Walt Disney Company could withhold signals of ESPN or even its ABC network from TCI. "Little Mickey had us by the throat," he complained to anyone who would listen.[13] Undaunted, Malone turned the tables: he could always yank a channel off the air if it tried to charge TCI too much. He put programmers on notice that instead of their charging TCI's cable systems for their content, the channels would have to start paying TCI for getting access to the cable dial. Murdoch's Fox News Channel had already begun paying as much as $13 per subscriber to be carried on cable systems; in addition, he offered TCI an option to buy 20 percent of the channel in exchange for TCI systems reaching at least 10 million homes. TCI anounced that it would be kicking off channels that don't pay in order to make room for new ones that do, and it set about dropping WWOR, Comedy Central, Nostalgia, and the Travel Channel, among others, to make room for Home & Garden Television, the Cartoon Network, and Animal Planet.

TCI customers around the country howled. Letters poured in to local franchises. At the University of Kentucky Singletary Center for the Arts, comedian Jon Stewart hosted a benefit concert for Comedy Central and passed around a petition to bring the network back to their TCI systems. Later, when MTV and VH1 were dropped in certain markets, Viacom orchestrated protests in several cities, including TCI's home of Denver. Artists such as Jewel, John Cougar Mellencamp, and Don Henley stood on the stage at the Denver Center to protest the removal of MTV and VH1. Once again, Malone had raised the ire of the public. A columnist for the *Denver Post* excoriated Malone for the changes this new position made in his channel lineup. "We are not treated like paying customers; we are treated like livestock to be delivered to a slaughterhouse. If they really want to show me what I'm looking for, show me chairman John Malone in rags holding a tin cup and a 'Will work for food' sign, standing outside the headquarters, which the sheriff had padlocked in preparation for the auction."[14]

It was hard to underestimate the hatred that subscribers reserved for their cable operators, particularly for TCI. In a letter to the St. Louis cable regulator describing endless calls to TCI, Al Walser ended with this rejoinder: "Unforgivable! Get rid of TCI!" "This latest move is nothing more than a way to decrease the value of our viewing pleasure and fertilize their money tree," wrote Roy Horton, miffed that WGN was pulled. "I will go satellite before I swallow this load."

Malone's longtime rival, Sumner Redstone, trumpeted his feelings in *Business Week* after TCI announced plans to bump off a couple of Viacom channels: "I had an absolute, positive commitment from him. He promised it would not happen, but it did happen. I do not believe John Malone would cross Viacom. I just don't believe it." Redstone called Malone directly. A week later, Malone, true to his word, reinstated the Viacom channels where they had been dropped. The potential crisis was quietly averted.[15]

ひひひ

The fear that had gripped Malone 20 years earlier when he arrived at TCI squeezed him again. He tossed and turned at night and wondered constantly if he could pull TCI through. The severe drop in TCI stock price robbed him of credibility with shareholders and caused in him a profound sense of obligation, particularly to Magness. In their frequent and informal chats, Magness never showed the slightest sign of distress and gave Malone his unflinching support, even though on paper he had lost hundreds of millions of dollars as TCI's biggest owner. TCI had lost more than half of its value in three years and hit a low of $11 in 1996. More than 20 years before, Malone had galloped in and saved TCI from problems he hadn't created, but this time TCI's travails were because of what he had done, he and his lieutenant. This weighed heavily on John Malone: "It was always Bob's company. I was running it for him kind of like a loyal son would run the family company, but didn't own any of it," was the way he looked at it.[16] This he would have to fix, and soon.

Days before the new year 1997 got underway, still in his office as the first stars appeared in the darkening sky over the Rockies, Malone told a reporter: "When it ultimately works—and it now does— when it ultimately turns out to be everything we hoped it would be and more, then I think we'll be vindicated. But the problem is we got a price to pay, and we are paying it right now for getting ahead of ourselves."[17] Malone's star was falling. "They've cried wolf too many times," Christopher Dixon, a PaineWebber Group analyst told the *Wall Street Journal.*[18] "The glow is off John Malone," said an analyst at STI Capital Management, which held 2.9 million TCI shares. "Skeptical best describes how we feel about him."[19]

10

DR. KEVORKIAN

In the months after John Malone woke up and retook control of TCI, he made it a point to back Brendan Clouston, publicly and without equivocation, but in the end Clouston's ouster was inevitable. It was a necessary bounty that had to be collected. He had committed the gravest of sins: He had let TCI's finances get out of control, he had disappointed Wall Street, and worst of all, he had *surprised* Wall Street with that disappointment. TCI's institutional investors needed to see someone pay, and Malone was disappointed and irritated with the man he had chosen to succeed him. After all, in 1973, an exhausted Bob Magness had tapped Malone to run the show, and Malone had pretty much never let the man down; 23 years later, an exhausted Malone had tapped Clouston, and now all hell was breaking loose.

Despite his annoyance in the first weeks after Malone rejoined day-to-day operations, the rapport between him and Clouston was cordial. He couldn't bring himself to fire Clouston, whom he regarded as devoted and loyal. That he allowed loyalty to come before performance was, perhaps, one of Malone's greatest weaknesses as a manager during his career at TCI.

Malone allowed the deposed executive to stick around, which made it all the more humiliating when, in February 1997, he tapped a new number two, a longtime cable partner named Leo Hindery, Jr. Hindery, 49 years old at the time, who was a serial deal maker, part-time racecar driver, and, as Daniels and Associates chairman Brian Deevy mused, "the hardest working man in cable."[1]

On his first day in the new job, Hindery entered the TCI building with his left arm in a cast, still aching after a nasty spill on a freshly waxed floor. He walked into a 10 A.M. staff meeting that was run by Brendan Clouston, who by this time had assumed the new title of chief financial officer—reporting to Hindery. After Clouston opened the meeting, each executive around the table spoke up, telling what he had done the previous week. Arm throbbing, Hindery listened to the first two executives and couldn't believe that as TCI was crumbling, these guys were wasting precious time gabbing away in a conference room. Talk less, do more. He rose to bail out of the meeting before it was even over, telling the group, "This is the last meeting of this kind we will ever have."[2] He took up residence in Magness's old office, connected to Malone's by a doorway.

Three months later, Hindery's public debut as the new blood at TCI was a bit friendlier. In a session with big institutional shareholders at a hotel in New Orleans, Hindery strode up to the front and fielded questions from a small group of influential investors, most of whom were frustrated with the stock's performance. After three months on the job, this was the first time some of them had seen Hindery up close. After Hindery opened the meeting with a brief introduction of himself and his solemn promise to fix TCI, Gordon Crawford, who had harangued Malone about TCI's stock price, pounced. "Leo," he began, "you're coming into a company that is arrogant. Corporate arrogance is pissing off the customers, it's pissing off the government, and it's pissing off your investors. What are you going to do to change it?" Uncomfortable silence followed. But then Hindery disarmed Crawford with his self-effacing humor and apologies for mistakes made at TCI before his arrival. He recited his track record in running Intermedia, the seventh-largest collection of cable systems in the United States, and gave a peek at TCI's recovery plan. If Malone had any doubts that Hindery was the best possible choice, they vanished quickly. This was the tonic that TCI so badly needed.

Hindery was a veteran driver in NASCAR races and a student of Richard Petty, whom he called an "old and trusted friend." Racing cars was the only hobby that could keep his mind off business. His fastest speed on the track was 196 miles per hour, and he wanted to match it in the office. He made a point of arriving for work in Denver by 5 A.M., every day, placing calls to Wall Streeters back East before some had even crawled out of bed. Hindery had worked in San Francisco at Chronicle Publishing Company, which owned a portfolio of TV stations, cable systems, and newspapers, and he had left the company to form his own cable firm in 1988. In the mid-1990s, Hindery crisscrossed the country chasing cable deals and building his Intermedia into a cable company reaching 1.4 million subscribers. Often he had blue-chip partners such as the Bank of New York, General Motors, and New York Life, but his most important partner was invariably TCI. Focusing his efforts mainly in the Southeast, Hindery quickly built up a portfolio of systems in Tennessee, Georgia, and the Carolinas. Over the years, Malone realized that Hindery would consistently wring more out of his systems than TCI. Intermedia's cash flow was stronger, and his profit margins were much higher.

A hard-driving executive, Hindery attributed much of his work ethic to the Jesuits. As a boy, he picked crops on a farm with his family in the Pacific Northwest, then left home when he was 17 to join the merchant marines. He worked odd jobs, including a stint as a sheet-metal journeyman, and earned a bachelor's degree from Seattle University, a Jesuit institution. He then graduated with honors from Stanford University's Graduate School of Business in 1971 and spent nine years at Utah International, a mining company. Malone knew of Hindery's reputation as deal maker and a consensus builder in the industry. In 1990, Hindery had led an industry consortium of companies, which included TCI, that bought Jack Kent Cooke's cable properties for about $1.5 billion. In the convoluted negotiations with the famously cantankerous Cooke, who also owned the Washington Redskins, "Cooke would slam the door and tell us to go away, Leo would come back with an alternative," said Marc Nathanson, owner of Falcon Cable, which participated in the deal.[3] And he had helped to negotiate some of TCI's infamously complex deals. In 1995, Hindery led the $2.2 billion buyout of Viacom's cable TV systems with TCI, a deal that would finally lay to rest Redstone's suit against TCI from the Paramount battle.

Hindery settled into TCI, and came to enjoy Malone's company. He found his new boss to be, if not remote, then terribly complex. "John is the *Three Faces of Eve*," Hindery said later. "Most of us don't live our hidden personalities so publicly. John has this wonderful ability to be several things in one day—contemplative, mathematical, or all business."

ᘮᘮᘮ

Hindery's favorite analogy for TCI's problems was that TCI was a gas station company acting like a pipeline company. Pipelines deliver fuel in bulk. But gas stations *sell* it to retail customers, a far more service-oriented business. Customer service would win the day, and no one could argue that TCI didn't need to pay more attention to its customers. "Running a pipeline business is a pretty easy business—you just turn on a pump. Running gas stations is a really hard business," Hindery liked to say.[4]

After a quick survey of TCI, Hindery saw what Malone had come to see: The company was top-heavy with managers trying to lay out plans to launch a battery of futuristic services that currently brought in no money. Meanwhile, the core business was withering. Too many corporate chiefs and not enough Indians. Too centralized. Instead of scores of TCI cable systems taking orders from Denver, Hindery wanted to put marketing and purchasing decisions back in the hands of local operators. "You market from the bottom up, and not the top down. What works in Birmingham doesn't work in Bozeman,"[5] he told the troops. With haste, Hindery lopped off the heads of 25 executives at TCI, including Brendan Clouston and his team, and replaced virtually all of the positions from within. He began remaking TCI into a collection of local companies that tended to their own markets, based on the simple idea that no single manager can manage more than 2 million subscribers. He also brought some marketing managers who were fired earlier, and asked at least one old-timer, Marvin Jones, to become COO of the cable division. Jones had begun his cable career in 1958 and was president and CEO of United Artists Cable Systems, which had merged into TCI in 1991.

A born politician, Hindery was approachable whereas Malone was aloof, assiduously modest whereas Malone was seen as arrogant. He cultivated a certain humility even in the presence of secretaries and mailroom clerks. Where Malone had angered and antagonized regulators in the hearings on reregulating cable, Hindery offered olive branches in his many trips to Washington, D.C. He delivered cable's message with a peace sign, where Malone had often used a fist. And he seemed to enjoy talking to the press, verboten in years past for all TCI employees, including Malone. Hindery worked to polish his reputation, mend fences, and change the company's image. He needed as many friends as he could get. He removed Ultimate Fighting Championship, the controversial no-holds-barred fights between amateur thugs, from all Intermedia and TCI cable systems. He pushed programs to hire minorities, supported promotion of women in cable, and in 1997, he was honored by Cable Positive, an AIDS awareness group.

He demanded to see copies of customer complaints for weeks at a time. Once he challenged a manager who was balking at refunding $20 to an irate woman who felt she had been ripped off. "Let me just get this right—subscribers are selling for $2,000 apiece. You think you are right, she thinks she is right." What mattered was 20 bucks versus losing $2,000. Weeks later he replaced that manager in Chicago and nearly every system in TCI's universe. Hindery visited with U.S. Senators Hollings and McCain and every other congressperson where TCI ran a cable system. He vowed to free TCI from its status as the whipping boy for the industry; if politicians wanted to bash cable, let them take on the entire industry, not just TCI.

♘♘♘

While Hindery worked on smoothing relations with the rest of the world, John Malone was plotting war against one of the most fearsome moguls in the media business: Rupert Murdoch. For years Malone had done business with Murdoch, the legendary mogul who built a media empire on the back of a struggling Australian tabloid. Murdoch's News Corp. not only defied conventional wisdom by creating a fourth national television network, Fox, but he'd stormed into cable, starting FX and Fox Sports with Malone's help, and later, Fox News.

When Malone first met Murdoch back in the late 1980s, U.S. bankers were ready to call in short-term loans on News Corp., which many thought to be near bankruptcy. Malone, who by then sat on the board of the Bank of New York, persuaded the lender to back off. Malone, sensing a good buy, even threw Murdoch an early lifeline, buying about $70 million of a $140 million private placement in convertible preferred stock by Allen & Co. "Rupert was aggressive, willing to bet everything, and John liked that," said Paul Gould, an investment banker at Allen & Co.[6] Malone walked away from the incident impressed by Murdoch's frank discussion of his problems and convinced of his drive. "He has a strategy and he will do almost anything to execute it," he said later. "Rupert is my hero."

They were fast partners. Malone needed content, Murdoch needed carriage. Together, News Corp. and TCI jointly owned a chain of regional sports channels, the FX cable channel, a joint venture in TV Guide Onscreen, and a direct broadcast system in Latin America. And TCI's Liberty Media and its international arm, TINTA, worked with News Corp. to buy and distribute global rights to televised sports. Malone had the edge, for TCI could instantly add millions of homes to the reach of Murdoch's Fox Broadcasting network and the fledgling Fox News Channel, not to mention the Family Channel, which he was hoping to purchase. The idea, Malone liked to think, was to collaborate even with your enemies—especially with your enemies—to avoid the large and costly fight of real competition. "It's like mutually assured destruction: Both sides could really hurt the other if they did something really stupid," Malone once said. "We have to treat each other with civility to avoid all-out nuclear war."[7]

Yet, for much of 1996, Murdoch's people had been saying unkind things about TCI and plotting an outright assault on the cable industry. They aimed to start a new DBS service, Sky, in the fall with

500 channels of crystal-clear TV pictures and CD-quality sound. It would sell service and pizza-sized dishes to U.S. homes, and every home that ordered Sky would have no need for TCI, or any other cable operator. As Murdoch made his plans clear, John Malone grew nervous. It was one thing to have to face satellite competition from a newcomer like Hughes Electronics and its parent, GM; it was a much more difficult thing to face an assault from Rupert Murdoch. Few promoters were better at building something out of nothing.

Murdoch had pretty much started this latest fight. On the afternoon of February 24, 1997, he gathered 250 people, an assortment of securities analysts and investors from around the globe, on a soundstage on the Twentieth Century Fox lot in Los Angeles. The audience had endured 10 hours of financial presentations, and Murdoch wanted to end things with a bang. So he made some news: Murdoch read aloud a hastily written press release announcing that News Corp. would contribute $1 billion in cash and assets to Echostar Communications Corporation, a minidish service with 500,000 subscribers run by a maverick named Charlie Ergen. To the astonishment of most attendees, Murdoch said he and Ergen would become 50-50 partners in Sky. Unlike its other satellite minidish rivals, Sky would offer local TV channels, thereby creating the first meaningful threat against cable.

Then Preston Padden stepped up to the podium. He was Murdoch's top lobbyist and the chief overseer of the nascent satellite venture, and he launched a vitriolic, populist harangue against monopolistic cable companies that only a veteran of Washington could have pulled off. He promised that Sky would be a "cost-effective overbuild of the entire American cable TV industry." In one carefully rehearsed line, Padden boasted that Sky would have the cable operators "calling Dr. Kevorkian," a reference to the infamous doctor who assisted suicides. The rhetoric held some truth for many who heard it. Details of the plan shocked Wall Street, frightened investors, and enraged cable operators, particularly Malone. Investors dumped cable stocks in droves the following day, wiping out more than $1 billion in market value for the cable TV industry. In a few cable circles, the venture earned the nickname "Deathstar."

A furious Malone called Murdoch after Padden's comments. "We have a real problem," Malone began, and then he pulled out the most serious threat he could conjure up. He suggested to Murdoch that the two companies get out of their jointly owned cable channels—the sports outlets, FX, and still more.

"We should cut the sheets on the programming, because if you go down this road, it's not going to work the cable side," Malone told Murdoch. "You don't walk into a guy's office and piss on his desk and expect him to sign a contract. Padden is yelling 'Dr. Kevorkian!' at the same time I have people trying to sign an FX agreement," he said.[8] Murdoch promised to tone down the rhetoric but press ahead with Sky.

With the new venture, Murdoch hoped to close the final and most crucial link in his global dish-TV strategy. Following the success of its British progenitor, BSkyB, and the launch of Star TV in Asia, as well as a new service in Latin America, the new venture was a way to sink his talons in the U.S. market. To these far-flung corners of the globe, particularly in the United States, Murdoch would beam News Corp.'s Fox network, Fox News, movies, sports, and children's shows. Murdoch's political timing looked superb. President Clinton had just signed into law the Telecommunications Act of 1996, which dramatically reshaped the nation's telecom boundaries in pursuit of a competitive free-for-all. For the first time, the law allowed true competition in both local and long-distance phone service, freed the Baby Bells to get into video, and tried to encourage cable companies to invade the local-phone monopoly. Still, cable was a monopoly.

In a full-page ad in the *Washington Post,* Murdoch and Ergen put their entire lobbying message in a dozen large, block words: "SKY. Finally—The Cable Competition the Telecom Bill Was Designed to Create." Murdoch had also accumulated ample political capital, particularly with the Republicans. News Corp., Murdoch, and his wife Anna together had donated more than $654,000 to the national Republican campaign committees during the 1995–1996 election cycle, not counting the $1 million Murdoch donated to state Republicans in California a few weeks before the previous November's elections. That spring, with regulatory hurdles in his way, Murdoch made an eloquent plea before the Senate Commerce Committee. Minidish TV "still has not made major inroads against cable," he said. "Why?" He gave three reasons: (1) the minimum $700 up-front cost was too expensive; (2) minidish services could not offer affordable rates for multiple TV sets in a single home; and (3) the program package didn't include local broadcast stations. He promised Sky would solve all three in a product that would finally bring competition to cable. "Sky is willing to risk a $3 billion capital investment to bring consumers a *better* choice *now* . . . If you give us the legal authority to compete, the rest is up to us," Murdoch declared.[9] More important, Sky would bypass and undercut the U.S. cable TV industry, which controlled access to 65 million homes.

Padden unabashedly predicted that Sky would have 8 million subscribers and cash flow of $1 billion in six years, taking a healthy bite out of cable's subscribers. By combining their satellites, the new Sky would be the first to offer 500 channels. Murdoch would beat the cable cowboys at their own game. Congress and consumers cheered the news, hailing the News Corp.–Echostar team as the first serious threat to cable's monopoly over U.S. consumers. For the first time, the cable TV industry felt the sharp edge of competition like a razor against its throat.

Before he had ever heard the "Dr. Kevorkian" comment, Malone knew precisely the root of Murdoch's hostility for cable. Though on the surface it was born of a keen competitive spirit, at its heart was a personal and bitter feud. About a year earlier, Murdoch had shaken hands on what he believed to be a firm agreement with Time Warner Chairman Gerald Levin to carry the new Fox News Channel, a 24-hour news channel in New York, the single largest and most lucrative TV market in the world. But Time Warner, the nation's second-largest cable operator, reneged and flatly refused to run the Fox News Channel at all. Murdoch countered that Time Warner was unfairly favoring CNN, recently acquired when Time Warner bought Ted Turner's company; Time Warner shot back that it also carries CNBC. In October 1996, News Corp. filed a fraud and breach-of-contract suit against Time Warner in U.S. District Court in New York, seeking $2 billion in damages.

The disagreement quickly mutated into a caustic and very public spectacle between Murdoch and Turner, the new vice chairman of Time Warner, who frequently lived up to his old nickname, the Mouth of the South. Turner tirelessly tongue-lashed Murdoch in public, describing him as "slimy," and once comparing him with Adolf Hitler in terms of his control over the media for personal benefit. Murdoch is "crazed for money and power," he told a national audience one night on the CBS news program *60 Minutes.* "I fear him and don't trust him."

Not to be outdone, for several days running in the fall of 1996, Murdoch's *New York Post* spent an extraordinary amount of space needling Turner and other Time Warner executives. "Is Ted Turner Nuts? You Decide," read one headline—a reference to Turner's bipolar disorder, which he acknowledged and for which he was prescribed lithium. During the World Series in October 1996 between the Atlanta Braves and the New York Yankees, Turner attended the games to root for his beloved Braves, now owned by Time Warner. News Corp. hired a plane to pass over Yankee stadium pulling a message that read "Hey Ted. Be Brave. Don't Censor the Fox News Channel." Cameras covering one game for Fox network focused on Turner picking his nose. The *New York Post* also went after Turner's wife, Jane Fonda, running a picture of Fonda in Hanoi during the Vietnam War by a column referring to her as "just another scatty-brained Hollywood nude-nik."

Enraged at the snubbing of his family of Fox cable networks, and worried that other cable operators would refuse to carry his programming, Murdoch pushed ahead in his effort to take over the fledgling U.S. satellite minidish TV market. He would show the cable industry. But the window of opportunity was closing fast—cable operators were racing to roll out their own version of digital TV to stave off satellite rivals. Murdoch had held talks with General Motors Corporation's DirecTV, the market leader with 1.7 million subscribers at the time, but nothing came of it. He had tried to link up with Primestar, the satellite-dish company owned by a consortium of cable companies, including TCI and its 1.8 million subscribers.

But Time Warner, a co-owner of Primestar, balked at letting Murdoch in. Malone appealed directly to Time Warner Chairman

Gerald Levin, arguing it was better to have Murdoch in the tent than outside of it. To no avail; Levin and others wouldn't budge. "Some of our fellow industry leaders had their heads up their ass," Malone would say later. Had his own agreement with Primestar not precluded it, Malone surely would have bolted from the cable pack and joined Murdoch's satellite venture—a possibility that still intrigued him a few years later. Malone had thought of Primestar as a safety net that accomplished two objectives: First, it was a way to catch the rural homes not reachable by cable, and second, in John Malone's eyes, if satellite competition was about to descend on the cable industry, it was better to be the competition yourself. Malone so trusted Murdoch, "I should have gone passive and let Rupert run it," he said later.[10]

When Murdoch realized he could not partner with the bigger, more established players, he settled for Echostar's Charlie Ergen, a Tennessee-bred entrepreneur who had broken into the dish business at the age of 27 by selling big 10-footers from a storefront in Denver. From a distance, Charlie Ergen looked like a teenager— fresh face, closely cropped and neatly combed brown hair. His dark brown eyes and wide smile were the finishing touches on an image he consciously projected: an earnest countryboy made good who never forgot his Tennessee roots. But his easy demeanor belied a wickedly sharp entrepreneur with a ballsy willingness to gamble— he had actually been banned from certain Las Vegas casinos for counting cards. In 1987, sensing a new opportunity, he had applied for a license to broadcast to much smaller 18-inch dishes. Ergen's Echostar started selling a service, Dish Network, offering a simple package that included 40 of the best cable channels, including MTV, USA, CNN, and the Disney Channel for $20 a month. Echostar had been hammering the cable industry in full-page newspaper ads ever since.

Ergen proved a nimble and combative competitor, even though he was two years behind GM's DirecTV unit. When asked who his competition was, Ergen liked to crack, "General Motors and General Malone." In the first nine months of business, Echostar signed up more than 300,000 subscribers at a rate of more than 60,000 a month. He straddled more than $1 billion in debt, then sparked a price war with his biggest rivals. In the summer of 1996, he cut the price to $199. In a full-page ad in *USA Today* in early 1997, Echostar ran ads that declared in bold letters: "Cable rates are on the rise again," with a bold arrow pointing upward. "Dish Network is your true alternative."

After years of casual conversation, Ergen and Murdoch quickly struck a binding agreement in a week of intense negotiations in Denver and Los Angeles. Murdoch's News Corp. announced it would buy 50 percent of Echostar Communications for $500 million in cash and the rest in satellites and other assets it owned with MCI Communications Corp.

ՄՄՄ

Murdoch's moves enraged cable operators. One of their biggest suppliers of programming was now fixated on becoming their largest competitor. They responded by openly blackballing him. Aside from Time Warner's refusal to carry Fox News in New York, other cable systems halted negotiations to add Fox channels, and some refused to meet with Fox executives at all. "It's like giving bullets to a guy who wants to shoot you," was the way one cable operator, Jeff Marcus, founder of Dallas-based Marcus Cable viewed it.[11]

Sometime in late March 1997, Malone and Hindery met with Murdoch to try to find a way out of the sordid mess. Murdoch was frustrated. Malone told Murdoch his plan to end-run cable was lunacy. "Well then, help me get out of it," Murdoch responded. "Help me find something else to do. What is plan B?"[12] Plan B included the enticement that TCI and other cable operators would carry Murdoch's cable networks.

"We concluded with both organizations saying, 'Let's talk. Let's not whale on each other'," Hindery said later.[13] During the spring, Hindery approached News Corp. chief operating officer Chase Carey about the possibility of bringing Murdoch into the cable tent. Both Hindery and Malone were playing the role of peacemaker, trying to convince the cable operators in Primestar that there was more profit in peace than war. Time Warner was the most vehemently opposed to the idea, still angry at the suit.

The cable operators' swarming opposition began to take a toll, and barely two months out of the gate, Murdoch's merger plans with

Charlie Ergen ran aground. Sky was falling, fast. The relationship had been strained from the start. Many within News Corp. were divided about Ergen. Chase Carey, COO at News Corp., told Murdoch he thought Ergen was a "small-time entrepreneur who would never rise to the level required by the venture."[14] But no matter. "He can't fire me and I can't fire him," Ergen, the chief executive said about Murdoch, the new chairman of Sky. "It's like a marriage."[15] Ergen's biggest enemy within Fox was Preston Padden, who had engineered several big regulatory victories for News Corp., including the nasty public battle over foreign ownership rules for Murdoch. Padden wanted to be a businessman, and Murdoch rewarded him by naming him president of Sky. But as Padden and Ergen planned the launch of Sky for the following year, Padden grew increasingly frustrated. Ergen, as chairman, repeatedly overruled Padden on everything from terms of a partnership to whether the office floors should be carpeted or covered with linoleum. Ergen, ever the penny-pincher, opted for linoleum.

At first, a genuine effort was made at bonding between the two camps. Indeed, Padden and Ergen vacationed in Phoenix together on Easter weekend at a local resort with their families. But back at the office, Ergen tightened his grip on Sky, often directly reversing orders made by Padden. For example, when Padden tried to buy two $8,000 emergency generators for its $150 million uplink facility in Arizona, Ergen nixed one of the generators in a cost-cutting move.

The breaking point between the two companies came when Murdoch sent a letter to Ergen insisting that the Sky venture use News Corp.'s News Datacom Ltd. security system. Ergen argued that Sky's own system was better. Padden pleaded with Ergen to "find it in your heart to give Rupert a break" and adopt the News Datacom system. Finally, Padden blew up, telling Ergen that the News Datacom system was "a very important business for News Corp. and to have our partner spurn it would not be good for our image." Ergen wouldn't budge. Two weeks later Padden quit, telling Murdoch, "You took my baby and gave it to an asshole!"[16]

On the day news trickled out that Murdoch and Ergen were having problems, in April 1997, Echostar's stock price dropped 14 percent to below $15. Curiously, TCI Satellite Entertainment, the separately traded company that represented TCI's 21 percent equity interest in Primestar, rose by 16 percent.[17]

♘ ♘ ♘

In a stunning about-face, Murdoch worked aggressively to heal his relations with the cable industry. His first peace offering would have to be aimed at Time Warner. The week of April 28, Murdoch telephoned Ted Turner to ask if a deal in which he could join Primestar might be possible. Turner curtly told Murdoch that he'd have to call Time Warner Chairman Levin. The following day, after each signed confidentiality papers, Levin and Murdoch met in Levin's office in New York City. The News Corp. founder said that he was willing to drop the lawsuit against Time Warner and that he wanted to pursue a Primestar deal, provided Primestar would guarantee carriage of News Corp.'s cable networks. But the fissures had grown too deep for Levin to see a reason to help a competitor. Levin said he wasn't interested. Levin and Turner, confident that Time Warner's big stake gave it veto power, were prepared to thwart any deal involving Murdoch.

Back in Denver, Malone wanted Murdoch in the partnership. TCI chief Leo Hindery enlisted Gordy Crawford, the closest thing to a diplomat and a major shareholder in both TCI and News Corp. Crawford had serious misgivings about Murdoch's U.S. satellite ambitions, believing the cable industry juggernaut was too formidable. He was also concerned about News Corp.'s balance sheet after a recent buying spree. News Corp. investors, spooked by memories of his brush with bankruptcy in the late 1980s, didn't want him to invest the additional $3 billion needed to launch a minidish service. None of this seemed to matter to Murdoch. In one week alone, he bid $350 million for the Los Angeles Dodgers baseball team and edged closer to a $1 billion bid for the Family Channel, owned by Virginia televangelist Pat Robertson's International Family Entertainment (IFE). But even Crawford, a longtime backer of Murdoch and a frequent guest of Turner at his Montana ranch, could not broker the peace. Turner could not forget Murdoch using his media outlets against him a year earlier. "They attacked my family," Turner said. "I'll never forgive him."

Malone and the other cable partners had better luck with Gerald Levin; they managed to convince Levin that the one approach that solved a majority of problems was allowing Murdoch in. The $1.1 billion in cash and satellite assets Murdoch would contribute meant that Primestar could become a powerful player in DBS, over time possibly the most powerful. Levin agreed, grudgingly, but not before exacting some quid pro quos: Murdoch's stake had to be nonvoting, and TCI's camp had to agree essentially to share control of Primestar with Time Warner. Finally, Dan O'Brien, who then headed Time Warner's satellite efforts, was to be put in charge.

It was a rare picture for media watchers: Rupert Murdoch, one of the shrewdest, most powerful media barons at the time, had misjudged the U.S. media market in a critical way. In Britain, Murdoch had successfully challenged a complacent broadcasting establishment by introducing satellite TV. He quickly signed up millions of subscribers by locking up exclusive movie and sports rights. By contrast, the U.S. cable industry was a far more antagonistic rival, especially when cable operators were aligned against a common threat. Moreover, the DBS market in the United States, though fledgling, already had three strong entrants. On top of arriving late to the market in 1998, Sky would have had to sign up 5 million subscribers to break even by some estimates. And Murdoch had other financial obligations, including a big check he had to write to keep the NFL with Fox. Murdoch had always known that the Sky venture would lose money. But even Murdoch had his limits.

Malone could also pressure Murdoch another way: Liberty was controlling owner in the Family Channel, a cable network owned by Pat Robertson that News Corp. desperately wanted. Pat Robertson, the chairman of IFE, continually asked for more money.

If he could pull off a deal with Primestar, Murdoch would extricate himself from his biggest strategic blunder in years. But it would cost him. It would mean Murdoch had broken a promise to the U.S. Congress to take on the cable industry, yet he had also angered the cable gang, the one group of businesses that could effectively castrate him in the United States. It was all becoming clear to Murdoch. He had rushed into the wrong deal with Echostar, without firm agreements on management or strategy. He had underestimated how much News Corp. would have to spend, and he had minimized the retribution of Washington lawmakers. Most of all, he had misjudged the ferocity of John Malone.

Finally, in May of 1997, Murdoch overcame Time Warner's objections and won a tentative agreement to join Primestar Partners. As part of the deal, Murdoch contributed the satellites that he and MCI owned in return for a nonvoting minority stake in Primestar. By buying peace with the cable operators, Murdoch secured a position more important to him—assurances to carry News Corp.'s myriad tentacles of programming. "When Rupert joined Echostar, they were scared shitless," Malone said of his cable brethren later. "It helped me bring people together."

♘♘♘

On June 11, 1997, Primestar admitted Murdoch and his satellites into the group of cable operators that ran Primestar. That same day, CBN sold the Family Channel for $1.4 billion to Murdoch, who would sell it to Disney three years later for $3 billion. The priority for News Corp., Murdoch said at the time, was "access to—not control of" distribution outlets. "It's our software that unites all of our activities." Echostar filed a federal lawsuit in Denver seeking $5 billion, alleging News Corp. reneged on its contract. News Corp. countersued.

The threat that Sky posed neutralized for the moment, John Malone had pulled off a huge coup yet again. He would be dealt a setback a year later when the Justice Department filed an antitrust suit against Murdoch, TCI, Time Warner, Comcast, and other partners in Primestar, blocking Primestar's bid to buy News Corp. and MCI's satellite business. "DBS presents the first real threat to the cable monopoly," said Joel Klein, Assistant Attorney General of the Justice Department's Antitrust Division. "Unless this acquisition is blocked, consumers will be denied competition—lower prices, more innovation, and better services and quality." Malone knew this wasn't the end of it: He would be facing Rupert Murdoch on the battlefield of business soon enough.

11

DEATH OF A COWBOY

"I've probably given a thousand speeches in the past 30 years. This is the toughest one for me." So began the eulogy John Malone chose for Bob Magness, his mentor, partner, and friend. Magness died on Friday, November 15, 1996, succumbing with alarming speed to lymphoma, a particularly deadly form of cancer of the lymphatic system. Two weeks later, on a bright, clear fall afternoon in Denver, almost a thousand mourners filed into the Church of the Nazarene to pay tribute to Robert John Magness.

When Malone ambled to the altar to speak, his hulking figure was heavy with grief. In his voice was a detectable vulnerability, as if the grief had forced a slightly unnatural rhythm to his normally casual baritone. "I came to love Bob," he said. "He was a man of enormous virtue. Quiet. Deep. Solid. Loyal. Brilliant in many ways. Self-effacing. We went through a lot of experiences together. We were partners. He was my mentor. In many ways, he was my father." Malone's own father, Daniel, had passed away several years earlier. "We were frequently unindicted [coconspirators]," Malone said, teasing furtive laughs from the hometown crowd. "We built a company. I joined a family."

His listeners included Ted Turner and his wife, Jane Fonda; Tim Robertson, son of televangelist Pat Robertson and head of the

Family Channel; longtime cable buddy Carl Williams; Glenn Jones, another Denver cable magnate; and legions of other business partners and competitors. "I hope there's this many people at my funeral," Ted Turner told the overflowing crowd mourning Magness. He heaped praise on Magness for stepping forward with Malone on the rescue of Turner Broadcasting. He credited Magness with igniting his own passion for the West, parcels of which Turner had since accumulated in such large numbers that he'd become the largest individual landowner in the country. "He was just about the finest man I ever met," Turner said. "I used to say, 'You build the wires and we'll make 'em sing'."

Sharon Magness, 47 at the time, had been married to Bob Magness only seven years by the time of his death. She planned the funeral and strictly abided by what Magness wanted. Only a few people saw Magness's remains before the funeral, just family members, John Malone, and longtime aide Larry Romrell; that's the way Bob had wanted it. There were no 21-gun salutes, because he hated the army and the way those bastards had bossed him around. His military career was noted by the simplest touch: an American flag, which Sharon had made sure was nicely ironed, draped over the coffin. Yet the service struck a decidedly patriotic chord. A Boy Scouts color guard presented three flags: one each for the United States, Colorado, and TCI. Country singer Lee Greenwood's version of "God Bless the USA" echoed softly about the arched ceilings of the church. Magness's body lay in its casket at the front of the church, near pews swathed in white roses. Near the front doors, a black show saddle studded in silver sat near a photo of Bob with one of his Arabian horses. On a corner of the frame hung his cowboy hat. Outside the church, Magness's horse, Thunder, the high-spirited mascot of the Denver Broncos, ate hay and pranced around. A choir led the mourners in "Battle Hymn of the Republic."

It was inspiring and comforting, but as Malone witnessed the service, a dark fear intruded on his fathomless gloom: that the single largest block of voting stock in TCI, Bob Magness's supervoting shares, might go up for grabs, giving any outsider considerable control of TCI. When Malone had first visited Magness at the hospital, Malone asked whether Magness had updated his will, but he couldn't bring himself to raise the issue again. He should have: Bob Magness did, indeed, have an updated version of his will, but it was unsigned. Malone and Sharon Magness had talked briefly about asking Bob to sign the document and make it all official, but they worried that the hospital's doctors would never allow it. Now they were stuck, and Malone had a gnawing, uneasy feeling about what might happen next.

ʊʊʊ

On the day of the funeral, two of Magness's oldest friends, Donne Fisher and Dan Ritchie, whom Magness had named as executors of his will, met with Bob's widow, Sharon Magness, and his two grown sons by his first marriage, Gary and Kim. Magness's legal will was a 22-page document peppered with notes and corrections. He crossed out sections he did not approve of, and wrote his initials where the revisions were made. He inserted multi-million-dollar changes in the upper and lower margins, and connected them to the text by long curvy lines that looped around paragraphs. Magness had left the lion's share of his estate to his two sons, about $225 million each. To his wife Sharon, he left $20 million and a $15 million trust; the couple's Cherry Hills Village home; Western artwork; and Magness Arabians, Incorporated, which owned about 400 horses. He left roughly $14 million to charity. On one page, in tiny letters barely big enough to read, he listed his charitable gifts: "(1) $500,000 to Colorado Ocean Journey; (2) $900,000 to the Denver Art Museum; (3) $2.5 million to the Boy Scouts of America; (4) $10 million to Denver University; (5) $1 million to such charities as my wife designates." Sharon had encouraged Bob's philanthropy in his later years, and he especially enjoyed donating and buying Western art. One of their latest donations had been his favorite: a 1906 painting by Charlie Russell of three Indians in a canyon, *In the Enemy's Country.*

Magness's estate was valued at around $1 billion, but one issue quickly outweighed all others upon his death, for it put the company he built into jeopardy: Much of his TCI stock would have to be sold to pay an estimated $500 million estate tax, a levy of about 55 percent, owed to the Internal Revenue Service. Shockingly, the biggest heir to the estate of Bob Magness, a man who so thoroughly detested paying taxes during his life, was the IRS. Magness made surprisingly little use of charitable trusts or other tax-sheltered means to transfer wealth to heirs, and for weeks following his death, newspapers pointed to his estate as a classic example of poor estate planning. Typically, wealthy individuals with Magness's kind of background took pains to structure their estates so their heirs wouldn't be bled by the IRS. It was as if one of the wealthiest men in the country had stashed his fortune in a sock drawer.

ՍՍՍ

Magness's will placed even more pressure on Malone to fix TCI. If he could raise TCI's stock price again fast enough, fewer shares would have to be sold to cover the estate taxes, and Malone could stay in control. But with TCI stock hovering around its all-time low, a large voting block might have to be sold on the open market, which might be disastrous for the company. Such a sale could depress the share price even lower and, more worrisome, allow outside investors unprecedented voting control in the company. For the first time, Malone publicly emphasized that he had the right to buy any TCI shares forfeited by the Magness estate before the stock could be offered to anyone else, sending a back-off signal to any would-be raiders. That right, which was given in a 1988 letter to Malone signed by Bob Magness, gave Malone some comfort. But a corporate raider could easily name a price that even Malone, with all his wealth, could not afford to match in a bidding war.

Magness's two old pals and executors, Donne Fisher and Dan Ritchie, jumped to seal Magness's last will and testament by a court order. The taxes were due in nine months by law, and the executors didn't want people to know they had this enormous pressure to raise huge sums of cash over what was a relatively short period of time. In court documents, the estate's attorney told the judge that potential buyers of Magness's stock would "have you over a barrel" if they knew of the duress to sell. Further complicating matters, Magness left no formal accounting of the estate of his late wife Betsy, though he was the executor and, in fact, had mixed some of their assets.

Adding another layer of complexity, Betsy's $26 million estate was to be divided between the boys upon her husband's death. When asked to describe the will in late 1996, Peter Barton, the Liberty Media chief, told his questioner: "You ever hear of the term FUBAR? That's what the estate is—Fucked Up Beyond All Recognition."[1]

Matters were made worse by how little time Bob Magness had to get his affairs in order. In the fall of 1996 he had seemed weaker than usual. On a lunch break at a TCI board meeting, Magness told Donne Fisher, his longtime friend and TCI board member, "I've just been awful goddam tired lately. I could take a nap right now." Fisher noticed his old friend looked pale. Balding and gray himself, he chuckled and said, "Hell, Bob, we're both getting old." A few weeks later, Magness dropped by Malone's office, with its striking vista of the Rockies, to say he was headed out to Santa Barbara, California, later that day. Though Magness was concerned about TCI's current straits and Malone's urgent return to set things right, it was also clear that Magness had no doubt that Malone would prevail over the current troubles. Magness shared a secret with his friend: He was about to bid a multi-million-dollar sum for a ranch that he had only leased in the past. The seller was asking too much money, but Magness, at 72, was willing to allow himself the extravagance of overpaying for the property. Ranching was in his blood, and his heart still leapt at the sight of the young Arabian colts he raised. His Arabian herd now numbered 900 and had achieved international acclaim. He told Malone a joke and walked out the door.

A few days later in Santa Barbara, a frantic Sharon Magness rushed Bob to the Eisenhower Medical Center in Colleacha Valley, believing he had suffered a stroke. They had been driving through the city when Bob made a comment about "how good the crops looked." Sharon looked around the highway and saw concrete, asphalt, and steel, but no crops. She noticed other non sequiturs in his speech and sensed he wasn't quite himself. Concerned, she took him to the hospital.

Like any good cowboy, Magness had never taken care of his body. Too much liquor and red meat, heaps of stress, and no exercise had made him a prime candidate for a heart attack. He had taken blood pressure medication ever since Malone had joined the company back in 1973. On two occasions in Malone's presence, Magness had fainted dead away, scaring the hell out of his protégé. Magness's frailty stemmed in part from cardiac arrhythmia, an occasionally abnormal heartbeat that can cause symptoms of light-headedness and, in some cases, death. In April 1991, Magness had gone to the hospital because of ventricular tachycardia, or v-tac, an abnormal heartbeat that originates in the pumping chambers. About a year later, Magness's ticker gave out again, and this time he nearly died. He fell on the kitchen floor and stopped breathing—no pulse—so Sharon whacked him hard on the chest, twice, to revive him and called 911. At the time, doctors installed a tiny defibrillator to stabilize any erratic episodes, but it was later removed.

Malone immediately flew out to the hospital to check up on his beloved benefactor, and Sharon Magness delivered the tragic news. Her husband hadn't suffered a stroke as feared, she told Malone. Instead, doctors diagnosed Magness with lymphoma, an aggressive and particularly deadly form of cancer. They found two tumors, one large and one small, on his brain. The prognosis: Magness would die within weeks.

Nothing prepared Malone for what he saw when he walked into Magness's hospital room. His friend and partner of 25 years, with whom he had joked only days earlier, could hardly speak. Although he could talk clearly on some days, Magness often searched in vain for the proper words to form sentences, more often than not speaking gibberish. Frustrated, he cursed and shook his head, furious that his mouth defied his mental commands. "Shit, shit, shit. . . ." was the only line he could recall easily in his exasperation. Malone could see that Bob understood what he said, even if he couldn't respond, and he could feel Magness's frustration. It was painful for everyone. Still, Magness kept a positive attitude in the next few days, as the list of visitors to his hospital room grew to include Larry Romrell and Bob's sons, Gary and Kim. When Sharon took Bob shopping a few days later in a nearby sporting goods store, Sharon offered to buy him several shirts he had picked up. But Magness stopped her. The message was clear: Let's wait and see whether I make it.[2]

Desperate to help, Malone called Michael Milken, the junk bond impresario who had pleaded guilty to breaking securities laws in 1990 and later staged a remarkable comeback from prostate cancer. TCI had been a client of Drexel Burnham Lambert's in the 1980s, and Milken's junk bonds had financed much of the cable industry. For the first time, Malone sought his counsel on a topic unrelated to financial deals. Milken urged Malone to rush Magness to the University of Virginia hospital in Charlottesville, renowned for its gamma-ray knife, a new tool that dispensed radical radiation to shrink tumors.

Very quickly, Magness's symptoms worsened. His liver began to fail, and his speech to deteriorate further, his brain unable to process the right instructions. "Occasionally an English word would come out, and his visitors would humor him as if they had understood: "Yes, that's right, Bob," recalled friend Larry Romrell.

Somewhere deep inside himself, John Malone struggled to quell the queasy feeling of going it alone, without Bob Magness to bounce things off and tell him everything would be okay. Malone was devastated by the diagnosis, and the laconic, hard-to-read cable cowboy became even more withdrawn than usual. On visits to the hospital, he doted on Magness and made like everything was alright, but he knew it was a lie, and the depression that had always been at the edges of his existence now overwhelmed him.

Everything that constituted Bob Magness had left the man's body—the sharp wit, the drawl, the sense of humor, the sheer appetite for life. In his last hours, he greeted visitors silently with his sky-blue eyes, which now conveyed his profound sense of loss. The 72-year-old Magness surely felt he was taken too soon.

ꙨꙨꙨ

In the weeks following Magness's death, Malone scrambled to consolidate greater control over TCI. In casting about for friendly investors, he approached Microsoft's chairman and founder, Bill Gates, as well as Comcast's controlling family, the Robertses, a longtime ally. He always had been interested in merging TCI with Comcast—the two companies had thrashed out the idea for years—and this could be a first step.

As he described it later: "They were guys I knew, they had plenty of money, and I had been trying to merge with Comcast anyway. I figured what the hell? They backstop me, and then we'll merge the companies later. I'll run it for a while and then Brian [Roberts] will run it. That's what they always wanted."[3] TCI lawyer Jerome Kern spent several days at Microsoft, and Malone spent a lot of time with Ralph and Brian Roberts at Comcast. Neither of them could make a deal stick. Microsoft wanted an ironclad agreement from Malone that he would retire and turn over control of TCI to Microsoft within five years, which Malone was unwilling to grant. And tax and regulatory issues made a Comcast investment impossible for Malone.

"We are extremely vulnerable," Malone thought to himself. "What if someone puts a bid on the table that I can't match?"[4]

In the summer of 1997, Malone devised a complicated offer to gain control of the Magness estate shares. It was classic Malone alchemy in its structure: complicated and logical, with plenty of upside for everybody. Under the plan, TCI would pay $529 million in cash, or $16.52 a share (a 10 percent premium to the stock price at the time) for the Magness estate's 30.5 million supervoting B shares.

Immediately, the Magness sons objected to the plan as unfairly benefiting TCI. Gary and Kim Magness thought the executors were selling too early and had shut off the chance for a higher bidder. The stock would eventually rise, they argued. Backstopping their position was a team of lawyers and advisors whose presence seemed to goad the boys into an aggressive stance. On the day before the planned sale to TCI, Kim and Gary Magness flew out to Maine to try to persuade Malone to change his mind. Having failed, they flew back to Denver to try, once more, to dissuade Donne Fisher, a coexecutor of the estate, from selling. The sons claimed Fisher and Ritchie hadn't genuinely solicited bids for the sale of the stock. The executors, they said, did nothing more than "thumb through their own Rolodexes." The Magnesses said the deal was a "fire sale" carried out by the executors at "breakneck pace" to discourage other bidders. All this was done, the boys claimed, because the two executors were fearful of "pissing off John Malone."[5]

The Magnesses' most enthusiastic objection was against Fisher, their father's longtime close friend. They claimed that Fisher was conflicted in his duties as executor, and they had a point: Fisher received $475,000 a year as a TCI consultant, reported directly to Malone, and was a TCI board member. The boys noted that Fisher and Ritchie's efforts would get only $16.52 per share, hardly a premium for the Magness estate's supervoting B shares. After all, Malone would have received the same 10 percent premium for his supervoting shares under the terms of the Bell Atlantic deal that was aborted in 1994.

Each meeting to resolve the dispute only aggravated the rift, as each side dug in. Although the dispute was, on the surface, about a business transaction, it was also personal for all involved. Gary and Kim Magness, the sole surviving children of Bob Magness, felt they knew best how to reconcile their father's will. Yet the two executors, whom Magness had requested in his own handwriting, had known Magness more than 25 years, and both men were intimately familiar with his struggles to build TCI. Fisher had little patience for the sons' complaints. He had indeed sought out deals with AT&T, software maker Oracle Corporation, and other possible suitors, to no avail. He faced a tight IRS deadline, he worried that cable stocks would fall even further on the stock market, and to pay the mammoth tax bill, he had to come up with more than $500 million that the estate simply didn't have. And TCI had agreed to pay a nice little premium over what he could get by just dumping the shares on the open market. Not to mention this: Just how greedy did Magness's progeny want to be? They would each walk away with nearly $200 million, and they had never done a thing to help build their father's company. Bob Magness would have liked this deal, Fisher felt; these boys ought to get out of the way.

♘ ♘ ♘

Neither of the Magness boys (they were still called "the boys" by everyone at TCI, even though they were now in their 40s) was particularly well liked at the company. Most people, including Malone, showed them respect in public, but it was painfully evident to most everyone that the two sons were not destined for the achievements of their father. Kim Magness, 44 at the time of Bob's death, was the older brother and eventually took Betsy Magness's seat on the TCI board after she died. The reclusive brothers pursued farming and ranching, and a family friend insisted that they were successful entrepreneurs in their own right, in businesses such as cattle, and later, casinos. Despite Magness's fortune, neither son was rich. If they needed money for a home or business, they took a bank loan, typically backed by Bob Magness's signature and collateral. Though Magness relished his role as grandfather to five grandchildren, his relationship with his two sons was strained. Several executives at TCI had watched the boys mature and had noticed with some distress that Gary and Kim openly challenged Bob Magness's carefully deduced decisions, exhibiting a lack of respect for a man who had achieved so much. In moments of anger, they cursed at him.

Neither did Magness's sons seem to have inherited much of the modesty or maturity from the shrewd and quiet cowboy they called Pop. Gary, two years younger than Kim, gave his father grief even as he grew older. About 20 minutes past midnight on June 6, 1994, Cherry Hills police officers spotted Gary Magness speeding down East Quincy Avenue in Denver in his 1973 red Ferrari, tires screeching, weaving in and out of lanes, and running red lights.[6] Gary had just left Bob Magness, with whom he had been arguing. When stopped by police, he failed all the roadside sobriety tests and cursed the officers, who noted how "belligerent and uncooperative" he was. Officers drove him to Arapahoe County East Jail, where he refused a blood test and shouted obscenities. Bob appeared in person to post bond for Gary, who was arrested on charges of driving under the influence of alcohol, speeding, and having no proof of insurance. Bob Magness personally apologized to the arresting office for his son's behavior.

In their younger years, the boys gave Magness his greatest aggravation. In 1973, the Colorado Bureau of Investigation arrested Kim Magness and three others in a drug bust in Garfield County, Colorado, for selling heroin to an undercover agent. Garfield District Attorney Frank Tucker said the arrests were for possession of heroin and conspiracy. Undercover agents bought what was believed to be a pound of pure opiate derivative for $40,000. Investigators estimated the street value of the seizure was $150,000.[7] The charges were eventually lessened, Kim did no hard time, and Magness took him back in. Kim later graduated from the University of Colorado. He once worked at a TCI cable system in Salt Lake City but was later fired because he failed to meet the stern expectations of J. C. Sparkman. Both Gary and Kim had taken on responsibilities intermittently at TCI at their father's request, but they were not cut out to be cable cowboys. "Why didn't Bob make those goddam kids grow up?" Fisher often asked himself. "I can't explain it."[8]

On June 16, 1997, as Fisher was making preparations to go ahead that day with the sale of Magness's stock to TCI, the Magness boys called and demanded that he halt the sale. Another bidder had stepped up to pay even more money for the shares, they claimed, and Kim Magness and his lawyers were on their way to the office of TCI. Fisher told him point-blank: "Don't stop for lunch, because this deal will be closed."[9] He knew he was being a smart-ass, but he meant it. Fisher viewed the whole thing as yet one more attempt by the boys' lawyers to manipulate the process. He could have easily gone back to John Malone and pressured him to sweeten the offer to, perhaps, $20 a share, but he didn't, because he believed Malone's offer was fair, and he viewed the alleged rival offer in simple terms: "Pure bullshit," he said to himself. Neither Magness showed up that day, never showed up at all.

The sale to Malone proceeded that day as planned. The money made a circuitous journey from TCI to the estate. TCI was loaned the $529 million for the 30.5 million supervoting shares by two New York investment banks, Merrill Lynch and Lehman Brothers. TCI bought the estate's class B shares, and then gave Merrill and Lehman the same amount of newly issued A shares; both classes of stock traded at similar prices, though the B shares had 10 times the voting power of A shares. Malone, through TCI, had the luxury of buying back the class A shares from the two banks over time, with interest. Most important, Malone still held hard control of TCI because he had the right of first refusal to buy the B shares, which were now locked securely in the company treasury.

♘♘♘

In June of 1997, Sharon Magness sparked a free-for-all for Magness's fortune when she sued to have his will rescinded by the court, igniting already incendiary emotions among the survivors. Sharon Magness argued in probate court that she was due 50 percent of the estate, around $500 million, instead of the $35 million, the house, and the horse farms she had been bequeathed in Magness's will. Sharon Magness's case was built around a provision in Colorado law that lets a widow claim up to 50 percent of a mate's estate. Sharon requested a jury trial on the issue, pitting herself against her two grown stepsons. On the surface it seemed unlikely the quarrel could unwind the sale of the Magness shares to TCI, but it made Malone nervous nonetheless.

The following month, the boys answered the suit by declaring war. They cited the couple's 1989 prenuptial agreement, which limited Sharon to $5 million in cash and $60,000 for six months' living expenses—significantly less generous terms than she ended up with. They battled in the court of public opinion, too, and it took a heavy toll on Sharon Magness, a woman they had once held in great affection.

Sharon moved in powerful circles in Denver and cultivated her image as a philanthropic socialite. In June 1997, she hosted President Bill Clinton and First Lady Hillary Rodham Clinton at the Magness home; later, at a meeting of the Summit of Eight, a financial conference of world leaders, Sharon rode a white Arabian horse into the arena, hoisting an American flag. Despite her good intentions, she was portrayed as a sly gold digger by her two stepsons. Magness, who in his life never gave interviews and assiduously avoided the press, was now making banner headlines in newspapers. The wealth he had worked so hard to create was now the centerpiece of a lurid sideshow that involved the family he loved and the very people he had tried to shield from the media during his life. "Magness Family Feud: Widow Wants $500M" screamed the *New York Post* headline on June 26, 1997. Under the subhead "Battle Royale" was a list of "Who Got What." "You can draw your own conclusions, but I don't think any of us really know who she is," Shelley Magness, Gary's wife, told the *Rocky Mountain News.* "She just kind of popped into the family years ago. We accepted and loved her, and now she has literally turned her back on us. None of us saw it coming." [10] The animosity grew.

When Sharon Costello first started dating Bob Magness, the boys were naturally suspicious of her motives. After all, she was more than 20 years younger, and Bob Magness was one of the richest men in the United States. She met Bob and Betsy while working with Arabian horses at a horse farm in Arizona. Several months after Betsy's death, Sharon met Bob again at a horse auction in Phoenix, where they struck up a conversation that lasted seven hours. They began to date seriously, and at Magness's suggestion, she moved into his Denver home in December 1986. "I'm gonna find you a younger man," he kept telling her. Finally, after a year went by, he said, "If you're gonna be silly enough to date an old man like me, then I'm just gonna have to keep you."[11] They married in St. Thomas, the U.S. Virgin Islands, in 1989.

Sharon's marriage to Bob was her first. Much of the Magness sons' mistrust and skepticism evaporated, though, when they saw how contented their father was in her presence. Despite the difference in age, Sharon seemed to be the ideal companion for Bob. She loved working with the Arabian horses, she delicately mediated in family squabbles and, despite Magness's wealth, she cooked regularly for Bob—usually filet mignon, baked potato, and Caesar salad. They spent almost every day together, traveling to their horse operations in California and Colorado. Sharon also helped Bob loosen up his pursestrings, and together they gave frequently to charities such as the Boy Scouts, Volunteers of America, the Denver Art Museum, the University of Denver, and the Colorado Women's Foundation. During his last days, Sharon and the boys stood side by side at Bob's bed. Only weeks earlier, Sharon had attended a Mother's Day brunch with the two brothers and their wives, and on the first Christmas after Magness died, they had sailed together on a holiday cruise. But now the goodwill was gone.

The family feud made Malone all the more wary, and he scrambled to consolidate greater control over TCI. He didn't have the financial muscle to do this by sheer force of capital, so Malone resorted to creative alliances and structures, arguing that his shareholders would come out better off in the end. Magness's shares accounted for 26 percent control of the company, even though he owned only 7 percent of the company's stock. Most of Malone's holdings, by contrast, were in Liberty Media, TCI's programming arm. Together, Magness and Malone effectively controlled TCI and Liberty through the supervoting class B shares, each of which counted for 10 votes, while class A shares held only 1 vote apiece—so long as they remained in the right hands. The key to holding on to control of TCI was clear: Buy more class B shares; put other B stock into friendly hands; swap single-vote A shares for supervoting B.

In an effort to grab more B shares, Malone bought 7.3 million TCI class A shares from Knight-Ridder, a newspaper business and TCI investor, then swapped those shares with TCI for the same number of supervoting shares.

In another complicated swap, TCI issued more than $700 million in new TCI stock to buy Kearns-Tribune Corporation, the publisher of the *Salt Lake City Tribune* and one of Magness's earliest investors. Not that Malone and TCI had suddenly found the press a likable enterprise; nor were they particularly fond of the publishing and real estate businesses of closely held Kearns-Tribune Corp. But the deal would enable TCI to buy back the publishing company's 7 percent supervoting class B shares, with 10-to-1 power in any shareholder vote. Kearns was run by chairman Jack Gallivan, a longtime Magness partner who had invested in TCI in the earliest days and had held on to most of his stake. He was a friend, sitting on the TCI board for years. Brilliantly, Malone designed a transaction that insulated TCI and shareholders of Kearns from taxes, yet also promised a small group of managers there the right to buy back the company in five years at fair value—a vow Malone later would end up breaking, to his utter regret.

TCI gave Kearns-Tribune about 47 million shares of its class A common shares. In return, Kearns-Tribune turned over its TCI supervoting shares, as well as its TCI A shares and Liberty shares. Immediately following the deal, Liberty Media bought back the newly acquired Liberty shares from TCI.

The stock swaps, the Kearns-Tribune merger, and the Knight-Ridder deal—all tax-free—boosted Malone's TCI voting power to 25 percent from about 18 percent.

ՍՍՍ

In September 1997, Malone's grand plan to save TCI from corporate raiders hit a wall. The Magness brothers filed a lawsuit against the estate, claiming they were shortchanged in their father's inheritance due to a scheme concocted by Malone and the two executors to gain control of the company. In the suit, the boys asked an Arapahoe County Court judge to overturn the estate's sale of Magness's stock back to TCI for more than $500 million, citing Colorado law that allows heirs to void sales of estates in which the executor has a conflict of interest. The boys petitioned the court to remove Fisher and Ritchie, who they claimed were motivated by loyalty to Malone. At the time the suit was filed, nearly a year after Magness died, TCI stock had climbed considerably, to the low $20s.

"TCI stock has been trading recently (October 29, 1997) at as much as $24¾ per share," the petition read. "This represents an increase of $8 a share or approximately $256 million more than the price received for the Estate's stock just four months earlier. Given that increase, Fisher and Ritchie should have borrowed money against the stock's value to pay the IRS." In the petition, the two boys said that the "unalterable hostility between the personal representatives and the two principal beneficiaries dictates their immediate removal."[12]

The suit created an even greater storm of publicity in the local and national press, further alienating the players involved. The ballyhoo was particularly troublesome for Ritchie, who served as chancellor of the University of Denver and was responsible for fundraising. The shy Denver philanthropist who once ran Westinghouse Cable had donated $16 million of his own money to the university, served as chancellor without pay and was crushed by news of the lawsuit. Fisher took it more in stride—he just didn't give a shit, basically. But one part of the lawsuit concerned Malone the most. The offer that the Magness boys had received for the stock was real. From Steven Rattner, deputy chief executive of the New York investment house of Lazard Freres & Co., the offer came in the form of a two-page letter. Rattner represented an unidentified buyer who was "willing to pay in excess of $20 a share" for the estate's 32 million series B shares.[13] That would have been north of a 25 percent premium for TCI stock, a fact that startled Malone. And what was worse, nobody at TCI had an inkling of who the raider was.

TROJAN HORSE?

As John Malone combed through the clues in trying to determine who TCI's unwanted suitor might be, he had the comforting knowledge that, if this escalated to war, at least he had lined up powerful allies on his side. Two of the most potent were Brian Roberts of Comcast and Bill Gates of Microsoft. He trusted Roberts implicitly because they had done business together for so many years; he didn't so much trust Gates as he admired the younger man for his brilliance and for being a self-made billionaire. Soon, Malone would learn he had been betrayed by both of them.

That unpleasant revelation came in October 1997, a month after Malone had learned the Magness sons had been telling the truth about an unsolicited offer for their father's TCI stock. On a crisp fall evening, at Morton's steakhouse in midtown Manhattan, executives of CableLabs sipped wine and prepared for the carnivorous feast that lay ahead, when suddenly Leo Hindery, well ensconced by now as Malone's number two, felt a hand on his back. It belonged to Brian Roberts, who leaned over and quietly said: "I should probably tell you something before you hear it from someone else: We were behind the offer for control shares." [1] Translation: Comcast was the secret bidder for the Magness stock. Maneuvering the previous June and working with his new partner, Bill Gates, Roberts had tried to buy the TCI supervoting stock right out from under Malone. He had done this in part at Bill Gates's behest—and without so much as a courtesy call to John Malone, a man Brian Roberts had admired for much of his career. Microsoft could have used the stake to force TCI into using Windows software to run its cable boxes; or worse, Gates could have tried to wrest control of the entire company from Malone.

Hindery nearly choked on his Chardonnay. "Brian, how could you do this!?" Suddenly Hindery realized he was in a crowded room and pulled Roberts to a quiet corner after dinner. "Jesus! Call us. There's only six of us left! We *are* the industry. All you had to do is call. Don't you think I'm smart enough to handle Bill Gates?"

♘♘♘

In June 1997, Bill Gates had become cable's savior in one simple, decisive move: He had shocked Wall Street by having Microsoft invest $1 billion in cash in Comcast Corporation at the behest of Brian Roberts. Until then, cable had been left for dead; the reregulation effort had crimped cash flow, the industry faced huge investment to go fully interactive, and cable stocks were near all-time lows. Suddenly everyone wanted to know the answer to the same question: Just what does Bill Gates know that we don't know? Gates had bought on the cheap. His $1 billion (a mere one-tenth of the cash on hand that Microsoft had at the time) bought an 11 percent stake in Comcast, while an equal slice of Microsoft would have cost about $18 billion (and far more in later years).

Gates's investment came after a behind-the-scenes courtship that was initiated largely by John Malone, who organized a cadre of cable cowboys for a technology tour to Silicon Valley and elsewhere. As the new century crept closer, new technologies from the cumulative innovations of the recent past—microprocessors, wireless, cable, fiber optics, the Internet, and digital compression—were coalescing, forcing unparalleled change in the way products and services were bought, sold, and used. Malone wanted to put his industry at the epicenter of this tectonic shift. In particular, he was looking to hook up with the computer industry and position cable as the preeminent pathway to high-speed Internet access. Wall Street had cut itself off as a source of new cash, and cable operators needed billions of dollars to rebuild their systems for the digital age; high-tech companies could help.

Malone had saved the best visit for last, and in April 1997 he and his entourage spent a long day at Microsoft's campus in Redmond, Washington. Present were about a dozen major cable executives united under the industry's research consortium, CableLabs, which had corralled the industry's efforts on key issues such as digital standards, cable modems, and, of course, cable boxes. They included Malone and Brian Roberts, Time Warner's Joe Collins, Cox Communications' Jim Robbins, and lab chief Dick Green. At one point, they met with Bill Gates in a large conference room and unveiled a single chart, revealing the precise timelines for rebuilding their systems to accommodate high-speed access to the Net. Gates was impressed: Roberts's Comcast was spending $600 million that year to upgrade its systems and soon would launch its first Internet-access service. And TCI, Comcast, and Cox had every intention of making their high-speed service, At Home, the biggest and the best; Time Warner Inc. had started its own service called Road Runner. Consumers sure seemed to like it—high-speed Internet access over cable had the additional advantage of being always on, unlike telephone dial-up Internet connections, opening the way for new applications for e-mail, news, and stock alerts.

Excitement built in the room as they began discussing what they all knew to be the undeniable facts. Chipmakers were producing faster chips, with memory and power doubling every 18 months under the axiom known as Moore's Law. Americans were bona fide data hogs, with voracious appetites for rich graphics and text on their screens. But the wait to download files and video from a distant site, using dial-up access over phone lines as most Americans did, could be interminable. The critical bottleneck wasn't on either end—it was in the middle. You could have a home computer with the latest, most powerful new Pentium chip, but it was like driving a high-speed drag racer down a dirt road. No matter how fast the PC or even the Web site, the data bogged down over the telephone line. The patience of American computer users, whose channel flipping on TV didn't transmute so well on the World Wide Web, had worn thin. America Online (AOL) became America Waiting Online (AWOL), and the familiar prefix of millions of World Wide Web addresses, www, became synonymous with the World Wide Wait.

Gates rallied behind the cable operators as if he were a cheerleader. Gates saw, as his guests did, that the notion of interactive TV, which had been tossed aside as all hype and failure, was very much alive. The viewers would be interacting with their TV sets, but in a way that connected them to the Internet. Gates talked excitedly about his latest prize, WebTV, a new device that allowed viewers to surf the Internet and exchange e-mail over their TV sets, which Microsoft had bought a week earlier for $425 million. These are the services that the cable and computer industries should be creating, Gates proclaimed, and the best company to supply the cable group with an end-to-end software package for the next generation of cable systems was, of course, Microsoft.

That night, the cable group and a contingent from Microsoft gathered for dinner, and it was one of the few sessions that Malone actually looked forward to attending, for he knew there would be a dearth of chitchat and an emphasis on technology and finance, subjects that whetted his appetite and loosened his tongue. He could ruminate over matters for hours with the right crowd, and so could his cohost for the evening, William H. Gates III. Bill Gates was the embodiment of Microsoft, the largest software maker in the world, a company that had made him a billionaire by the age of 31 and the richest man in America by the time he was 40. Through its Windows software, which hosted an infinite number of other software programs, Microsoft already dominated the computer industry with a 95 percent share of the PC market. Now the Internet was at the beginning of its transformation into a ubiquitous means of communication, and like Malone, Gates wanted to dominate as much of this new world as antitrust laws would allow. And then some.

Gates believed the cable delegation's message—that the industry was serious about providing the main pipeline for surfing the Internet. He gave a few more words of encouragement, and then Brian Roberts spoke up: "If you really believe in us, why don't you buy 10 percent of everyone in the room tonight?" Grins broke out on the faces of the cable brass at Malone's table, but Bill Gates was suddenly intrigued.

"How much would that cost?" Gates asked.

"I don't know, let's say $5 billion," Roberts offered, off the cuff.

"You know, I have around $10 billion in cash," Gates replied. "I could do that."

The group laughed off Gates's comment as a boast, and the subject quickly changed. "Tell us about your next big trip," one of the cable operators asked Gates. They all knew Gates was a traveler to exotic locales; two years earlier he had taken a three-week tour of China with Warren Buffett, visiting the Great Wall, the Forbidden City, and a local McDonald's. "Funny you should ask," Gates replied. "I'm due to go to the Amazon tomorrow with Paul Allen," the billionaire cofounder of Microsoft who would himself amass a cable empire years later. Allen would escort Gates and his wife on a trip to see a rare species of chimpanzee in a rain forest so remote it was best viewed by helicopter. He then turned to Brian Roberts and said, "Would there be any regulatory problems?" They discussed a Microsoft investment in the cable industry some more, but no one took Gates seriously. After dinner, Malone ribbed Roberts along with the others about his entreaty to Gates. "Brian, it sure was a sad thing to see you on bended knee asking Bill Gates to bail out the cable industry," he said as the others laughed.[2]

Funny, but all too true. The cable industry certainly needed bailing out, if not by Gates, then by someone. However strategically sound they found their position to be for the future, the present was killing them. For the investing community and for viewers, too, cable's single largest problem could be summed up in a single word: *credibility*. In the 1980s, the industry expanded at a breakneck pace, raising rates with abandon. But by the start of the 1990s, after TCI and other cable operators had failed to deliver on promises of new digital services and interactive TV, Wall Street and viewers had lost faith. Some months before, Brian Roberts had dinner with an investment banker in New York who had asked him how many subscribers he would have to lose to direct-satellite rivals before going bankrupt. Things were that bad—this guy is actually thinking about bankruptcy, Roberts thought. Even his own father, Ralph, the

77-year-old founder of Comcast, had considered selling out or merging with a telephone company.

What the cable operators failed to realize at the moment was how truly strong their position was. Only the cable industry's fat pipes, where the electrical signals danced along lines passing 95 percent of American homes, could launch the American PC industry into a new level of what Malone verbosely called "two-way broadband digital connectivity," which translated to a cornucopia of online news, entertainment, and shopping. All of the hundreds of new dot-com companies starting up would not have a chance unless Internet service providers could deliver pictures and sites instantly over a broadband network. For that reason, the future of the computer industry in the United States was largely reliant on the future of the cable industry. By linking America's computers to its high-speed or so-called broadband networks, cable promised to be the bridge so many people were depending on to reach the next phase of development in America's digital economy.

After dinner, Gates said goodnight to his cable friends, and the delegation dispersed and flew home. The following day, there was a message waiting for Roberts back in Comcast's Philadelphia office from Greg Maffei, Microsoft's vice president of corporate development.[3] When Roberts got him on the line, Maffei said he just received an e-mail in Redmond from Gates in the Amazon. "Bill wants to follow up on the deal," he said. Roberts returned to Seattle with his investment banker, Steven Rattner, the deputy CEO of Lazard Freres, a banking boutique in New York City. On a Tuesday morning four weeks after the dinner, Gates and his deal-making lieutenant, Maffei, met with Brian Roberts in Rattner's suite at the Woodmark Hotel on the shores of Lake Washington, where, over muffins, they discussed a Microsoft investment in Comcast.[4]

Gates had found a kindred spirit in Roberts, another baby boomer running a large technology company in the media spotlight. But while Gates had started his company on his own, Brian Roberts had taken the reins from his own father, Ralph, who founded Comcast in the 1960s. Ralph Roberts was a former Navy lieutenant who ran a suspender and belt manufacturing company in his beloved Philadelphia. Ralph left the business in 1962 because he feared that Sansabelt beltless trousers would render his business obsolete. A year later, Ralph bought his first cable system, in the unlikely hamlet of Tupelo, Mississippi. He expanded into Pennsylvania, Florida, and Michigan in the 1970s and 1980s, with the help of Julian Brodsky and a crack management team, building Comcast into the fifth-largest cable operator in the United States. Ralph Roberts was the perfect made-for-TV grandfather, with white hair, a soft voice, and a friendly chuckle. Those traits belied an aggressive deal maker.

Brian learned the business at his father's side. Ralph would let young Brian sit in the corner as he negotiated contracts, and the father was proud to see that his son was so eager to perform. Brian would sit in on a meeting, mute, and ask his dad a list of questions once it was over. During college vacations, the young Roberts worked as a cable installer and door-to-door salesman and moved up the ranks. By 1990, with Comcast serving some 2 million subscribers, a new era began as 30-year-old Brian, a Wharton graduate who now knew how to hang wire, began to lead Comcast into new businesses as president of the company. No one could accuse Comcast of being a rusty old cable company; before most anyone else, it branched out into the cellular market, serving the Northeast corridor, and was active in cable in the United Kingdom.

The Microsoft investment showed Wall Street that Comcast, and by extension, cable TV, was ready for the big time. Malone welcomed Comcast's newfound prosperity mostly because it gave TCI and others a bounce in stock price. Comcast was a frequent partner in big deals with TCI, and Malone enjoyed young Brian's inquisitiveness about the business. In 1986, in one of the first deals in which Comcast and TCI teamed up, a consortium bought pieces of Group W; Comcast's share of the deal doubled the company's size. Later, the two were investors in QVC, together owning 57 percent of the home shopping network. Both TCI and Comcast owned a 20 percent stake in Teleport Communications Group, a business telephone service, and a 15 percent position in Sprint PCS, a wireless service. Comcast also owned the NBA's Philadelphia 76ers and the NHL's Flyers, and a 69 percent piece of E! Entertainment cable network. But with a debt load of more than $7 billion, Comcast needed cash to finance the costly upgrade of its cable network.

Privately, Malone cautioned Brian Roberts about Gates's intentions and the possibility that he would push for control. Malone said that TCI was willing to accept an equity contribution from a high-tech company, but not if it meant that company had a role in setting policy. Don't trust Gates too blindly, Malone hinted. "After six years of negotiating with Bill Gates, I can tell you that everything he negotiates comes with strings attached," he said at the time. As for TCI, Malone said, "We'd be happy to take a contribution from a strategic partner, but we're not going to allow them to take any control for that equity."[5]

Brian Roberts listened attentively, for he had the highest respect for John Malone. A year earlier, they had traveled together to Japan to tour the Consumer Electronics Show, and one of the most memorable moments for Roberts came when he boarded the plane before the 14-hour flight. Malone slapped the seat next to his own and looked at Roberts. "Brian, have a seat," he said. From the time they took off, neither man took a nap, watched a movie, or had a drink of anything stronger than coffee. Malone gave Roberts an earful, sometimes in excruciating detail: the tax logic of Liberty, where cable stocks were headed, and a strategic analysis of the DBS industry. It was the kind of high-level briefing that would have driven Bob Magness crazy—why let our rivals know all this sophisticated stuff? "We talked about the future of the world, and it was fabulous," Roberts said later. "It was like going to business school."[6]

What impressed Roberts most, though, was Malone's unassuming manner. He projected a confidence that required no artifice. And because there was no need to boast, Malone appeared modest by conventional standards. He discovered in Malone a shrewd mentor, like an old college professor who had taken an interest in a bright student. "He's giving you a lot of theories, a lot of them are conflicting, and you get the feeling he's working them out with you while he's talking to you, and that's part of the engaging style he has," Roberts told a reporter. "He's really there with you, at that moment. And it's also the knowledge that there's a lot going on inside that brain that you're not totally on the same plane with. People say John has a 'three-dimensional-chess'-type of mind, and it's true, and a lot of time you feel like you're still playing in one dimension."[7]

ぴぴぴ

Cable operators wondered aloud whether Gates's investment might be a Trojan horse. Gates had built a reputation of his own as a monopolist. Already the U.S. government's antitrust division had its eye on Microsoft. "It's not just our lunch, but our carcasses that Microsoft wants to eat," Gary Reback, a Silicon Valley lawyer representing Sun Microsystems and others, told reporters.[8] Gates would enter the industry via Comcast and, eventually, buy his way into dominance of cable. Those fears turned out to be well founded. Not long after investing in Comcast, Gates was in New York, speaking to top executives of several major cable companies at Time Warner's boardroom in Rockefeller Center. He mapped out details of how Microsoft could provide the one-stop solution for cable. At the meeting, Gates proposed a system that operated exclusively with Windows software, on the servers and in the set-top box, with Microsoft collecting not just a licensing fee but a cut of what the cable companies charged for the interactive services—a clearly arrogant and unpopular suggestion. The sales pitch left some of the cable operators flabbergasted.

At TCI's annual meeting in Denver a few months later, Malone, ever calculating, told an attentive crowd in the bluntest language yet that the cable industry should keep a tight rein on the technology inside the box. Gates should be thanked for his cable investments from a distance, he told his shareholders, but "Bill Gates would like to be the only technology supplier for this whole [digital] evolution. We would all be foolish to allow that to happen. Bill has to accept the fact that he cannot have quite the dominance in supplying our industry that he developed in supplying the PC industry." "We have to push [the standards] in Silicon Valley, and when the smoke clears we still own it," Malone told his audience. At the same time, said Malone, a host of other Silicon Valley leaders, including Oracle and Netscape, were looking at the standards, and "there is going to be a tug of war. There needs to be a single, open standard, and it doesn't have to be Windows CE, or whatever Bill

Gates is calling it. It can be from a David, any number of other operators out there. Bill has got to accept the fact that he can't set the standard that the rest of us are going to use."

All along, Malone and the cable gang were struggling to adopt standards with Open Cable, a system administered by CableLabs, the cable industry's research and development arm, which would ensure that all digital set-top boxes would be compatible with one another whatever their manufacturer or operating system. Malone wanted a layered approach that would allow many companies to provide different pieces of the complex system. It followed the cable industry's, and Malone's, longtime reliance on healthy competition between hardware makers. Scientific Atlanta has always been the number two to GI. The cable industry liked having them compete with each other. But the boxes needed the firepower of the computer industry. Malone and the other cable operators steadfastly refused to be tied to Microsoft; they earnestly courted rivals Sun and Oracle Corporation, just to keep Gates honest.

With TCI on the mend, Malone was allying with other major cable operators to close ranks, swap systems, and take its overall debt leverage down. His top lieutenant, Leo Hindery, built on an idea that Malone had pushed, putting clusters of cable systems (i.e., contiguous cable systems that had a large footprint and that could be operated together at lower cost) together with rival companies. If another cable operator could run a cable system more cheaply than TCI, Malone figured, then let's make a deal. Hindery quickly set about striking joint ventures with other companies, usually those that had better profit margins and leaner operations. It was a quick and effective way to improve TCI's wobbly balance sheet and anemic stock price.

In what he would describe as the "Summer of Love," in 1997, Hindery struck a dozen new partnerships and nearly as many system trades with fellow cable operators. "Once there were a hundred of us cable operators, then there were fifty of us, then there were twenty of us, then there were ten of us, then there were six of us," Hindery told a reporter at the time. "That's why everybody's enjoying the Summer of Love, because it's like the old days, but they know it's over. They know that this was one last time to fix your sins.

Next year, Time Warner will do its thing and is not going to call me and ask what I think about it."

In the summer of 1997, Hindery unveiled the most important of them all: a major deal with Chuck Dolan's Cablevision Systems. Cablevision got TCI systems serving 820,000 subscribers in lucrative markets that meshed perfectly with Cablevision's base in metropolitan New York. Cablevision's New York properties would jump to more than 2.5 million from 1.7 million paying customers. In return, not only would TCI receive a 33 percent stake in Cablevision and two seats on the Cablevision board, but more important for the moment, TCI would get to unload $670 million of debt linked to those systems. Chuck Dolan was on an all-out crusade to dominate the New York market, taking on his former employers at Time Warner's cable division. Malone had known Dolan since his earliest days in the industry, and he regarded himself as a friendly advisor to the family rather than an actual competitor. He saw cockpit problems from time to time in the Dolans' operation, but they were solid operators. He and Hindery were betting that TCI shareholders would benefit more by simply owning a piece of the Dolans' action than by having TCI run the systems itself. It was a nice move: Malone's 33 percent stake in Cablevision shot up in value on the day the deal was announced, as Cablevision's stock price jumped nearly 30 percent.

Cablevision was just putting the finishing touches on a $1 billion upgrade of the New York systems to offer 100-plus digital channels, video on demand, and high-speed cable modem linkups. "Cable is the most efficient platform for TV and computer services. Period," Dolan's son, James, the company's chief executive, told reporters when the deal was announced. "Bill Gates sees it. TCI sees it. We see it. I hope investors see it. I know my consumers are going to see it."

TCI also struck several deals with Comcast, notwithstanding its earlier role as spoiler. On the night in October 1997 that Brian Roberts brazenly told Leo Hindery that Comcast and Microsoft had been behind the secret offer for the Magness estate's stock, Hindery moved immediately to let John Malone know of the revelation. Malone was livid, particularly with the Robertses, with whom he had been partners in deals that shaped the industry. Hindery, typically calm, yelled in anger one afternoon on the phone with Malone as he portrayed the secret bid by Roberts and Gates as a rape-and-pillage attempt. "They're going after our wives, after our children on this," Hindery screamed into the phone, momentarily losing it. Malone felt particularly betrayed because he had gone to Comcast and Microsoft, separately, more than six months earlier to line up support on the estate fight. Yes, business was business, but Malone viewed this offense as an unforgivable breach of what was right. When he got Brian and Ralph Roberts on the phone after learning of their treachery, Malone chastised them. "You shoulda told me, guys—all you had to do was come through the front door." Even the calloused Darth Vader seemed hurt. "They had lobbed one in as soon as Bob died," he told one listener later, bitter with resentment.[9]

Malone especially disliked the underhanded way Roberts and Gates had gone about it; there was no need to go hostile—hell, if you want to do a deal, just call me and let's work out something good for everyone. That was the Malone way. "Who knows what would have happened had they called me up on the phone and said, 'We'd like to buy all or some of the estate's shares?' I'd have probably said, 'Come on in.' The only thing that bothered me was these are guys I know. They should have picked up the phone," Malone said soon after. "It affected our relationship for a little bit. . . . I felt they owed me something—because they screwed me."[10]

For Hindery, the real betrayal was Brian Roberts. "Bill Gates was never an issue—he has a right to go after anyone, that's business," Hindery told one interviewer. "But Brian broke the code—there will come a time when I will make that son of a bitch pay, but right now I need some stuff done. They broke the code. I was furious because it was a shot at John Malone." You don't do that in an insular business like cable, Hindery believed. "In this industry you don't screw with your friends. We're all joined at the hip. Brian said Bill was going to do it anyway." After the veil of secrecy had lifted, Roberts assured Malone and Hindery they had had no malice in their intent. Gates placed a personal call. "I owe you an apology," he told Malone. Malone forgave him on the phone, as he had forgiven Roberts, but he would never forget it.

Malone would find a way to exact revenge, for he and Gates were elbow-to-elbow in too many endeavors. TCI already was an investor in Microsoft's online venture, MSN. And Gates badly wanted the primary piece of TCI's cable box business, hoping to provide the software and take a cut of cable revenue. That was where Malone had him, and he made sure to put the software titan through an ample amount of hell. By the fourth quarter of 1997, Malone intensified talks with hardware vendors and computer companies about providing a new, single device that would handle a variety of video and audio services, including high–speed Internet access, phone calls, e-mail, games, sophisticated on-screen programming guides, and electronic shopping and banking.

Gates had told Malone that Microsoft could make the new boxes for $300. Malone went back to his long-delayed, ever-disappointing supplier, GI, and told the brass: "Gates can make 'em for three hundred bucks." GI executives warned Malone that Microsoft was not to be trusted, and that Gates would take losses to subsidize the real cost and get the price down initially—and ask for too much control in return. Malone countered: "Okay, let's get serious about it. How many do you have to be buying for and by when, to get your price down to this three-hundred-dollar mark?" Malone had recalled that in Orlando, the terminal server in Time Warner's Full Service Network cost tens of thousands of dollars, while set-top boxes alone ran $7,000. "Everybody was sitting there saying, 'Oh, well we can demonstrate it technologically, we just can't implement it as a consumer product, it's too expensive.' But I disagreed. I could add up a components list and say, 'Why should these be so expensive?'" Malone told associates.

There was a simple reason: scale. In December of 1997, Malone struck a deal to break the logjam of digital boxes. TCI led a consortium of cable operators representing nearly half of the industry in a deal to buy some 15 million digital set-top boxes over five years from GI. The $4.5 billion order was for boxes that would cover the gamut of cable-driven video and audio services. Though the group had chosen GI, Malone and others took pains to point out that GI was simply supplying the *boxes,* which would comply with the industry's

Open Cable standards so different companies could contribute software to the devices.

In a single day, GI looked like the new dominant manufacturer of digital boxes. The boxes themselves were far superior to the set-top boxes ordered in 1992 at a cheaper price. The original digital boxes were capable of digital decompression, essentially getting lots of channels, but beyond that, there wasn't much firepower. The brains in the new box from GI had the processing power of Intel's lightning-fast Pentium II, and it was capable of displaying high-definition TV, routing Internet phone calls, browsing the Web at high speeds on a cable modem—all simultaneously. Most important, the box would allow for the first time meaningful interactive advertising, such as hot transfers to Web sites. "The vision of five and a half years ago is real, with more power and reach than we contemplated five years ago," Malone said at the time.

From TCI's point of view, 10 million boxes for every customer, at $300, was $3 billion. If Malone could offset that by getting a $1 billion stake in GI, and another $2 billion from other sources, it was like an equipment pool, building a massive platform with little economic risk. As Malone would explain it to colleagues later on: "It becomes self-fulfilling. If you can get the scale economics, you can get the costs down. If you get the costs down, you get the scale economics. If you get the scale economics you can develop applications that are really important to a lot of people. If you can get applications that are important to people, you get people to buy the boxes, and you'll get more scale economics."

Under the terms, GI agreed to grant stock warrants to the cable operators buying the boxes, a group that included TCI, Comcast, Cox, and Time Warner, enabling them to acquire 16 percent of GI. TCI agreed to swap part of a digital programming transmission service, called Headend in the Sky (HITS), to GI for an extra 10 percent of the company. While the details of the deal required engineers and lawyers, the crux of negotiations was carried out in a phone call to Ted Forstman, who would sell Malone his considerable stake in GI at a later date. Liberty would end up with 31 million shares and 21 million warrants, representing about 25 percent of GI, whose shares jumped $2 on news of the big order.

Computer companies would provide the processors and operating systems for the new digital boxes. "We bought a pop can and we can fill it with any kind of soda," a spokeswoman at TCI said at the time. Meanwhile, Malone held intermittent talks with Oracle, Intel, and Microsoft, among others.

Malone and the other cable operators adamantly refused to be pulled into Microsoft's orbit. "This keeps Microsoft trying hard to get our business," Malone told interviewers at the time. "This thing can support Windows or other operating systems, and our agreement with GI lets us make those decisions, not them—so we get to decide graphics chips, microprocessors, all of which gives us the negotiating leverage we need to line up Silicon Valley. I'm trying to structure it so as many people as possible are supportive of the program and will be eager to continue."[11]

On Christmas Eve that year, Scott McNealy, chief executive of Microsoft's major competitor, Sun Microsystems, flew to TCI's Denver headquarters for an audience with Malone. After a brief meeting, they reached an agreement in principle to supply TCI with Java software in its newest cable box. Java was a software application created by Sun in an effort to render Microsoft Windows obsolete on the World Wide Web. Now that Malone had an attractive proposal from Sun, TCI was in a position to press Gates for concessions. And press Malone did. When he talked again with Gates, Microsoft gave up a bit on licensing fees for every cable box that contains the Windows CE operating system. To sweeten the deal further, Microsoft agreed to provide TCI's hardware suppliers with some key WebTV chip technology at low cost. Right up until the end, Microsoft attempted—unsuccessfully—to convince Malone that Java was an unnecessary waste of computing resources.

Gates didn't want to appear before an upcoming consumer electronics show crowd empty-handed. In a hurry to eclipse some of Sun Microsystems' glory, Gates called Malone on January 8, 1998, and pressed hard to cinch the deal in time for his own keynote address the next morning.

Through clever maneuvering and an intuitive sense of what buttons to press at Microsoft, Malone remained in a position to call the shots. "I told Bill, 'Look we just don't have a deal yet.' You know, it's always a problem when you try to limit Microsoft to just a piece of things." [12]

"If you are in the role that I am in, where I am basically going to be writing the checks to develop this stuff for my applications, the best thing I can do is balance commercial forces," he said later of McNealy and Gates. "Let them keep each other honest. Make them all perform. Let them watch each other, as it were, and do not let them meet when I am not there." [13]

Around the time the deals with Sun and Microsoft were struck, Malone reaffirmed TCI's commitment to buy new boxes, then crowed to the press: "I don't think I've been as excited about our cable business since Universal gave us *Jaws* for HBO."

For all the posturing, Malone privately felt he could have just as easily taken Gates's offer, with conditions, of course. Malone already had a history with Gates through its investment in the MSN joint venture. "My own judgment was that if we had given it to Microsoft in a clear, straightforward way, they would have run with it and we would have been further down the road, faster," Malone recalled later. "On the other hand, maybe the skeptics are right and maybe Bill would end up owning the economics as well. Who knows?"

Later, TCI cut deals both with Kraft Foods to deliver targeted advertising through the cable box, and with Intuit and Bank of America to provide financial services on the TV screen. TCI's deal with Intuit was part of Malone's strategy to open the doors to all players in the computer industry. Other big cable operators were singing in tune with Malone. "Silicon Valley will now play a critical role in the development of what we used to call the cable industry," predicted Gerald M. Levin, chairman of Time Warner Inc., which owned the nation's second-largest cable system.

Malone believed the technology would revolutionize Madison Avenue. "Stop and think about what it means for Amazon to be the exclusive [bookstore] of the platform, or Blockbuster to be the exclusive video supplier. What would Phil Knight pay every time you watch a game to click a button and have the sports scoreboard brought to you by Nike?" [14]

ʊʊʊ

Cable was shedding its skin again. It had begun as a low-cost antenna service to tune in the big networks. In its second evolution, cable was the fount of dozens of new programming services, from HBO to CNN. Now the wire had found a life that no one would have dreamed of just a decade earlier. It would make PCs and TVs a lot more alike and a lot more functional. The marriage of high-speed lines and powerful chips would finally bring high-speed online access to millions of U.S. homes. Once again, technology—or at least the promise of technology—had saved the cable industry.

WHAT POP WOULD HAVE WANTED

The new year 1998 began with a good omen. Fourteen months after the death of Bob Magness, the rancorous battle over the TCI stock in his estate had ended. John Malone pulled this off in a masterfully accommodative way, essentially enriching the Magness sons by close to $200 million more than they otherwise would have received—in exchange for their agreement to let him vote their father's stock as if it were his own. This ended up giving Malone almost absolute control over TCI's future, with a grip on 40 percent of all outstanding stock, without requiring him to put up any more of his own money to do it.

Malone accomplished this consolidation of power largely by doing what he always did: picking up the phone and reaching out to the other side to look for the common ground where he could put together a mutually agreeable deal. The tug-of war tore at the fragile bonds of a family, threatened control of the largest cable operator in the United States, and nearly fractured an industry; it was settled in a complicated resolution worked out two days before Christmas and announced on January 5, 1998. Malone thereby sidestepped a hearing in a Colorado state court scheduled for February 2 to air the Magness boys' grievances and evaluate the stock deal, avoiding the distinct possibility the shares would be sold on the open market to the highest bidder.

The settlement unwound half of the original sale of 32 million shares of TCI stock for $529 million on June 16, 1997, which had been made under the pressure of a tax deadline. The Magness brothers argued that holding onto the shares was a better investment than selling them, and had initially asked for all 32 million shares to be returned.

But in returning 16 million shares, which had appreciated some $12 each to trade since the June 16 sale, the brothers reaped a $192 million windfall. Indeed, the price of the stock had skyrocketed from around $10 at the time of Bob Magness's death to about $16 in June to a near record of $28 in January. And it was certainly easier to make all the contestants happier by dividing a bigger pie. The value of TCI had more than doubled in the 14 months since Magness's death, creating more than $18 billion in additional value.

As part of the deal, the Magness boys granted Malone the right to vote their shares. Combined with his own stock, Malone now had control of 76 million shares, or about 40 percent, of TCI and its related companies, TCI Ventures and Liberty Media Corp. Never again would Malone, or TCI, have to worry about losing control of the company to an outside raider. Sharon Magness, meanwhile, agreed to drop her claim for half of the estate in return for a confidential amount estimated at about $100 million. "Sharon deserved everything she got," Donne Fisher, a coexecutor, told an associate. "She really took care of Bob. She loved him. She was more than a wife, almost like a nurse."

In further evidence of how well Malone fared in making sure everyone walked away happy, the settlement also called for Magness's coexecutors, Fisher and Dan Ritchie, to resign and be paid $1.5 million each—hefty pay for a one-time job, which the pair donated to the University of Denver. Finally, TCI, Sharon Magness, and Magness's sons each agreed to donate $1 million toward a new Volunteers of America building named in honor of Robert Magness. "This is what Pop would have wanted," the Magness boys said in a statement. "We have a significant block of the stock back, we have added significant value to the estate, and we can now continue to participate in our family's legacy." At the hearing on January 5 in Arapahoe District Court in Denver, Gary Magness told the *Rocky Mountain News,* "We still have a few family issues to work out."[1]

One of the more controversial aspects of the settlement was TCI's agreement to pay $150 million to Malone, and $124 million to the Magness boys, merely for first-refusal rights to spend even more money to buy their shares in the event of death or sale. TCI got the right to buy Malone's class B shares (roughly 42 million supervoting shares he now personally owned) at market price plus a 10 percent premium. Shareholders howled at paying Malone, an insider, a $150 million windfall. Many shareholders balked, and some filed suit within days in Delaware state court to block both payments. "The arrangement is an unearned and unwarranted windfall for defendant Malone . . . [that] cements Malone's domination and control of the company, with TCI's money. It constitutes a waste of TCI's assets."[2]

The local and national press shined a harsh spotlight on the payment. "Malone's payday a rip-off" screamed the *Denver Post. Newsweek* columnist Allan Sloan sniped: "You can see where selling 16 million [supervoting] shares back to the Magnesses at a bargain price makes sense for shareholders: a judge might have voided the whole deal. But the $274 million of option payments to Malone and the Magnesses— ostensibly to ensure stability—smells like last week's fish."

But Malone might never have received the payment had the TCI board not learned of the takeover feelers from Bill Gates and Brian Roberts. Malone cited the hostile possibilities to make the board realize that he could sell control of the company, without so much as demanding a premium for all other shareholders, and simply notify the board he had done so the next morning—there was nothing the directors could do to stop it. The idea that, all of a sudden, Microsoft could take control of the company without owning all of it stoked the board's enthusiasm for a sweetheart payment that would lock in Malone's shares. Pressed to defend the arrangement, Malone told his hometown paper, the *Rocky Mountain News:* "I'm not selling my soul for a few bucks. I've made all the money I need to live as well as I can think how to live . . . I'm not motivated by money." He used the payment to buy more Liberty shares.

That assertion was not entirely true: Of *course* it was about money. And value, the most efficient use of capital, not to mention the right to reap the rewards of his effort—with John Malone, it *always* was about those things. And if Malone wasn't motivated by the extra $150 million, why hadn't he simply signed away those first-refusal rights to his beloved company free of charge? For Malone, turning down $150 million was like turning down a drink of water in the desert; you just don't do that.

Looking back on the whole mess, John Malone would come to view the timing of events (i.e., the startlingly accelerated death of Bob Magness when TCI stock was at a low, the fight over the estate, the big comeback in TCI shares) as if it all were scripted. Once again, luck had played a big role in the outcome of Malone's fortune. In the end, the play by Microsoft and Comcast for TCI had strengthened Malone's hand in two critical ways: First, he had been forced to find creative ways to tighten his grip on TCI, and second, he had put a lot more money into his own pockets. Malone had bested the potential hijackers, and in lighter moods he referred to the Microsoft-Comcast overture as a "Polish takeover." "I got what I wanted—voting control. Sharon got what she wanted (a doubling of what the initial will called for). And the boys got what they wanted. Everybody pretty much got what they wanted," Malone told people later.

Some weeks after the Magness estate was settled, Malone made a surprise announcement to the public, almost as a postscript to the deal he had just orchestrated. He would form a new educational charity, the Malone Family Foundation, and fund it with part of his $1.5 billion fortune, the bulk of it in TCI and Liberty stock. Some years earlier, Malone had begun donating to the Hopkins School in New Haven, Connecticut, which he once attended, to support math and science programs, and to construct a new science center that would be named after his father. He would give some $23 million to Hopkins, and nearly the same to Yale University, another alma mater, for a new engineering building. But the new foundation was on a far larger scale, and it stood a strong chance of someday ranking as one of the largest private foundations in America.

"You know, after the zeros and numbers get so big, you just can't really comprehend them," Malone told a local newspaper. "What are you going to do with it? How many cars and vacation homes can you own?"[3] The two main tenets of the foundation: (1) "To promote the secondary and liberal arts education of the most able young men and women of our society and train such individuals as future leaders of society," and (2) "to acquire and preserve land and open space, preserving forever Nature's natural and pristine beauty."

But Malone's real motivation for the Malone Family Foundation ran deeper, and it was more personal: The trustees of this new entity were limited to John and Leslie Malone, and their two grown children, Tracy and Evan. And once every quarter, all four of them would get together to act on foundation issues; it was John Malone's way of ensuring they would all have to get together at least four times a year beyond holidays. He could meet with his daughter, who took a special interest in the foundation, at education conventions, stealing lunches and dinners with her between seminars. Given the pace he kept and the family he largely gave up to build TCI, it gladdened his heart.

Malone's children were not covetous of wealth, a fact that pleased him but did not surprise him. In fact, his son and daughter had settled into a comfortable and surprisingly middle-class life. After the frenzied battle over his best friend's estate, he was even more convinced that not only would money not buy happiness, too much left in the wrong hands could generate immense pain. Wealth, if bestowed for no other reason than inheritance, had more power to destroy than to strengthen one's character.

But Malone still felt unsettled with his TCI holdings. The good news was that he had taken full equity control of the company now—and that was, unfortunately, the bad news, too. He had tired of the hassle of dealing with irksome regulators at so many levels of government, and he knew that for TCI to truly deliver on the information highway hype that Malone himself had helped to create, it would need outside help. TCI, Malone concluded, would need to be bought. And so after the dust had settled on the Magness family feud, Malone instructed his loyal lieutenant, Leo Hindery, to begin the search for a new buyer.

⊍⊍⊍

Hindery had done a remarkable job painting and patching up Malone's company. In two and a half years since joining the company, he had largely repaired relations with Congress, replaced most top managers, soothed the doubters on Wall Street, and even placated angry customers. Hindery had logged 900,000 miles in the air since going to work for John Malone, who once referred to Hindery as the "Energizer Bunny." Hindery had a special alacrity for deals, and he worked on so many in his 18-hour days, seven days a week, that Malone began to feel if he didn't check in with Leo twice a day, he'd fall behind on what was going on. Not only did Hindery surprise Malone with some decisions, but he rarely gave Malone the downside to a deal he had brokered. "He really is a whirling dervish," Malone would tell other TCI staff.

One Hindery decision that riled Malone like no other was the proposed sale of the *Salt Lake City Tribune*. The *Tribune* was the morning paper and the lone secular voice in a Mormon community. TCI had merged with the *Tribune*'s parent company, closely held Kearns-Tribune Corporation, as a way to cash out a partner and gain a slice of control during the Magness estate battle. Under pressure to slash costs, AT&T first tried to sell the paper to the *Deseret News,* raising for the first time the very real possibility that the Mormon Church could wind up buying some or all of the *Tribune,* owned and published since 1901 by descendants of Utah mining tycoon Senator Thomas Kearns. No one at TCI had wanted to publish a newspaper, much less one that had taken on the Mormon Church for more than a century. Still, Malone had promised to protect the editorial independence of the *Tribune* and to sell it back to the management team. Malone said he learned of the *Tribune*'s potential sale at a board meeting. The *Tribune* management group sued AT&T in federal court in Salt Lake City, claiming that AT&T ignored its exclusive option to buy back the newspaper in 2002. Nonetheless, in a sale supported by the church, the paper was sold in December 2000 to a Denver-based company called MediaNews Group, Incorporated.

"We were very close to TCI," says Dominic Welch, the *Tribune*'s publisher and president. "None of this would be happening now if John Malone had kept TCI."[4] But Hindery argued that a sale of the

Tribune back to the management team was complicated by terms of the newspapers' joint operating agreement, which ultimately precluded the sale and opened the gate for a lawsuit against AT&T by the Mormon Church.

"It was a breach of the intent of the contract," Malone said later. "And Leo should have known better." Still, "Leo did us a hell of a job—and not just me and the TCI shareholders, but the whole cable industry," Malone conceded later. "I'll forever be in his debt for that."

Betting on the odds, Hindery and Malone moved to link up with Rupert Murdoch in the fight for an interactive program guide. They merged TCI's United Video Satellite Group with Murdoch's *TV Guide* in a deal valued at $2 billion in cash and stock. The strategy: to gain control of the nation's remote controls, quite literally, by adding the huge name recognition of *TV Guide* magazine to United Video's on-screen listings channel. Two years later, Malone's and Murdoch's TV Guide Inc. would merge with another powerful electronic guide company, Gemstar International Group, Incorporated, in a deal valued at $9.2 billion, giving Malone and News Corp. each 20 percent in the new Gemstar–TV Guide International, which would become the undisputed owner of precious electronic TV guide patents.

Cable stocks had surged since Bill Gates's investment in Comcast. Microsoft went on to pump $400 million into Rogers Cablesystems of Canada, and Gates's cofounder, Paul Allen, paid $3.2 billion to acquire Marcus Cable, a Dallas-based operator with 1.2 million subscribers—and then ponied up $4.5 billion more to buy Charter Communications of St. Louis, with 1.1 million households. Cable wasn't just piped-in TV service anymore—it was basking in the buzz of the Internet. TCI's stock price rose accordingly; mired at $16 after Magness's death, it was at $28 by early 1998 and was flirting with $40 by early summer. What no one dared ask was this: How long could the miracle last?

Even Hindery felt the pressure to sell out at the top. What bothered him was that TCI stock was rising sharply based not on its ongoing business but on what it hoped to become—an Internet-ready digital powerhouse. Wall Street was running earnings models predicting how much more cash flow would be thrown off by new inter-active services such as digital video, digital data, and digital phone calls, "but more than two-thirds of this stuff isn't done yet," Hindery said later. When more than 25 percent of the value of your stock is something that you haven't done yet, get real nervous—real fast."

Hindery felt that he needed to act quickly to sell TCI into some-one else's hands, someone desperate enough to pay a big premium over TCI's already-lofty price and deliver "this last big slug of value for my shareholders," as he liked to call it. If he and Malone didn't bail out soon, "when we start the downhill slide, it isn't going to be pretty," he'd warn his boss. That someone, Hindery came to believe, was an awfully familiar face: AT&T, where John Malone had begun his career more than 25 years earlier, and the same company that Malone had approached about merger possibilities back in 1993 before his ill-fated hookup with Ray Smith and Bell Atlantic. This time things might be different, for AT&T had recently ousted the old guard that had spurned Malone five years earlier in favor of a dynamic and decisive new leader who was determined to push AT&T into broadband services (a.k.a. high-speed Internet access). AT&T had hired C. Michael Armstrong.

Armstrong had arrived at AT&T in the fall of 1997, a 30-year vet-eran of IBM fresh from a five-year stint as chief executive of Gen-eral Motors Corporation's Hughes Electronics unit. At Hughes, he oversaw the emergence of cable's biggest rival, the DirecTV mini-dish service. Upon arriving at AT&T, Armstrong showed what a dis-ciplined manager he could be. He slashed 18,000 jobs, worked out kinks in AT&T's global operations, and made AT&T a major Inter-net service provider. He sold the credit card business for $3.4 bil-lion and the customer care business for $625 million. His efforts would bring badly needed credibility back to AT&T, sending the stock soaring to an all-time high of nearly $90 after only a year and a few months at the helm. "Surprise, surprise—Armstrong is emerging as AT&T's long-awaited promise keeper," *Business Week* rhapsodized.[5]

Malone was one of the first people Armstrong sought out after taking the top job at AT&T, flying out to Denver to confer with the cable titan to talk over industry issues. The two men quickly hit it off and began delving into possible areas where they might do business together. Malone told Armstrong they should partner in three areas: (1) Teleport, a local bypass company that sold phone services to businesses in competition with the Bells; (2) At Home, the hot new Internet broadband service that TCI owned with other major cable operators; and (3) cable telephony, the effort to zap local phone calls over cable TV wiring.

The new AT&T chief needed the advice, for the company he had just taken over was headed, inexorably and inevitably, for profound trouble. Though AT&T held a 60 percent share of the $80-billion-a-year market for long-distance services, the market was declining amid commodity pricing and a raft of new competitors. Per-minute rates had plunged by two-thirds in just two years, from 15 cents to as low as 5 cents, and prices were likely to fall even more once the Baby Bells entered the business. (The Bells, local phone monopolies spun off in the antitrust breakup of AT&T in 1984, had been banned from long distance since then, until the Telecommunications Act of 1996 razed the barriers separating local and long-distance markets.) Long-distance revenue made up more than 75 percent of AT&T's $51 billion in annual revenue when Mike Armstrong arrived at the company; in four years, it was expected to plummet to just 35 percent.

Armstrong needed to find other revenues to offset that sharp decline, and the most likely targets were local phone service (a $110-billion-a-year market) and the booming new business of Internet access. But while builders of the fabled information highway sped by, Ma Bell seemed to be in need of a walker. AT&T's biggest weakness: It didn't own "the last mile," the wire going inside each home and business; only the local phone monopolies had control of the ubiquitous copper wires that linked millions of customers to service providers. To complete a long-distance call from, for instance, New York to Los Angeles, AT&T had to pay a toll to the local Bell at each end, totaling up to 40 percent of what AT&T was able to charge for the call. Laying its own new wires would be prohibitively expensive, requiring $100 billion or more by most estimates. AT&T could lease local lines from the Bells and resell local service, but there was no profit in that. A takeover of a big local phone company might help, but it would probably get scuttled in Washington, given AT&T's monopoly past. AT&T looked at a plan code-named "Angel," to use wireless devices to sidestep the Bells' networks altogether, but it never materialized.

AT&T needed a last-mile play—and only one other industry had a pipeline directly into millions upon millions of homes: cable television. Racing to stay ahead of the deterioration in AT&T's core business, Armstrong began looking for alliances with cable companies to deliver local phone service and high-speed Internet access over their networks. TCI, the nation's largest, would be key to any such efforts. Malone and Armstrong had kicked around several partnership ideas, including bundling their current services together and selling them as a package, but both men knew that the real prize was At Home.

At Home was the cable modem Internet service that was first sketched out by John Doerr (a renowned West Coast venture capitalist) and TCI's Bruce Ravenal that embodied the crucial last mile into customers' homes. A central element of the plan, in one variation, was to put AT&T's consumer long-distance business into a company with cable's assets. But because of At Home's various cable owners, and their different business agendas for the high-speed service, they couldn't reach a quick deal.

From Malone's point of view, Armstrong was asking for way too much. AT&T wanted to contribute its Internet service, WorldNet, and the AT&T brand name—but pretty much no cash and no capital—in return for a big chunk of the combined company. Cox Communications, a part-owner of At Home, argued that AT&T should pay cable operators to use *their* brand names, rather than the other way around. Others felt that AT&T's budding Internet-access service was worth far less than AT&T maintained. None of the complex structures offered TCI an upside—and TCI always had to have an upside.

Malone was getting frustrated. "We could never really agree on who controlled what, or what the values would be," he told an associate later. His interest in a big deal began to flag. Armstrong floated an even bolder idea: AT&T would sever its consumer long-distance business and combine it with TCI and hold a controlling stake in the merged concern. Armstrong argued that TCI needed a lot of cash flow, and long-distance service would generate enormous cash flow while TCI's operating losses would shelter much of the proceeds from taxes. Again, the deal fell apart on valuation and on control. "I wasn't going to give up control of TCI," Malone said later.

Soon the direction of the discussions, led by Leo Hindery for TCI and AT&T's president, John Zeglis, began to focus on Teleport Communications Group. The business services phone firm was started by TCI and cable partners Cox and Comcast back in 1992 on an initial investment of $70 million by TCI. They agreed to sell Teleport Communications Group to AT&T for $11.3 billion, giving the long-distance giant an instant entry into competing with the Bells for business clients at the local level. Teleport, with half a billion dollars in revenue, owned local fiber-rich networks in more than 60 U.S. markets, between and including New York and Los Angeles. Malone, in character, structured the deal as a tax-free stock swap that valued Teleport at just under $60 a share, making TCI's 30 percent stake worth $2.9 billion. Malone at TCI, Roberts at Comcast, or Robbins at Cox never really thought of Teleport, a public company that they controlled, as critical for their survival in the cable TV business. But the timing was perfect. The previous year, WorldCom, Incorporated, bought Teleport rival MFS Communications for $14 billion in stock.

The Teleport deal done, Armstrong continued searching for a way to get hold of what he considered to be the real key to the kingdom: the At Home broadband service. Though At Home could claim only 100,000 customers after three years in business, it held enormous potential in the race to provide home users with high-speed Internet access. With cable's fat pipe and AT&T's brand name and bankroll, the promise for Internet-based services was limitless. Even more important, At Home's reach went far beyond just TCI's 10 million customers; it had exclusive rights to provide Internet service to a total of 55 million households in cable systems owned by At Home's owners—TCI, Cox Communications Inc., Comcast Corp., Cablevision Systems Corp., and Rogers Cablesystems Ltd. TCI was the key: It controlled 72 percent of the vote on major strategic decisions.

Leo Hindery took part in all the lengthy nuts-and-bolts meetings with AT&T executives, and he reported to Malone that Mike Armstrong was eager to do a bigger deal. "Bullshit," Malone said to himself. Frustrated, Malone at one point called Armstrong for a blunt conversation. "I don't see how we ever get anywhere," Malone told the AT&T chief. "We will never reach an agreement. You are basically asking TCI to take the guts out of its company and put it into a joint venture that you control. I don't see how we ever get anywhere on that model." And then Malone dropped the handkerchief: "The only thing I could think of would be you could just propose to buy TCI. And if you were interested in that, we could discuss that."[6]

Armstrong agreed to think about it, but he also was looking at other possible merger partners. He had tried unsuccessfully to link up with America Online and had looked at trying to acquire Bell-South, with more than 17 million local telephone customers. All around AT&T, phone rivals grew bigger and bigger through mergers and alliances, part of the revolution unleashed by the Telecommunications Act of 1996. SBC Communications, Incorporated, the Texas Bell, gobbled up Pacific Telesis Group in 1997. Bell Atlantic, TCI's onetime mate, bought Nynex the same year to form a company called Verizon. MCI, the number two long-distance carrier, agreed to merge with WorldCom, and SBC agreed to buy Ameritech Corporation, the Midwestern Bell. Back at TCI, Hindery heard whispers that Armstrong was talking to BellSouth and almost panicked. "I'd have killed myself if AT&T had gone to BellSouth, because I had no exit," Hindery told an interviewer much later.

♘♘♘

In May of 1998, Hindery hatched a plan to bring Armstrong running into TCI's arms. He arranged a secret meeting of the largest cable operators at the annual industry convention in Atlanta to meet with Armstrong about the cable industry coming together to sell AT&T-branded phone service. Though he discussed it with none of the men in attendance, Hindery cultivated a hunch about how his cable colleagues would react to Armstrong's partnership plans. He escorted Armstrong to the meeting, where Brian Roberts of Comcast, Joe Collins of Time Warner, Chuck Lillis of Media One (a spin-off of the Bell company U S West), and Jim Robbins of Cox waited. Armstrong made a passionate pitch, and then the cable heads spoke up. "They eviscerated him," Hindery later told a reporter. "It was so deliciously rude, and I knew they were going to be rude. I mean, it was calculated, but the risk that I ran was that it wasn't rude and they agreed to a deal—at which point there was no reason to buy TCI." If there was a deal to be made, the group assured Armstrong, AT&T would have to pay for it. Armstrong left Atlanta shaken by the chilly reception and frustrated that he couldn't do the deal with the cable industry as a whole.

One day Hindery called Malone with good news: The hook was set. "I think they will go for this with a premium (to the current price of the stock). Mike wants to do the deal and he wants to do it really fast."

"I don't see any indication of it. I don't trust it," Malone replied. Any big purchase would cut AT&T earnings in half, and AT&T investors demand good earnings, unlike those investors willing to buy cable stocks and ignore losses, focusing instead on cash flow. "It will kill them," Malone thought.

But Hindery's skills as a deal maker were substantial; he had a knack for sensing what the other side wanted, and even Malone had marveled at this ability, which he would later call invaluable. Hindery knew Armstrong looked at TCI as his entrée into the entire cable industry: In addition to TCI's 10 million customers, it had deeply intertwined agreements with nearly a dozen other cable operators, representing around 75 percent of all cable subscribers in the country. All of them, perhaps, might be persuaded to join AT&T to offer local phone calls over their wires. TCI looked liked a good bet from where he stood. Malone had 48 percent voting control of TCI and 41 percent of Liberty. TCI, in turn, owned 72 percent voting control of At Home, which Armstrong believed would bring AT&T to the Promised Land.[7]

Finally, Armstrong flew to Denver in the spring of 1998 and met with Malone and Hindery. He had made an earlier trip and discussed with Malone why and how cable technology could trump telephone and satellite technology in the race to consumers' homes. Now, in the boardroom on the eleventh floor of TCI headquarters, he proposed a deal that would rock the telecommunications world: AT&T would buy TCI. The conclusion was mutual, and Malone started spinning ideas for tracking stocks that would represent the disparate parts of the business.

That way, old-line investors who demanded strong earnings growth in AT&T's old business could own one stock, and more aggressive investors could take more risk on a cable tracking stock that was judged by cash flow, despite producing annual losses. Malone drew up several financial models for Armstrong and his CFO, Dan Somers, showing how they could eliminate the damage that the deal would do to AT&T's earnings by offloading cable's losses onto a tracking stock. Armstrong warmed to the idea of trackers and sold himself on being able to buy TCI without hurting the main company's earnings. Within AT&T, Armstrong and others discussed how much of the tracking stock to distribute to the shareholders, and how much to retain. At one point, Malone suggested an issue of preferred stock, which typically paid a special dividend above and before regular common shareholders got anything. He even offered to come in personally and become a substantial shareholder.

In selling Teleport to AT&T months earlier, Malone and Hindery had learned a lot about Armstrong's due diligence and negotiating style. Deals are courtships in the business world. Each sale or investment is different, a reflection of the personalities involved and the strengths and weaknesses in their logic and motivation. "They were smarter than we were," Hindery said later. "They know *everything*. It was very helpful." Malone and Hindery thought some assumptions they made about business were absurd. Once they decided to proceed on a plan largely of Malone's calculations, the entire deal took eight days to pen, a whirlwind for any merger, but especially miraculous for lethargic, deliberative AT&T. Armstrong later told a reporter that he was tired of waiting and watching deals appear, then vanish. "Time was closing in on us," he said.[8]

♘♘♘

On June 24, 1998, flashbulbs strobed furiously as Malone and Armstrong stepped upon the stage. At the turn of the century, the oldest telecommunications company with the most widely held stock in America had just placed its bet on the cable industry as the single fastest way to hop on board the Internet. AT&T had agreed to pay dearly for TCI and its Liberty Media sibling: $48.3 billion in cash, stock, and assumption of debt. For TCI shareholders, Malone won a premium of more than 30 percent over the value of the shares before the deal was announced—$50.71 a share compared with the $30 range in which the stock had been trading. TCI stock had hit a high of $32.87 at the time Bell Atlantic proposed to buy the company in the fall of 1993. Now TCI shares were at the $50 mark. At Home, the cable Internet service, rose in total market value by nearly one-third to more than $6 billion with the AT&T deal, At Home's shares rising almost $12 to more than $51 apiece on the day the accord was unveiled. Fittingly, Malone had struck the best deal for himself and other holders of class B supervoting stock, including the Magness estate; for them, the premium was 10 percent, or $55.78 a share. The financial press viewed the latter move as "pretty tacky." ". . . even in the moment of his greatest triumph, Malone can't resist creaming off about $170 million of extra goodies for himself at the expense of most of TCI's other shareholders," wrote one financial columnist.[9]

Malone had always found a way to avoid paying taxes, and his swan dive from TCI proved no exception. Instead of cash, the currency of the deal was AT&T stock. It would be one of the largest sales in the history of telecommunications, and Malone had structured it so that the Internal Revenue Service had no choice but to treat it as a tax-free stock merger. Basically, Malone had exchanged his personal stake of $1.7 billion in TCI and Liberty for $2.4 billion in AT&T and Liberty stock. When the merger was announced, Malone told reporters, "We've been accused of our vision exceeding our grasp. But when Mike came along, he clearly shared our vision and brought the resources needed to reach the goal, at least in my lifetime." The deal sent the value of cable systems soaring to unprecedented levels; Cablevision Systems Corporation surged 23 percent to $76 per share in American Stock Exchange trading. And cable giant Time Warner Inc. rose 6.5 percent to close at $88.625 on the New York Stock Exchange. The value sent other systems in better shape to $5,000 a subscriber, a figure that would have been laughed at just a year before.

On the surface, the terms of the proposed merger seemed simple. AT&T would gain control of TCI's domestic cable operations, its high-speed Internet company At Home, the National Digital Television Center in Arapahoe County, and TCI's microwave business. AT&T also bought back the stock it had paid TCI when it acquired Teleport earlier that year. The biggest prize was TCI's cable assets, a collection that had been painstakingly assembled over a quarter of a century, granting Ma Bell direct access to 11 million subscribers, and a few million more through minority stakes in some of the most lucrative markets in the country, including Chicago, Dallas, Denver, and San Francisco. By their own estimation, the companies said they could potentially reach 33 million homes passed by their wires.

Heavy debt and other distractions had caused TCI to fall behind some other cable companies in rebuilding their systems, but executives at AT&T and TCI promised to accelerate the upgrade of TCI's cable systems to handle two-way Internet data transmissions. With time and money, AT&T would be the consummate one-stop shop for an entire panoply of communications services in the twenty-first century. AT&T could now reach directly into U.S. homes and businesses, selling long-distance and local phone service, as well as Internet-access services, interactive video, and new electronic services not even invented.

For himself, Malone had reserved an extraordinary amount of freedom and power to run what was most important to him: Liberty Media. Liberty would remain, for all practical purposes, independent, with few restrictions. It could issue as much as $10 billion in debt without having to seek AT&T's approval. Malone held 4 percent of its outstanding stock, 33 percent of the vote, and six of nine seats on the board; AT&T shareholders held the rest, but AT&T itself didn't own a single share. AT&T could use any losses to reduce its own taxes, but it had to pass on the savings to Liberty. Perhaps most important, Liberty won exclusive rights to a dozen digital channels on AT&T cable systems, and the exclusive lock on the on-screen guide that would greet AT&T cable customers, worth a fortune in future ad revenue. AT&T had also agreed to pay a monthly fee to Liberty for the Encore movie channel as if it reached all 12 million TCI subscribers. Never mind that some of the systems were too small and overcrowded to carry the service. And whenever AT&T acquired any other cable systems in the future, it was stuck in the same deal.

AT&T also agreed to funnel $5.5 billion in cash to Liberty Media, to use as the subsidiary saw fit. Prior to the formal acquisition, TCI's Ventures unit, which oversees digital and Internet-related services including At Home, would be merged with Liberty Media. Liberty would then sell some TCI Ventures assets, including the National Digital Television Center, AT&T stock from the earlier sale of Teleport, and its 39 percent At Home stake (which TCI acquired in 1995 for a few million dollars), to AT&T for $5.5 billion. That cash would be the start of a hefty war chest for Malone. At his behest, Liberty also had the explicit right "to take actions that may not be in the best interests of AT&T or holders of new Liberty Media Group tracking stock."

It was, hands down, the best deal John Malone had ever negotiated in his entire career. The financial press all but said it: Malone had outsmarted Mike Armstrong, an impression that made Armstrong and his CFO, Somers, bristle with indignation. But it was true: Malone had run circles around them. Now if only he could make the deal stick.

GIVE ME LIBERTY

Freed from the shackles of TCI and the headaches that came with running a regulated monopoly, Malone set sail with *Liberty*, quite literally. In the fall of 1998, his spirits high and his craving to be on the open water strong, Malone told Marty Flessner, the polite and protective redhead who kept his schedule, to block out a week. Winter was creeping along, and the harsh weather of Maine would force him to take his 80-foot powerboat, *Liberty*, on a long voyage south to Ft. Lauderdale for winter storage. He and the boys were going sailing. *Liberty*—Malone had always loved that word. He was as libertarian as a man could be, fiercely proud of what he had accomplished. A man who believed that wealth creation was a noble, moral achievement, he was pushing 60 with Calvinist roots and capitalist beliefs. As a boardmember and donor of the Cato Institute (the libertarian think tank that espouses limited government and individual liberty), Malone believed the definition was not freedom *from* obligation, but freedom *to* choose which of those obligations to take on, which roles to play in business and life.

Malone's home life was shockingly middle-class for a man of such enormous wealth. He filed his own taxes, washed his own clothes, cleared the table, and until the mid-1990s, mowed his own yard.

The moorings of diligence and self-denial came from his father. But at 57 years old, Malone was finally beginning to enjoy the possessions and playthings that came with wealth—boats, houses, and even a tiny island in the Bahamas. Unless these material artifacts could efficiently shelter income or increase in value, he felt conflicted about owning them. It had taken his painfully shy wife, Leslie, 40 years to convince him to retreat, occasionally, from his inborn urge to analyze, tinker, and apply set theory to nearly every aspect of his life. Her attitude was, "You've earned it. Let's enjoy it."

Headstrong enough to get her way occasionally, Leslie was also an affectionate wife who could soothe even Darth Vader. She supplied the ballast to Malone's business career, particularly now. He focused on financial efficiency so much, he often wondered whether he wasn't simply stingy and cheap. One day, when Leslie opened a package of raspberries she had just bought at the market, Malone looked at the price and gulped. "How could you pay $5 for raspberries?" His reaction was the same when Leslie bought a horse she fancied. "My God, how could you pay so much for a horse?" he asked her. "Who are you ever going to resell it to?" But he backed off more and more now, giving in to her modest indulgences.

At the dock in Portland where *Liberty* was tied, Malone and Larry Romrell, now retired from TCI, met with Paul Gould, TCI's longtime Allen & Company adviser, whom Malone had chosen to replace Bob Magness on TCI's board, and Jeff Lowell, a burly, bearded man who was Malone's trusted first mate and caretaker of the boatyard in Boothbay Harbor. They eagerly jumped aboard the *Liberty,* whose remarkably rounded black keel reflected the low light of the day like a smoky mirror. At around 3 P.M., Malone scoured the overcast skies, glanced down at the bank of dials and electronic charts embedded in the mahogany dash, then nudged the throttle levers forward. The diesel engines beneath him purred in response, and in seconds, a thin sheet of water flew up on either side of *Liberty*'s sleek, black bow. The sun sank over their inland horizon, and Lowell warmed up a big pot of chili.

Malone loved to be on the open water; it recharged the undefinable creative force that seemed to power him. He treasured Denver and the West, but he was most at home in the East, especially when he could inhale the salt air. The new Liberty headquarters reflected this dichotomy: the earth-tone building was nestled at the foot of the Rockies, but it was round, and inside, the hallways were marked by compass readings in degrees embedded in marble floors.

With *Liberty*'s engines humming, an open sea ahead of him, Malone smiled at nothing in particular. He waxed on about the stock market and the weather, a powerful little storm was in the works, in between big bites of crisp red apples picked in his own orchard that day by Lowell's young sons. He especially loved this boat. At his encouragement, *Liberty*'s maker, Hogdon Yachts in Maine, had deployed every possible advanced construction technique using a combination of the strongest and lightest wood, resins, and carbon fiber. Unlike the ever delicate 1928 *Ragtime* that Malone had restored, the *Liberty*'s hard-chine bottom was light and tough, representing a new era in boat building. "She is, to my way of thinking, the highest quality wooden boat ever built," Tim Hogdon, a fifth-generation Maine boatbuilder who oversaw the three-year project, liked to brag to *Liberty*'s admirers.[1] As the sky turned darker, the winds kicked up, and Malone inched the throttle forward.

Malone had never liked sailing with a hired crew. He preferred the privacy of friends and the responsibility of charting a course, with little more than intellect and experience to pull him through to the other side. He enjoyed the whole challenge of seamanship, of running his own boat. The longer the journey, the better. *Liberty* sailed through the Cape Cod Canal, then sped through Buzzard's Bay off Massachusetts. From there, Malone set the boat's course by global positioning satellite to east of Long Island and drove harder. Rain and spray now slammed against the windshield. Visibility was bad, and Malone could steal only a few seconds of vision cleared by the pass of giant windshield wipers before the glass was covered again. The sea rolled, and *Liberty* bounced. "It's coming down now . . ." Malone said to Gould. "What about shifts?"

"Larry and me . . . ?" Lowell asked Malone. Romrell nodded.

"And Paul and I will start," Malone said, finishing the sentence.

For the rest of the night, the seas tossed *Liberty*. In driving rain and pitch darkness in the Atlantic Ocean, Malone peered through the windshield, never once looking tired or terribly concerned as he hung on to the wheel. Gould, an amiable and regular sailor on Malone's boats, was less talkative than usual as he squinted out the side window, then back through the front windshield in search of any lights that moved in the blackness—a sign of another ship. A practical joker who made long trips bearable, he had stowed in his bag a blow-up doll to throw overboard, but now was not the time. He was glad just to hang on to his chili.

Around daybreak, the seas calmed. *Liberty* cruised the open sea until Malone brought her inland, away from the choppy waters. The following afternoon, with Annapolis just 50 miles away, he set the course for the naval base. At port, docking wasn't left to the crew. Working the twin diesels, Malone brought the 80-foot-long *Liberty* up to the dock as gently and precisely as if he were putting a baby in a cradle. Back on terra firma, the men showered. They were clean but exhausted from the strain of the previous eight hours. Starved, they set out on Main Street to grab dinner. After passing several elegant restaurants, a neon sign caught Malone's attention. "Buddy's Crabs and Ribs," he read aloud. Inside, the joint was boisterous, filled with a mix of families, college kids, and military. Malone, with his angular, beefy physique in a polo shirt and khaki pants, could have been mistaken for an aging Annapolis naval captain, sipping nothing stronger than ice water after getting tossed about so rudely by the ocean. As the young waitress delivered a tray of boiled and fried seafood for the hungry crew, Malone spent the rest of the evening talking about the politics, boat building, and the next day's weather. Business, for the moment, was not on the menu.

ᘇᘇᘇ

Perhaps it should have been. Since John Malone had stood onstage with C. Michael Armstrong to announce AT&T's daring acquisition of TCI the previous June, the signs weren't all that encouraging. The AT&T guys just didn't seem to get it—they didn't understand how cooperative the cable industry was, with archrivals laying down arms to team up in joint ventures in order to make a bigger profit. Nor did they respect the financial structures that sought cash flow over earnings and pounded taxes down as flat as was legally possible. "It was a joke," Malone told a friend later, annoyed. "They'd ask, 'Have you *ever* paid any taxes?' like that's a crime. I said, 'Sure I've paid taxes—as little as possible, and as late as possible.' I'm serious! Then I make them a speech. 'I regard that as my share-holders' money. It is not the government's. It is my job to save as much of that as I can for my shareholders.' " The message, which Malone proselytized, never seemed to take.

For the first time in his career, Malone was in a particularly weak position: He had huge financial exposure but no control. Virtually all of his wealth was tied up in the AT&T stock he had received for selling TCI and Liberty, yet the decisions affecting the stock's value were being made by a bunch of AT&T executives who didn't know the cable business. And it was beginning to look like the decisions they were making were the wrong ones. Malone was expected to watch politely from the sidelines. This he tried to do, holding his tongue as miscue after miscalculation accumulated. Increasingly, he came to feel like these guys couldn't shoot straight. He lamented the absence of cable pros and knew that soon, none of the old cable gang would be left; all the old-timers were dying out or selling out. Malone knew the other board members were waiting for him to meddle, and he vowed to stay out of it.

And so Malone dutifully kept his mouth shut when he got a call from Mike Armstrong in the opening days of 1999, revealing what Malone took to be bad news: Armstrong had elected to renege on the Malone-inspired plan to issue a separate tracking stock for AT&T's cable business. AT&T's shares were roaring, and Wall Street was loving the TCI play, Armstrong said, so why mess with it? Malone wanted to go along, and he stopped himself from saying what he really wanted to say:

"Here's why you should mess with it, Mike: You've just issued more than 400 million new shares of AT&T to buy a business that produces no earnings. It will be a huge money-loser for years, given how much you'll spend on broadband. That's going to sharply dilute your earnings per share, and your old shareholders *like* earnings. That will hurt your stock price, and then you can't use stock to make more acquisitions, then you're stuck. If you create a tracking stock to track the performance of cable, you separate out the losses we produce and show better earnings for your main shareholders; and you can use the tracker to buy more cable interests in tax-free deals."

That's what Malone had *wanted* to say, and when Michael Armstrong looked back on the moment much later, after all his plans ended in disastrous consequences, he would admit that he wished Malone had convinced him to issue the tracking stocks after all.[2] To buy TCI, AT&T had used two forms of currency, its own AT&T stock and a new AT&T-issued Liberty tracking stock (basically a pass-through to original Liberty and TCI Ventures shareholders). AT&T's stock had long been known on Wall Street by its ticker symbol, T, and the original plan was to have three: T for the old-line company, one for Liberty, and one for the new tracker for the cable business. Tracking stocks don't represent an actual ownership interest in the underlying assets, which remain owned by the parent company; instead, a tracker is tied to a business's performance, and it lets investors bet on how good that performance will be by buying or selling the stock. It also lets other investors figuratively buy the piece they like in a company, without having to invest in the whole thing. Armstrong had seen trackers before at Hughes Electronics, which traded as a separate tracking stock from GM's common stock; that was one reason he had gone along with Malone's logic, initially.

Armstrong surprised Wall Street with his no-tracker decision on January 8, 1999, saying investors now had so much confidence in AT&T that they were willing to accept short-term losses for long-term gain. AT&T's share price so well reflected its cable future (its stock now traded near the $60 range) that a separate cable entity with its own stock was unnecessary, Armstrong maintained. The move concerned Malone, who had told reporters when the TCI takeover was announced that he planned to swap his AT&T stock for the cable tracker once it was issued, and maybe for a wireless tracking stock that should be issued, too. Malone had been fixated on the trackers. "Look, you have the [number one] cable company in the U.S.," he said in meetings. "Give it its own identity, its own currency, its own focus and management growth. And support it every way you can as part of a big [semiconglomerated] company.

And find what synergies you can. Do the same thing with wireless."

As conceived by Malone, AT&T's cable assets were a stand-alone entity with a separate balance sheet. The idea was to insulate cable, valued in terms of cash flow, from the consumer long-distance business, which is valued on earnings. From his early days in cable, Malone had preached that you couldn't mix a growth-oriented, capital-intensive company valued on a cash flow basis with a traditional earnings company. Malone went along with the plan for now, but it bothered him, and he consoled himself with the knowledge he could convince Armstrong and CFO Dan Somers later of the need to issue the trackers as they had first planned.

U U U

About a month later, on the night of Tuesday, February 16, 1999, top TCI executives met for dinner in Denver. In just one week shareholders would vote on AT&T's final takeover of the entire company. The commanders who had helped Malone and Magness build TCI were there trading jokes and sipping wine. Most of the old gang had shown up: J. C. Sparkman, 32 years with TCI; Don Fisher, 30 years; Larry Romrell, 38 years. The dinner was held at the elegant Swan Restaurant in Denver, where TCI executives nibbled on pepper-seared beef carpaccio and crab cakes before sitting down to dine on choice of chateaubriand, tuna steak on ginger rice with Asian pear salsa, or breast of capon on wild mushroom cake. It was an oddly stylish place for a group that had built a reputation around a no-frills management style. Off to the corner, at John's side, was Leslie Malone, there to celebrate her husband's departure from TCI. After dinner, Malone spoke to the small gathering and praised his longtime supporters. "We're going out absolutely on top," he told the group. "We were like Rodney Dangerfield, we never got any respect. Finally, we're getting respect." He praised Leo Hindery, in particular, saying, "He really has made this merger possible—a lot of us were skeptical a deal could get done. He did it with sheer energy. He drove it and drove it and drove it, and brought the deal home. Thanks, Leo, I appreciate it."

Looking back, TCI's record was undeniably impressive. A $10,000 investment in TCI when Malone joined in 1973 would have grown to nearly $3 million by the end of 1999. Looked at another way: If an investor had bought $100 worth of TCI stock in 1973, participated in the spin-offs and splits, mimicking Malone's trades, he would have $181,200 by late 1999.[3] Longtime TCI investors were richly rewarded. TCI excelled not because it was a great cable operator and friendly corporate citizen. Those were promises Malone never felt compelled to make or keep. True, it was the largest cable operator in the country, but Malone never pretended to be the best cable operator. TCI built wealth and made its shareholders wealthy by investments and complex financial engineering.

A week later, the merger moved three steps closer to completion. As Mike Armstrong talked to owners of the most widely held stock in America on a giant videoscreen at a meeting in Secaucus, New Jersey, 99 percent of AT&T's shareholders approved the merger. The same day in Washington, the FCC gave its unanimous blessing. And on a bright clear morning in Denver, in the cavernous halls of TCI's National Digital Television Center, Malone convened the 26th and final annual TCI shareholders meeting. Sharply dressed in a dark suit and red tie, he announced to the gathered shareholders that they and their colleagues had overwhelmingly approved TCI's $48 billion acquisition by AT&T. As he called the meeting to order, Malone stood against a blue curtain on a stage he shared with Leo Hindery and Liberty Media President Dob Bennett. "We've had a helluva run, and now we're going off to a new adventure," he told the standing-room-only audience of 300 loyal investors, all of whom were now much richer thanks to their association with TCI.

"Bob Magness would have loved this. The run-up of TCI stock and Liberty stock is close to $100 billion—which I think would even get Bob's attention. What a great run," Malone told the crowd. When Hindery spoke, he lavished praise on Malone and the shareholders. "I'll go to my grave grateful for these shareholders," he said, his voice shaking. "What John Malone did for me personally meant more to me than I can ever express." At the press conference that followed, Malone said he felt like the Denver Broncos after their second straight Super Bowl win. "It's like, Wow! We did it! Now what do we do?" Reporters hounded Malone about his future plans for Liberty. What was his next deal? What would he buy with so much money? Malone played coy. "Like they say, you've got to kiss a lotta frogs before you find a prince," he said.

Not everyone was as nostalgic about the deal, or as reverent of John Malone's place in business history. AT&T "will have to spend a fortune to rebuild the TCI network," David McCourt, chairman and CEO of RCN Corporation, a start-up telephone and cable company, told reporters. "AT&T paid too much for too little."[4]

♘♘♘

A month later, John Malone was in Fort Collins, Colorado, working another acquisition—this one in cattle, not cable—when he was tipped to some startling news. It was a Friday, and he immediately called Mike Armstrong at AT&T to reveal the secret: Come Monday, Brian Roberts of Comcast would announce a stunning $58 billion bid for Media One, the third-largest cable company in the nation. Media One, with 5 million subscribers nationwide, had been spun off by U S West, the Denver-based Bell company, and it also owned a coveted 25.5 percent stake in Time Warner Entertainment, the subsidiary encompassing Time Warner's cable and HBO businesses. Comcast wouldn't pussyfoot on this—only months earlier it had swooped in and bought control of Jones Intercable through purchase of Bell Canada's stake in the company. Armstrong had few contacts in the cable industry and was clueless about the cataclysmic event.

Malone looped him in for one main reason: He knew AT&T had been looking at Media One for months, and Armstrong needed to know AT&T simply couldn't afford to bid for Media One, even though he might want to. "Mike, I don't believe, given the prices that are being talked about and the currencies that are being used, that you can really justify competing for them," said Malone, ever direct. His unspoken point: If Armstrong had kept his word and issued a tracking stock for the cable business, maybe he could have used those shares as the currency for going after Media One. Instead, AT&T would have to issue still more of its own common stock and a lot of cash, rupturing its balance sheet. This it should not do.

Armstrong thanked Malone for the heads-up and got off the phone. On Monday morning, April 22, 1999, Brian Roberts surprised his fellow cable operators by announcing that Media One had accepted his $58 billion takeover bid. Roberts had bought Media One right out from under Armstrong's nose, some people said, but Armstrong swallowed his pride and called Brian Roberts to congratulate him. Just a few weeks later, Malone, at an AT&T board meeting, was stunned—and stung—to learn that Armstrong has a rich counterbid for Media One in the works. Mike Armstrong had taken Malone's call—and ignored his advice. Two weeks later, AT&T jumped into the bidding, offering $62.5 billion for Media One.

To Malone, AT&T's bid was the zenith of stupidity. The price was simply too rich, by billions of dollars, more than $5,000 a subscriber when the typical industry deals were closer to $3,000 per subscriber. And worse yet, AT&T had to use a mix of stock and cash to bankroll the massive sum—that meant Media One holders were taxed by the IRS on the cash portion, a ridiculous waste of money. An all-stock deal would have wiped out any taxes owed entirely, which would have meant the price paid could be that much lower because the sellers kept the entire proceeds. But Armstrong had unwisely eschewed a cable tracker, so it had to put up $24 billion in cash and issue 603 million more AT&T shares and take on an extra $4.5 billion in debt, pushing AT&T's total debt load to almost $60 billion. The way Malone saw it, Armstrong had done nothing more financially creative than go to the bank and borrow short-term money for a highly taxable deal, a grave sin in Malone's mind. Also, Armstrong had chosen to make a rival hostile bid when he should have just called Brian Roberts and asked to participate in the offer—he used a battering ram when he should have simply knocked politely on the door. Malone never did things this way, there was no need to; it was why he competed with, but also shared ownership interests with, such lethal rivals as Rupert Murdoch, the Robertses, the Dolans, and Time Warner.

Ultimately, AT&T did cut a deal with Brian Roberts, winning the Media One battle (and ultimately losing the war). AT&T agreed to sell Comcast 2 million (nearly half) of its Media One customers, including a 1.5 million swath of customers in the Philadelphia area long coveted by the Robertses when it was owned by TCI partner Lenfest Communications. The Robertses at Comcast walked away with $1.5 billion in breakup fees, and ended up with a total of 8 million customers—the nation's third-largest cable TV operator. And if AT&T ever sold phone service to Comcast customers, Comcast was guaranteed AT&T's most generous terms. Comcast also agreed to provide AT&T with cable-phone access, so long as AT&T first signed up at least two other cable operators for similar deals. That condition would prove to be far more difficult to honor than Mike Armstrong had ever anticipated. Moreover, AT&T was stuck with Media One's 25 percent interest in Time Warner Entertainment, which it would have to divest.

From Malone's point of view, Armstrong was making major missteps. Armstrong didn't have the kind of support he needed to help the company really do a first-class deal. He wasn't in contact with the accounting department, whereas Malone talked to his accountants every day. "They killed the pig, and they didn't use the blood, the skin, and the guts," Malone told someone later. "So they ended up with a couple of nice hams, which they paid way too much for."[5] He traced the failure back to the lack of a tracking stock. "He [Armstrong] could then have used this new currency to consolidate anything else in the cable industry he wanted to buy. And he would have been king. But he didn't see it," Malone told a colleague.

The Media One deal was one of the few times Malone and Leo Hindery parted company, for Hindery was all for it. He had stayed with TCI after the AT&T deal to become the combined company's top cable executive, and he was charged with trying to sign up the entire cable industry to team up with AT&T on local phone service. He looked at Media One as offering him more latitude to strike alliances, because he would have more cable systems available for horse trading. In exchange for promises to carry AT&T's brand, Hindery thought he could cut generous swaps and trades. The new AT&T-TCI could offer New York subscribers to Chuck Dolan, Cleveland systems to Adelphia, neighboring systems to Comcast, and St. Louis systems to Charter Communications. "I had to get those properties—no one was going to do a phone deal with me if I didn't give them something," Hindery told an interviewer later. "Time was running out."[6]

As Hindery raced around the country trying to sign up cable operators to the AT&T phone plan, he continued to bang heads with the bureaucrats in AT&T headquarters in Basking Ridge. His newest nemesis was John Zeglis, the smooth AT&T veteran who was to have been Hindery's boss until Hindery demanded to report directly to Armstrong.

Armstrong, too, had become oddly obsessed with the minutia of management, approving low-level hires, pricing, and even ad copy. "It was just so bizarre," Hindery said later. The meetings with top brass "would go interminably every Monday out in Basking Ridge," he said.[7] When he refused to be present physically for the mini-summits, attended by as many as 50 people at a time, Hindery, who kept his home in San Francisco and an apartment in Denver, was told he could attend via an elaborate videoconferencing system that AT&T had installed back at TCI headquarters. Hindery literally pulled the plug on the contraption and claimed he had encountered technical difficulties.

The infighting got worse when Hindery discovered that AT&T had commissioned a background report on him a year earlier, later sharing its sometimes uncomplimentary findings with the board. In June 1998, the *New York Times* ran a profile on Hindery that questioned his character and included family interviews that ran counter to Hindery's description of a tough and miserable childhood. The timing—three days before AT&T's announcement of its TCI acquisition—seemed odd. "It got really ugly. The report said that even his own mother and sister say you can't trust him," was how Malone viewed it. "Three or four people say lots of energy but no integrity. And then that report gets written up clearly in a venal anti-Leo way, instead of a balanced way. And it was leaked to the board."

Mike Armstrong, when Hindery confronted him about the report, looked Leo square in the eyes and said, "Leo, it was the wrong thing for AT&T to do. I destroyed it. It has never been shared with anybody. Don't worry about it." But months later, as

John Malone sat in a board meeting, the findings were shared with his fellow directors. As far as Malone was concerned, Armstrong was stretching the truth. "So now there is Mike with his nose getting longer, telling Leo a [bald-faced] lie," he thought.[8] Hindery called Malone to complain, telling him: "You know they have an expression at AT&T. It's called 'grin-fucking,' really sticking it to you while they are smiling at you. Armstrong was really grin-fucking me, wasn't he?"[9]

At the national cable show in Chicago in June 1999, where Malone was inducted into the Cable Hall of Fame, AT&T's Armstrong was the keynote speaker. He seemed confident, perhaps too confident, that the clubby cable fraternity would embrace him. After greeting the audience, he noted that in the past year alone, more than $140 billion in cable systems had changed hands, a testament to the health of the industry. He resurrected the notion of interactive TV, saying it had taken on a new life through the Internet, and that cable operators stood at the cusp of another era. Up on stage, squinting out in the darkness at some of the 30,000 cable faithful at the show, he proclaimed, "I'm proud to be a cable guy."

υυυ

In the summer of 1999, Hindery barely came up for air in his new role as chief executive of AT&T Corporation's cable TV and Internet unit. He flew from office to office of the half-dozen biggest cable operators in the United States, cajoling them to partner with AT&T in delivering phone service over their cable wires. But it was all proving to be much harder than Hindery, Armstrong, or anyone else had anticipated. AT&T desperately needed to form links to other cable operators to get access to the last mile into their customers' homes. Without this national linkup with other cable operators, the entire reasoning behind buying TCI was fallacious.

Hindery had exactly 12 phone-cable deals teed up with various operators, including, and depending on, Time Warner. "In each deal, I gave each one—Adelphia, Cox, Comcast, and Cablevision—something they couldn't get otherwise. And for that they were going to give me phone," Hindery told a colleague. Hindery wanted more than anything for AT&T to partner with Time Warner, the nation's second-largest cable operator, mostly because the other operators would fall in line like a high school band. In June, Hindery and Armstrong met with Time Warner CEO Gerald Levin and President Dick Parsons to discuss the matter. Time Warner, like others in the cable gang, was reticent to sign a deal on the logic that its own brand of phone service would sell as well as, or better than, AT&T's. Before the meeting concluded, the men briefly discussed another subject: America Online. At the time, Levin was terrified that AOL would use its pumped-up market capitalization to attempt a hostile takeover of Time Warner. Thanks to the Internet inflation in the financial markets, AOL had twice the market capitalization of Time Warner and had hired bankers in the summer to plot strategic possibilities.

Hindery, a longtime cable guy, closed ranks with Time Warner and promised that AT&T would never talk with AOL without talking to Time Warner first. The men even discussed a poison pill for Time Warner Entertainment. Armstrong also needed a pact with Cablevision Systems Corporation, the Long Island, New York–based cable empire headed by cable pioneer Charles Dolan. With 3 million customers, Cablevision had a stranglehold on the juicy New York metropolitan area, a potentially attractive platform for AT&T. But Dolan, famously shrewd and tough in negotiations, along with his son James, Cablevision's CEO, wouldn't accept AT&T's phone terms, even though AT&T owned one-third of the company through its TCI purchase.

"Tell Chuck Dolan this is the deal, and if he doesn't do our phone deal, we'll overbuild him with fixed wireless," Mike Armstrong told Leo Hindery one day, as Hindery recalled it. Leo shot back: "Wait a minute! You don't *tell* Chuck Dolan anything. You *beg* Chuck Dolan, you *plead* with him, you *ask* him, but you don't *tell* Chuck Dolan he's doing anything." During these increasingly heated discussions, Hindery told Armstrong, "Mike, you bought the company—you didn't buy the industry."

"You and your industry are going to have to learn that what's good for AT&T is good for your industry," Armstrong countered. Hindery got in the last word: "That's a message you should convey more than me."[10]

Indeed, AT&T executives weren't afraid to throw down the gauntlet, even in the industry trade rags, threatening to used wireless telephones in other operators' markets. Dan Somers, AT&T's CFO at the time, declared in *Cable World*, "If a cable operator doesn't want to partner with us, that market won't be left alone."[11] Threats to compete against another cable operator were verboten. No one in the cable gang had ever talked like this. For more than a quarter-century, the cable industry had done business without local competition. "Mike pissed off the whole industry, threatening to overbuild with fixed wireless," Hindery recalled later. The Dolans' reply was swift and pointed: Just try it. In mid-1999, AT&T predicted 800,000 phone-cable customers by the end of 2000, and "millions of customers" by the end of 2001. But AT&T couldn't hide the fact that the predictions were laughably optimistic. By 2000, it had only about 500,000 cable telephony customers and no clear plan to meet its goals.[12]

One of the deepest fissures between AT&T and its new cable friends was the contentious issue pitting cable TV operators against Internet service providers; AT&T, of course, owned both. Led by AOL, Internet service providers complained bitterly that AT&T and other cable operators with high-speed Internet service would hinder their access to the new high-speed lines. Never mind, for a moment, that these wires were not laid by some public utility—they were paid for by shareholders. Over cable, AT&T could offer Internet cruising speeds that were 100 times faster than phone lines, charging $40 a month for At Home.

Soon, a long list of consumer advocates and competitors began lobbying for regulators to force AT&T to open up its cable wires to all content providers, rather than granting exclusive opening-screen access to its partly owned At Home unit. City officials in Portland, Oregon, took AT&T to federal court to require the company to open its cable lines there to any Internet company on the same terms it gave At Home. AOL and other services lobbied the FCC and Congress for action largely out of fear that they would be left out of the high-speed future.

Hindery balked at opening up AT&T's network to just anyone, saying such a practice would turn a hundred-billion-dollar asset into little more than a dumb pipe. Like most cable operators, Hindery wanted the choice to sell to others, not a fiat from the government telling him to do so. Cable operators spent billions to build and upgrade their systems for two-way digital services, all without subsidies or aid from the government; it wasn't the government's place now to nationalize those systems and force the companies to take all comers. In this charged atmosphere, in October 1999, Hindery spoke to reporters at an appearance at Trinity College in Hartford, Connecticut, and was asked a question by a reporter: Was AT&T negotiating to give AOL access to its high-speed lines? "I don't usually respond to rumors but this one is absurd," Hindery retorted, strongly denying that AT&T was in talks with AOL about open access or any related issues. That would have been in direct violation of Hindery's promise to confer with Time Warner before ever talking with AOL; and it couldn't have happened without the knowledge of Hindery, head cable honcho at AT&T.

The following morning, Hindery heard from an AT&T lawyer who told him: "Well, we have a problem." To Hindery's surprise, Armstrong had held several discussions with AOL without ever notifying him of the overture. "*We* don't have a problem! *You* have a problem!" Hindery told the AT&T attorney. "This can't be true, because I'm not aware of it, and I am the CEO of the company!" he thundered. AT&T put out a statement confirming it was in talks with AOL, but didn't elaborate. Besides the momentary embarrassment of showing the business world the lack of communication between the chairman and his cable chief, it threatened to derail Hindery's tentative deals to offer AT&T local service on rival cable systems. Cable executives across the country were outraged. Days earlier, AT&T had met in confidential talks with top cable executives to discuss open-access issues, and the revelation that AT&T was talking with AOL behind their backs led many to conclude that AT&T wasn't to be trusted.

In Hindery's view, it showed Armstrong's arrogance, through and through; he thought that because he had bought TCI, he had bought automatic acceptance into cable's inner circle, but admission had to be earned first. In an industry with just six national players left, you didn't screw your neighbor. Hindery called Dick

Parsons at Time Warner to make amends and express hope they could still do a deal for AT&T-branded local phone service. Parsons was cold on the plan: "We'll meet you anytime you want, Leo, but the deal we agreed to last August is probably off the table." A few days later, news leaked that AT&T had been working on an open-access arrangement that could be used as a model for the industry with MindSpring Enterprises, Incorporated (an Internet service provider), the FCC, and the city of Atlanta. Cable operators erupted in anger over the news, branding the plan too generous to AT&T and too risky to cable operators.

Peeved with AT&T's hardball tactics, other cable operators followed in Time Warner's footsteps and turned cold on telephone deals with AT&T. AT&T's plan to build a nationwide local phone network through a web of other cable operators was faltering. For Hindery, it was the last straw. "These are the last days of Pompeii. When it breaks, it's gonna break big." Why put up with this shit? He had already sold stock that netted him $40 million, and he held AT&T stock worth $125 million and another $130 million in Liberty shares.[13] He was tired after clashing with Armstrong and the entire bureaucracy for months. On October 4, 1999, Hindery got his secret wish: He was fired, and eventually was replaced by Dan Somers, the CFO. A few years later, Hindery would become the head of the YES network, which aired New York Yankees games for Yankees owner George Steinbrenner—negotiating with old cable comrades for the same high fees he carped about as TCI president.

ひひひ

John Malone was having much more fun running Liberty Media, free to chart his own destiny. As if cued by the vernal equinox only days earlier, Malone chose the first week of April 1999 to act with a flourish: In 48 hours, he executed a series of deals that would top $6 billion in value and would send Liberty's stock through the roof. In one deal, Liberty set plans to swap stakes in various Internet companies that Malone had bought with TCI Music, a public company that was 86 percent owned by Liberty Media. Over the months, as the market's interest in the Internet grew, so had Malone's, despite his nagging suspicion that Internet stocks were overvalued. Liberty's TCI Music owned stakes in DMX, a music subscription service; Sonic Net, a music Web site with events, reviews, and streaming audio; and The Box, a jukebox-like cable network that allowed cable viewers to order specific videos at $1.99 each. TCI Music took possession of the Internet stakes, what Magness might have called "cats and dogs": SportsLine USA, Ivillage, drugstore.com and Priceline.com.

The swap lifted Liberty's stake in TCI Music to 94 percent from 86 percent. Malone renamed the company Liberty Digital, and gave it a new mission. Just as Liberty Media was a mutual fund of cable programming such as CNN, Discovery, and BET, so then would TCI Music be the new vessel for Malone's Internet investments. It was classic Malone: Take a tiny, near worthless stock, fill it with small stakes in several companies, watch them grow, then trade them for stakes in even bigger, more secure companies. Internet investors sent shares of the new TCI Music, whose symbol was TUNE, to more than double to almost $30, adding some $3.6 billion in value to TCI Music shares and $2.6 billion to the value of Liberty Media in one day. By the end of the week, TCI Music, which was worth less than $1 billion days earlier, was now valued by the market at an astonishing $10 billion. Malone knew it was only paper profits, but oh what fun!

The market loved the idea of Liberty Digital as Malone's Internet and interactive TV fund. A digital mutual fund, backed by Malone's investing reputation, a proven track record, and a $5.5 billion warchest. Almost overnight, he had turned TCI Music into the largest holding in the portfolio of Liberty Media, surpassing the value of the media company's 9 percent stake in Time Warner, its 21 percent share of USA Networks, and its 15 percent of a wireless telephone partnership with Sprint. By the end of the year, Liberty Digital had soared an astounding 1,400 percent. Nice while it lasted.

That same week in April 1999, Malone struck a deal for Liberty to pay $280 million to buy 5 percent, or about 10 million shares of the number-one cable TV box maker, General Instrument, the company with whom Malone had such a long and profitable relationship. By the fall, Motorola, a maker of high-speed cable modems for the cable industry, announced it would buy GI in an $11 billion deal. Malone agreed to sell his equity in GI to Motorola in a tax-free swap valued at $1.8 billion, leaving him with a 4 percent stake in Motorola, more than the founding Galvin family owned.

In a third deal, Liberty swapped its 50 percent interest in the Fox/Liberty Sports Networks for an 8 percent stake in News Corp., Rupert Murdoch's global conglomerate of movie, television, magazine, newspaper, and advertising businesses with assets of $36 billion and revenue of $14 billion. Upon signing the deal, Malone became the second-largest shareholder behind Murdoch. (Later, Malone would trade his 20 percent stake in the newly merged Gemstar–TV Guide International Inc., for News Corp. stock, which increased his stake in News Corp. to 18 percent.)

Only three weeks after closing the sale of TCI to AT&T, Malone had engineered a flurry of transactions that had added billions of dollars to Liberty's holdings. As the 1990s ended, Malone had managed to accumulate a number of large investments in media leaders: 8 percent equity interest in News Corp., 18 percent of General Instrument, 9 percent of AOL Time Warner, 22 percent of TeleWest Communications, 49 percent of Discovery Communications, 21 percent in USA Networks (still run by his friend Barry Diller), and a 43 percent share of shopping giant QVC. On May 20, the day Liberty shares hit $73, the company announced a 2-for-1 stock split. All the while, Malone's wealth grew. By mid-1999, his Liberty shares had nearly doubled in each of the previous two years, raising his personal stake to about $2 billion. With another $2.5 billion worth of AT&T shares, Malone's net worth floated close to $5 billion.

As for Liberty, "We are in the sweet spot of the media industry," Malone told Forbes magazine in 1999.

But while Liberty cruised along nicely, AT&T sputtered. By the third quarter of 1999, Wall Street had taken the wind out of AT&T's sails, knocking close to 30 percent off its stock price. Apparently, investors weren't as forgiving as Armstrong had expected. AT&T reported an 18 percent drop in earnings, a sign of falling long-distance prices and dilution of shares from the 440 million new shares issued to buy TCI. The massive outlay for upgrading TCI's lines and other costs had ballooned, and cash flow had dropped. Armstrong's biggest adversary was time. AT&T had spent close to

$80 billion on cable systems to transform an American business icon into a futuristic communications superstore, but it would require billions more to upgrade the lines.[14] AT&T's core long-distance business, meanwhile, eroded rapidly. One telling sign was a massive contract AT&T had with the federal government. For the previous five years, the federal government paid 13 cents a minute; for the next five years, it would be 2 cents.

As AT&T veered off course, Malone felt increasingly powerless to turn the supertanker. On his one-year anniversary on the board of AT&T, he wrote a five-page letter to Armstrong, marked personal and confidential, airing his thoughts on strategy and execution. Armstrong knew how Malone felt about AT&T's reticence to create a new tracking stock. Malone had always anticipated that AT&T would create a tracking stock for cable and another for consumer long distance. "Mike, you have to give cable its own currency," Malone had told Armstrong more than once. AT&T couldn't simply throw cable systems into a bigger company and hope that they were going to get swept up in the growth of the parent company. "In my bones, I know damn well that if they had done the tracking stock stuff right up front, they wouldn't be facing any of these issues today," Malone told a reporter in late 1999. "That's frustrating."

First, Malone suggested in the letter that Armstrong needed a first-class CFO, and Malone urged Armstrong to involve AT&T's tax department in more transactions before they were negotiated with an outside party. Malone began to realize, in conversations and in the details of deals, that Armstrong lacked a strong financial background, and could not see financial efficiencies the same way he did. Malone also acknowledged that timing was critical for AT&T to bid for Media One, but he criticized the structure and execution, largely because of the vast amount of cash required and because it was not tax-advantageous. Finally, Malone declared that he still believed in the idea of four tracking stocks representing all parts of the AT&T empire. Malone thought he could still keep the company intact, structuring the four units very much like Jack Welch structured business units at General Electric, as "autonomous units with a total delegation of operational parameters within budgeting controls," as he precisely described it. "If you do these things," Malone said in his letter to Armstrong, "you will have a great company, and you will maximize shareholder value. If it turns out that shareholders' interests are better served by those tracking stocks eventually becoming independent companies, you will have lost nothing."

Malone got a friendly note in the mail from Armstrong that said he had read the letter and was thinking about it. Shortly thereafter, he did take Malone up on one piece of advice, hiring a new CFO in December 1999—Charles Noski, the former president and COO of Hughes Electronics Corporation. Malone still believed that Armstrong could pull AT&T out of the doldrums, and publicly went out of his way to defend him and Somers. "You never get blamed for what might go wrong. Anytime he makes a decision he gets a desk full of memos, six or seven basketfuls, and the weight of all that staff pressure can really get to you," Malone told an associate one afternoon. "I don't fault Mike. In fact, I say, where would the AT&T shareholders be today if Mike hadn't done what he had done then? Well, they wouldn't have seen their stock go up to like $90 from $30 and had a chance to get out at it. So he gave them something, real assets that are going to put a floor under their values."

After outlining AT&T's problems to a visitor one day, Malone smiled. "I think what happened was he failed to heed the old Latin saying, '*Illegitimi Non Carborundum*' ('Don't let the bastards wear you down'). I think the bureaucracy wore him down. I think he went native. He got in there, into that bureaucratic culture, and all of these people warned him about don't get blindsided by this, or don't do this, don't do that."[15] Armstrong and Somers were always wary of Malone, suspect of his advice, as if it would somehow end up helping Malone. It was all the more reason for Malone to be diplomatic in his critiques. "What I learned to do was, I just float these things. If Mike wants to take them, he can take them. Often, they just go right by him."

One example: Control seemed more important to Mike Armstrong and his legion of lieutenants than financial upside. That's why AT&T ended up paying huge sums of cash to push its cable partners out of the At Home cable modem service, at a time when Malone felt keeping the co-owners involved would encourage their cooperation in extending At Home's reach. At Home was responsible for designing the high-speed network and providing services such as e-mail, and a home page featuring news, entertainment, sports, and chat groups. Cable operators were required to upgrade their local systems to accommodate two-way transmission, as well as handle marketing, billing, and customer complaints, for which they would get 65 percent of the revenue. But early on, the company struggled to bond the cultures of cable cowboys and the digerati of Silicon Valley. Leading the computer camp was Tom Jermoluk, At Home's 42-year-old Hawaiian-born chairman and chief executive, known in the Valley as "T.J." Though he was an energetic believer in the new company, several cable operators, particularly Hindery, bristled at his relaxed and arrogant operating style. Still, Wall Street fell hard for the idea of cable operators interconnected into a digital backbone that allowed high-speed customers to tap in at $40 a month. At Home's stock price had rocketed past $100 in early 1999, inflating the company's market value to more then $20 billion—not bad for a firm that never turned a profit.

With this ballooning currency, At Home struck a deal to buy Excite, Incorporated, one of the World Wide Web's busiest sites, for $7.5 billion in stock, almost twice the price that the stock had been at only months earlier. After the Excite acquisition, Jermoluk insisted on giving Excite prominence on the opening screen of At Home service, rankling rivals like Yahoo!, but more important, cable operators that wanted to choose the opening screen themselves. Jermoluk would butt heads with his cable operator partners repeatedly on the issue, but operators had no allegiance to Excite, an Internet portal. They had signed on, in Malone's own words, "to build a scale-efficient data-transport company." Period. "It was *the* home run and it would have essentially mooted the power that Microsoft and AOL wanted to have," Malone said later. "But they were at cross-purposes." Though he couldn't see the collapse of the Internet coming, he knew that the Excite deal had poisoned the partnership, in part because they had overpaid, but more important, because it diluted the ownership of cable operators, from around 85 percent of the company to about 50 percent. Suddenly, the cable partners began to wonder if they couldn't make more money from their high-speed lines on their own.

Cable operators realized it was a better business proposition to have several portals paying to get access to their pipes than to be hemmed in to an agreement with a single provider, even one they owned, like the newly crowned ExciteAtHome. Besides, it was bad politics; the FCC would step in if they weren't careful. When Hindery began unilaterally negotiating a deal with Yahoo!, Jermoluk and other execs became enraged, and ultimately, Hindery backed down. Another pressure point: cable operators had agreed to sell the high-speed service under the ExciteAtHome brand until 2002—after that, the cable operators were free to sell as they wished, which made their allegience tenuous. Then customers of Excite-AtHome began to report service problems. Installations weren't moving as fast as planned. At one ExciteAtHome board meeting, Malone got fed up with the bickering. "This is a slam-dunk! You guys have one vehicle that you have any chance of competing with, and that's this! I wish to hell somebody would suggest the solution and everybody get behind it," Malone finally said in frustration. Ever so gradually, it was dawning on Malone that he no longer had the same power he once did among the old cable gang. Before this, TCI had typically led the biggest cable operators in highly complex—and profitable—partnerships, such as the purchase of Group W cable systems, the Turner bailout, the Sprint wireless alliance, and Teleport. In the old days, Malone would have banged heads together to get everyone to go the same way.

Tired of the spats with cable partners over the direction of ExciteAtHome, AT&T agreed to pay founding partners Comcast and Cox Communications Inc. $1.6 billion each in cash, or $48 per share to get out of the way. The stock was trading at less than half that at the time and would fall even further. With Excite-AtHome shares trading at around $10, AT&T would owe roughly $3 billion to Comcast and Cox for shares that were worth about $550 million at the time.[16] The deal infuriated Malone further. Although AT&T now could claim a solid majority on the board at ExciteAtHome, it had proven too costly. AT&T had spent more than $4 billion in two different transactions, including the original AT&T-TCI merger, to become the controlling share-holder in At Home. "They are sitting there at the table with their peer groups, in the same industry, building a business they will all profit from—and they can't get along?" Malone bellowed one day in his office. "They have got to go pay Brian Roberts and Jim Robbins to get off the fucking board! All because they don't understand partnerships. It's ridiculous!"

As AT&T untangled itself, its rivals seemed to grow stronger. On January 10, 2000, AOL paid a stunning $165 billion to buy Time Warner in the largest merger in history and the most striking testament to the influence—and inflated values—of the Internet. Later, when Internet stocks crashed, pundits would question whether Time Warner really needed an Internet partner as much as AOL needed cable. But for the cable cowboys, it was proof positive of the supremacy of cable wires as a medium. No other service could provide quicker lines into homes. In a deal that Armstrong could only envy, AOL, the biggest Internet service, with 25 million subscribers worldwide, joined forces with one of the world's biggest cable and media companies to take advantage of the very access it claimed to have been denied.

For Malone, the new merger was just too much to take. His critiques of AT&T management were progressively more harsh. He believed that much of the core problem with the company was that the managers of AT&T were not owners. "A guy who rises to the top of a big corporation and owns none of it is much more interested in control than he is in economics. It is just the nature of humanity. A guy who owns his business is used to control. He never has to fight for control. What he has to fight for is economics. But a bunch of entrepreneurs find it much easier to collaborate and create economic value. They have something beyond control—they have economics," he ruminated. Back in the day, Malone said later, any one director of TCI owned more company stock than the entire AT&T board. It was not complicated, he said: You've got to have some skin in the game.

Malone could empathize with Armstrong on the decline of the long-distance business, which dropped like a stone. What bothered Malone most was the unwillingness of Armstrong and Somers to explore unique ways to avoid taxes, save the company money, and reap the most reward for an asset. As time passed, Malone became more outspoken about issues, particularly short-term debt. He went ballistic when he heard at a board meeting that Dan Somers, the former CFO named president and CEO of AT&T Broadband, proposed to sell 1.2 million cable subs in Montana and Iowa for around $3 billion—part of a plan to hack away at its $62 billion debt load. It didn't bother Malone that the buyers were acquaintances of Somers as much as the fact that AT&T was taking a note on the sale, and worse, the sale was totally taxed. Malone called Armstrong, uncharacteristically furious. "Certainly if you can't sell them to anybody else, sell them to Liberty. We can buy them tax-free, and I will pay you $50 million more than the after-tax proceeds of this deal, whatever it is."

Then he unloaded: "I am not doing this because I want to go into the cable business. I am doing this because I think this is the most stupid fucking thing. What are the headlines going to say? Buy them for $5,000 a sub and sell them for $1,700 and make it up in volume! Excuse me, but this is the guy that brought you the Media One deal! And he may be a good operating guy, but he is the worst dealer that I have ever seen in my life! You guys are nuts! You are actually going to take your leverage up by selling these assets. I am not telling you not to sell them. I am just telling you don't sell them this way." The deal was shelved for the moment.

ひひひ

AT&T's stock price gradually began to sink roughly 50 percent from the fall of 1999 to the fall of 2000—and with it fell the value of Malone's 33-million-share portfolio of AT&T stock—what he hadn't sold or given away. Meanwhile, his Liberty stock zoomed up, then down, but held steady. Still, he was anguished, forced to watch as the remaining stock in AT&T dropped in value from $1.5 billion to about $744 million.[17] Many of the institutional investors had bailed out of the stock immediately after the deal. What bothered him most was that some TCI retirees had not cashed out at the time of the merger—saw their life savings evaporate. He winced occasionally with guilt when good friends whose biggest asset was their 401(k) called to ask: When is the stock bouncing back?

Meanwhile, the Internet bubble had reached maximum capacity, and by April 2000 it burst, taking the air out of so many new media stocks. ExciteAtHome's stock, too, began a steady decline in 2000 that would not stabilize. The implosion of Internet values had affected the portal side of the company, Excite, more than anything else. But Comcast and Cox were protected: AT&T had contracted to pay them $48 a share for their stock, no matter how low the ExciteAtHome stock fell. By the following year, the venture that held so much promise to be the first national high-speed cable modem service declared bankruptcy. AT&T, which controlled the venture, lost a bundle. At its peak, the company was valued at more than $20 billion, with shares trading around $100 on the Nasdaq market in 1999. In the end, it had dwindled to a mere $2 million, with shares trading between 1 and 0.6 cent on the OTC Bulletin Board.

Liberty Media had pumped billions of dollars into highflying wireless, Web, telephone, satellite, and TV companies, and much of it came to an unpleasant end. Malone would pay $3 billion in stock for control of Associated Group, whose major investments included Teligent, a fixed-wireless service for businesses. Malone would extinguish a large chunk of Liberty supervoting stock held by early TCI investor and Associated CEO Myles Berkman in the deal, bumping his personal Liberty voting control to around 47 percent, but the stock of Teligent sank until the company went bankrupt. Others fell in varying degrees. Online airfare auction site Priceline lost most of its value, and ICG, which provided the systems—networks of switches, modem banks, and fiber-optic cable—that linked people to the Internet, would seek bankruptcy protection, too. (Malone would eventually turn over Liberty's stakes in ICG and Teligent to IDT Corp., a scrappy communications company whose ambitious founder, Howard Jonas, reminded Malone of himself in younger days.)

Even rocket-fueled Liberty Digital fell to earth, from around $70 at the beginning of 2000 to less than $10 by year's end. Two years later, Liberty Digital, having lost its value as invasion currency, would be folded back into Liberty Media.

In the case of ICG, Malone ran a loss on the investment bigger than anything ever before in his career: Liberty invested a massive

$500 million in February 2000 when ICG was trading around $30; by November it had filed for bankruptcy protection, and Malone could only find consolation in the tax write-off. Malone was angry with himself and his men for lack of vigilance over the troubled company, but he was more upset with Texas high-roller Shelby Bryan, the CEO of ICG who had assured Malone and TCI that ICG would meet its numbers only a week earlier in a personal visit to TCI. Malone felt snookered. He believed Bryan withheld relevant information about the company's financial condition.

ICG lost investor confidence when the stock plunged on news of severe network problems. Bryan called Malone. He said, "I hope you don't think I was sandbagging you," Malone recalled. "He said, 'You can't believe how many things came together to go wrong right at the last minute.' "

"I said, 'Yeah, sure, Shelby.' And that was it."

Later in the year, he would realize a welcome gain: Sumner Redstone's Viacom agreed to pay $2.3 billion for Liberty's 35-percent-owned BET Holdings, which owned the BET cable channel, a Jazz channel, a book-publishing venture, and a thriving Web portal. The Viacom deal made Johnson, the onetime cable lobbyist, the country's first black billionaire. Because top black BET executives held stock options, Johnson said that "John can take credit for creating more African-American millionaires than any other white guy in the country."[18] Johnson owned 63 percent of BET; Liberty Media, 35 percent. Liberty's cut of the deal: 15.2 million shares of Viacom stock valued at more than $850 million—not bad for an initial investment of $180,000 in 1979.[19]

Still, he could not shake AT&T from his thoughts. At home, Leslie noticed her husband's agitation, too. "You're around physically more, but I know where your mind is," she said.[20]

By July 2000, Malone dusted off the letter he had sent to Armstrong months earlier, and sent him another copy. "Mike, I still fundamentally believe this would have been the right thing to do," Malone told the AT&T chairman, "but it may be getting too late in the game now for this to work."

15

DÉJÀ VU

In the end, the collapse of C. Michael Armstrong's grand plan to turn Ma Bell into a broadband powerhouse came with dispassionate quickness. On October 26, 2000, Armstrong announced what looked like the final chopping up of the final remnants of AT&T, along lines eerily similar to what John Malone had mapped out two years before. Liberty Media would become entirely independent. AT&T's wireless business would be spun off, and a tracking stock for cable would be created with the intent of spinning that business off, too. What was left of AT&T—plain old telephone service—would be represented by two stocks, one for business services and the other for the fading consumer business. The breathtaking retreat held up the very real possibility that AT&T's core long-distance service would end up getting gobbled up someday by a rival.

Malone had wanted Armstrong to issue the different tracking stocks and keep the entire empire together, empowering it to offer a one-stop bundle of local and long-distance phone services, wireless, broadband, cable TV, and more. Armstrong, having lost the faith of Wall Street and the support of his board, went much further, agreeing to chop up the entire company into separate limbs. Shareholders had fared exceedingly well betting on past breakups of AT&T. When antitrust regulators busted up the original Ma Bell in 1984, the seven Baby Bells were spun off and went on to achieve great financial results. When Chairman Robert E. Allen broke up AT&T a second time in 1996, spinning off Lucent Technologies and the NCR computer business, Lucent went on to create enormous riches unheard of in telecommunications. Shareholders who held on to all the stocks they received, and stood pat as the Bells then began buying up one another, benefited handsomely: From year-end 1983 to October 2000, their investment rose an astounding 774 percent, almost 50 points better than the rise in the broader stock market. One hundred shares of AT&T, worth $6,150 before the 1984 breakup, had grown to 1,250 shares in nine companies, worth $53,765 plus dividends.[1]

This last breakup of AT&T, however, looked different—it was born out of weakness and self-inflicted injury, not government edict or the drive to unlock wealth. By late December 2000, AT&T's stock, having lost 60 percent of its value over the year, hit a new 52-week low, $17.06, as it announced plans to cut dividends. And even as Mike Armstrong tried to bring a breakup to pass, the cable cowboys were getting in his way. In July 2001, Brian Roberts of Comcast threw AT&T into a new round of disarray by bidding $58 billion in stock and debt for the cable assets that AT&T had assembled at a cost of more than $100 billion—roughly $80 billion after sales of particular assetts. AOL Time Warner and others immediately descended, ready to fight over the pieces for themselves. For a storied institution such as AT&T, and particularly for Michael Armstrong, an unwelcome takeover of the nation's largest cable operator would be an ignominious end to the assets for which he had paid so dearly. Now Armstrong would have to publicly resist the shame of accepting Comcast's bid.

By this time, John Malone and Leo Hindery had briefly considered bidding for AT&T's cable business. It would have given them the sweetest revenge of all: vindication. Such a move might let Malone salvage his fortune in AT&T and set the business right. Hindery was keen to execute a takeover of AT&T broadband and suggested making their move just as AT&T was dividing its four main business units into separately traded companies. But after several conversations, they both decided to scrap a bid because they would be doing it for the wrong reasons, mainly retaliation and vindication—not for money or a desire to operate a regulated monopoly.

Comcast's Roberts wasn't nearly so circumspect. If Comcast succeeded, the combination would create the largest cable operation in the United States, giving it the scale and leverage in a family-run company, the same as Malone once had. And why shouldn't Comcast take over the assets of AT&T, the Robertses argued, given Comcast's operating margins of 41 percent compared with AT&T cable margins of 18 percent. The market showed enthusiasm for the deal initially, bumping AT&T's depressed share price up 12 percent in a day. But AT&T's board rebuffed any deal that allowed Comcast voting control of the company.

If Armstrong had hoped for a more honorable ending than selling AT&T's cable assets to the highest hostile bid, he had only himself to blame. By breaking up the company into four separate units aside from Liberty (i.e., business, consumer, broadband, and wireless), he had practically put a For Sale sign on the cable assets, which would almost certainly be better managed in the hands of a more experienced owner. Three days after Brian Roberts floated the unsolicited bid, a somewhat muted but angry Armstrong made a speech to the Boston Chamber of Commerce and gave reporters the latest on his plans to "recognize AT&T to unlock the value we invested in and were creating." As for Comcast's offer, Armstrong said he got a first look at it that Sunday at his house—"about the same time that it appeared on fax machines of newspapers across the country." A week later, AT&T summarily rejected the offer, but in a nod that the company would entertain other bids, Armstrong indefinitely delayed his plan to spin off the cable assets as a separate company.

John Malone was involved, behind the scenes, and was well aware of what Brian Roberts was up to—and he was shut out of the AT&T board's discussions about how to respond. In a slight to a cable warrior of such high stature, Malone was told he shouldn't take part in the Comcast deliberations because he was soon scheduled to leave the board anyway, upon the final spin-off of Liberty Media in August. The official version was that actions the board was about to take might lead to litigation long after Malone had departed, so it was better to insulate him from the decisions. True, Malone was conflicted in several ways, but his money was still in AT&T. The hidden message was all too clear: Armstrong didn't trust Malone, given his knowledge of the industry and his close relationship to Brian Roberts, a lifetime member of the cable gang and still a friend of Malone's, never mind their quarrels. So Armstrong invited Malone to leave the room.

A few days later, on July 12, John Malone resigned from AT&T Corporation's board of directors. He quit a month earlier than planned, in part because there was no point remaining once he had been excluded from the AT&T discussions about the Comcast offer. Moreover, it freed him to pursue other options, uninhibited by conflicts.

Malone did not regret selling TCI to AT&T, despite the outcome. Looking back, he had found the best buyer, but perhaps not the best partner. What he regretted was failing to negotiate the right to sell his stock at the time of the deal—a move that would have certainly raised eyebrows among AT&T shareholders—then watching it lose close to half a billion dollars before selling most all of it. "Like I told Turner," Malone said later, "'When you sell, sell! Get out!'" Turner, like Malone, would lose a paper fortune in AOL Time Warner stock after AOL's values evaporated with the Internet crash.

The same day Malone resigned, Malone went to war with AT&T, essentially having an AT&T-owned entity turn around and sue AT&T itself. Liberty-owned Starz Encore Group, the premium-channel business, sued AT&T's cable unit in federal court, saying it failed to pay Starz Encore $44 million in programming fees. The money represented AT&T's share of Starz Encore's programming fees, the legacy of a 1997 deal between TCI and TCI-owned Encore Media Group. In the 25-year agreement, TCI agreed to pay a flat monthly fee to Encore, but with a twist: If programming costs were more than projected, TCI and Encore would split the difference. The actual costs, as it turned out, far exceeded projections, as Encore had struck some of the richest deals ever for films from Disney and Sony Pictures, among others. Now, as chairman of Liberty, which fully owned Starz Encore, Malone was in a position to reap the benefits.

Freedom for Malone finally came a month later when AT&T spun off Liberty Media as an independent company, completing the next orderly step in the breakup of Ma Bell. Because of net operating losses that Malone carried on the old TCI books and the terms he had imposed letting Liberty make use of the losses to reduce its tax bill, AT&T had to make a cash payment of $850 million to Liberty as it was saying good-bye.

While Armstrong put AT&T on the auction block, Malone could do nothing but let the smoke settle, and therein look for new opportunities to put Liberty's money to work. He tended to more deal making, like a great white shark swims in order to breathe. Just three years after ceding to AT&T the cable empire he had spent 25 years building, Malone suddenly was on the way to making Liberty the largest owner of cable systems in the world. With AT&T breaking up, the U.S. cable TV industry mature, and TV companies of every stripe facing new competition, Malone turned his sights overseas.

After a string of successive deals, Liberty Media initially agreed to pay the German phone giant, Deutsche Telekom, $4.8 billion for stakes in six regional cable TV companies that serve 10 million households. But Germany's Federal Cartel Office blocked Malone with a familiar impediment: regulation. Liberty Media refused to agree to invest more than $7 billion to upgrade the systems, a government edict that robbed the company of any flexibility. The refusal was a reflection of simple truths Malone had acquired from previous mentors, particularly Moses Shapiro: "Always ask, 'If not?'" He passed on another stake in a troubled United Kingdom cable giant, NTL—which he believed fit well with TeleWest—but these were minor delays. Malone decided on a familiar strategy he employed whenever he thought the market had undervalued his company's shares: He bought back Liberty Media shares. If you believe the share price is cheap, Malone liked to say, why not buy back your own shares at a bargain?

Much like his investing hero, Warren Buffet, Malone had assembled influential stakes in a portfolio of dominant media companies. Liberty owned 4 percent of AOL Time Warner, the world's largest media corporation; 18 percent of News Corp., second only to Rupert Murdoch; 20 percent of Sprint Corporation's Sprint PCS;

22 percent of USA Interactive, which housed Home Shopping Network, Ticketmaster, and an impressive media empire that Barry Diller built on the back of a group of TV stations that Malone had sold to him; and 3.5 percent of Vivendi, the French media giant that struck a deal to buy Seagram Co.'s Universal Studios. Liberty, with just 35 employees at its Denver base, controlled a global operation that also oversaw big stakes in hundreds of video channels, from Animal Planet Asia to UK Food, as well as the dominant U.S. brands (e.g., QVC, Discovery, and the Starz-Encore Group of networks).

As he scoured the globe, Malone had increasingly relied on an old friend and partner to do his bidding in Europe, Gene Schneider, an authentic pioneer of the U.S. cable industry who had built one of the nation's first systems in Casper, Wyoming, in 1953 with his brother, Richard. By 1989, after building the eighth-largest cable operator reaching 17 states, Gene Schneider, as chairman of United Artists Entertainment, sold the company to TCI for $2 billion. In what seemed like an afterthought, Schneider persuaded Malone to sell back to him United Artists' cable systems in Sweden, Norway, and Israel for $85 million. Those overseas leftovers would become the foundation of a new company specializing in building and buying overseas cable systems called UnitedGlobalCom, Incorporated (UGC Inc.), which by 2001 would be the largest international cable operator with systems reaching 11 million subscribers in 26 countries and annual revenue of $1.6 billion.

After informal discussions, UGC and Malone's Liberty Media agreed to combine their international operations. Liberty contributed its assets in Europe and Latin America, including its 25 percent stake in TeleWest, Britain's second largest cable-telephone provider, with some 1.2 million cable subscribers and 1.7 million telephone customers.

"This for me is déjà vu all over again," Malone told reporters at the time of his initial investment, taking time to note cable's potential in Europe. "We've been in business with Gene Schneider and United Cable for many years." By pooling his international cable properties with UGC, Malone hoped to give it the scale to expand farther, faster. Per subscriber, cable properties were selling for prices at less than half of those paid in the United States. UGC distributed video programming—including Liberty's portfolio of networks—and eventually, high-speed Internet services to millions of international consumers. Already, a UGC subsidiary operated a cable-modem service called Chello in Australia, Latin America, and Europe. Gene Schneider, the white-haired, cigar-smoking septuagenarian, installed his son, Mark, as head of United Pan-Europe Communications, UGC's main subsidiary. Mark would later resign his post after the company overextended itself, spending $5 billion on cable properties without the promise of quick revenues.

In 1999, Malone increased his stake in his old buddy's company from 7 to 45 percent. Malone's price got cheaper as the stock fell. Later, with UGC's and UPC's debt reaching $8 billion, a Liberty affiliate bought $1.4 billion of UGC's junk bonds at 40 cents on the dollar, lent the company more money, and bought more stock. The total price, as the financial press reported, was a mere $2 billion for a company that was valued at nearly $13 billion only 24 months earlier. Malone would end up with a 75 percent chunk of the equity and 90 percent of the voting rights.[2]

Though Murdoch's News Corp.'s satellite holdings could compete against UGC in some markets, Malone saw no problems when asked about the relationships. "Liberty likes to bet on winners," he said on a conference call with analysts one day. "We're perfectly happy to be betting on both UGC as well as News Corp."[3]

A day after the initial UGC deal, Malone looked East. Liberty and its Japanese partner Sumitomo Corporation, agreed to combine their cable company in Japan, Jupiter Telecommunications, with Microsoft's Titus Communications, which also serves Japan, creating overnight the largest cable operator in the country. Microsoft, which had acquired Media One's 29.9 percent stake in Telewest a year earlier, and was also a minority partner in UGC, was as eager as Malone to push overseas for new business.

ꖴꖴꖴ

When AT&T conceded that its cable systems were formally up for sale, AOL Time Warner and Cox jumped into the fray. Microsoft lurked in the wings, too, promising to back the Cox and Comcast bids in order to block the only other broadband behemoth it considered a real threat, AOL Time Warner. Handicapping who would end up with the TCI and Media One cable systems came down to this: Who could craft the most lucrative, face-saving offer for Mike Armstrong?

After sweetening its bid once more, Comcast ultimately won. For $47 billion in stock and $20 billion in debt, Comcast scooped away AT&T's hard-won cable holdings and became the nation's number one cable operator, with 22 million subscribers—zooming past AOL Time Warner. The Roberts family, who had a 33 percent voting control of the combined company, compared with an 87.5 percent voting stake in Comcast, promised not to sell the new company's stock for 10 years. Gates, who owned stakes in both Comcast and AT&T, would end up with 6 percent of the new company and get a favored spot on the cable systems for its MSN online service, which operated in the shadow of AOL. Through this and other investments in cable operators, it was gaining a way into the new digital boxes with its software.

In the merger agreement, Comcast and AT&T forged extraordinary provisions that ensured few shareholders could question management decisions after the deal. Moreover, it assured that AT&T Chairman Michael Armstrong would keep his post in the new company, and that Comcast President Brian Roberts would be CEO. Roberts would succeed Armstrong as chairman. If anyone wanted to remove Armstrong or Roberts, they'd need a vote by 9 out of the 12 board members. None of the board members could be replaced before the 2005 annual meeting, and no firm could amass more than 10 percent of the new company's stock without permission. Brian Roberts, it seemed, had learned a thing or two from Malone.

The new giant would not be without enemies for long. The big local telephone companies had largely surrendered the fight to offer video services, instead merging with each other and attacking long-distance and business telephone markets. But the satellite companies had grown up, and now threatened cable's core product of digital cable TV. The cable gang had successfully blown apart Murdoch's deal with Echostar by luring him into their camp, and likewise, the Justice Department had blocked Murdoch's subsequent deal to partner with the cable gang's Primestar. Cable operators, unable to forge ahead competitively without high-powered satellites necessary for tiny dishes, collectively sold Primestar to DirecTV in early 1999, much to Malone's disappointment. In late 2001, the shifting alliances settled, and where Murdoch had failed, Echostar agreed to merge with DirecTV in a deal valued at around $26 billion. Echostar and Hughes, which together would serve nearly 17 million subscribers, were suddenly a satellite giant. For the first time, the new service could overcome cable's primary advantage over DBS, offering all local signals. The merger partners found themselves on the same end of pointed questions from antitrust regulators as their old cable adversaries. And they answered in strikingly similar ways: A merger of the two largest satellite providers would increase competition with cable TV providers.

Comcast, a family company that started with a tiny system in Tupelo, was in some ways an anachronism in an industry where few original cable entrepreneurs were still around. AOL's acquisition of Time Warner Inc. capped a string of deals that collectively put well over half of cable subscribers in the hands of nontraditional cable companies for the first time. AOL, AT&T, and Paul Allen's Charter Communications were all considered outsiders, corporations with no ties to the first generation of cable cowboys. The new entrants were already splintering the once-clubby fraternity of owners with different and conflicting agendas. The cable industry had withstood surges of consolidation over the past 25 years, but the latest wave had swept enormous change throughout the ownership ranks.

"I don't think, going forward, it'll ever be the same as it was," said Gordy Crawford, one of the early TCI investors late one winter afternoon in his Los Angeles office after selling most of his cable TV holdings.[4]

From time to time, Malone felt the hollow ache of regret, not over the deal to sell TCI, for he had long wanted to leave that yoke behind, but more because he had failed to negotiate the perfect deal, one that would have allowed him to sell all his AT&T shares in a block trade at the time of the deal. The agreement disallowed such a sale, and Malone himself was convinced it could poison the relationship between Liberty and AT&T and weaken shareholder confidence in the deal. But he would lose hundreds of millions of dollars on paper because of the terms. After he left the board, Malone would begin unloading the bulk of his AT&T shares, all at a discount: roughly $400 million worth to pay off debt; an estimated $400 million worth to charity, primarily the Malone Family Foundation; and roughly $200 million worth converted into Liberty shares. Left with around 10 million shares, he had hedged on most of his position by collars, a combination of put options and call options that can limit the risk that values will decrease. Taking into account market losses, as well as charitable contributions, Malone's net worth approached $2 billion.

By the start of the century, cable TV, or broadband as it was increasingly known, was beginning to deliver on some promises made over previous decades; others it would never fill. Though perhaps not quite in the way furturists, or even the early pole climbers themselves, had predicted, the wires had taken hold in the country, and there was scant evidence they would be replaced by a more efficient delivery system. What began as a way to get a better picture was now a pipe—a very large pipe—that carried digital pictures, sound, and data.

More than 15 million subscribers received new digital cable services—and could count themselves as the first true beneficiaries of Malone's and the industry's 500-channel promise made a decade earlier. Interactive TV, however rudimentary, was sneaking into digital cable homes, with choices of watching 200 current hit movies, playing games, and checking local weather and movies—all accomplished by pressing buttons on an interactive remote control. In May 2002, still a believer, Malone agreed to pay $185 million in cash and stock for control of OpenTV, a maker of interactive software for cable set-top boxes. Around the same time, Liberty agreed to buy another interactive-TV software company it partly owned called ACTV as well as a firm called Wink Communications, and would form the Liberty Broadband Interactive Television subsidiary.

And despite the disintegration of ExciteAtHome, cable operators were well on their way to making cable modems the de facto standard for online delivery in a world ravenous for bandwidth, with some 7 million people paying $40 a month by 2002. The network of fiber and coaxial cable painstakingly strung and buried along

American streets by cable operators reached into 73 million homes by 2002, and had evolved into an electronic delivery system unrivaled anywhere. Cable networks numbered 225 and were expected to increase their average audience by an estimated 9 million homes, while their old nemesis, broadcast networks, were expected to lose some 2 million homes between 2000 and 2006. People in more than a million homes made local phone calls over cable wires.

Even as the industry began to deliver on its grand promises, cable seemed to take square aim and shoot itself in the foot. AT&T's problems were only the start. The stocks of all big public cable operators were down, some drastically, because of the heavy debt they carried. Cable stocks took another hit when news of a cable company financial scandal broke—the worst in industry history since Irving Berlin Kahn was convicted of bribery in 1971. In Coudersport, Pennsylvania, Adelphia Communications Corp. filed for bankruptcy protection after disclosures in the spring of questionable accounting practices by the Rigas family. Authorities uncovered secret loans to Rigas-controlled companies, falsified financial results, and abuse of fiduciary duties. By summer 2002, Adelphia founder and CEO John Rigas and two of his sons were hauled away in handcuffs and arrested on charges of looting the sixth-largest cable TV company—using it like "a personal piggy bank," according to prosecutors. Cablevision, another family-run concern, which traded in the $70 range two years earlier, was now in the teens. Each bit of bad news hammered cable stocks.

Liberty Media would lose about half its value in two years, hurt by risky investments in new companies and sharp declines in its portfolio of established media and telecommunications stocks. Though he was still licking his scrapes, Malone endeavored to recreate a new cable kingdom, this time outside the United States. In late summer, Liberty's bargain-hunting march across Europe yielded another prize: Dutch cable operator Casema NV. Through Liberty and its affiliates, Malone was already one of the world's largest cable operators, but bragging rights counted only when creating wealth. Liberty's footprint extended throughout Europe, Latin America, Australia, and Japan, giving it controlling interests in companies with wires into nearly 16 million homes worldwide—far larger than the audience TCI had served when Malone sold it to AT&T.

Even with the bad bets on the Internet companies, Liberty began 2002 in a comfortable position to deal, with more than $2 billion of cash and $25 billion in very liquid, publicly traded investments. True to form, Malone wanted nothing more than to build Liberty. Sailing past retirement age, he was still hell-bent on finding the right combination of partners, currencies, and desperation to put together another showstopper transaction.

To those who knew him best, it was a given: John Malone was nowhere near done yet.

EPILOGUE

"I've never seen it this bad," Malone said one morning in his office as summer of 2002 approached. "If we get hit any harder on this we may have no solution but to sell."

Malone was talking about cattle, not cable. A long drought had withered pastures across the West, prices for cattle were volatile, and beef consumption was down. "Unless we get some rain soon, these cows ain't gonna eat."

As his years at TCI had passed, Malone, the suburban boy who had grown up passionate for sailing along the shores of Connecticut found himself more and more comfortable with the cowboy lifestyle he had learned from Bob Magness. And though he still professed to enjoy the sea best, he certainly basked in the role of rancher.

Beginning in 1999, Malone spent more and more time in his ranch office, a small white house with green trim nestled in gently rolling hills southeast of Denver. Across the street, in a big red metal barn surrounded by large fences, Leslie trained her horses. Small streams laced the property, barns and big bales of hay dotted the pastures, and lazy Black Angus cattle slept in the afternoon shade. Above the door to his office, a sign read, "No one gets to see the wizard. Not no one. Not no how."—a gag gift from Leslie. The house was sparsely decorated, but it reflected Malone's tastes: a bronzed bull in a charging stance behind his desk; a picture of his boat, *Liberty*, on the back wall; Texas longhorns above the sink; and a figurine of an eagle gripping the arrows of war, the olive branch of peace, and an American flag. Some mornings, Malone pulled a frozen honeybun out of the freezer, plopped it on a plate, and warmed it in the microwave. In this office, a ranch hand was more likely to walk through the doors than a CEO.

And though he passed many hours on the phone, usually with Liberty President and CEO Dob Bennett, Gene Schneider, or Rupert Murdoch, he spent more time at home now. On a trip to New York for Liberty, Malone left a day early while Bennett stayed for a charity dinner representing the company. In the plane, as he scanned documents from his scuffed leather briefcase, suddenly Malone looked off in the distance. "Cats," he said aloud, remembering his chore to feed them. For Malone, pets were a welcome artifact of home life, and they could crack his straight stare with a smile. When one of the pugs died in the winter of 2000, Malone had a casket made, held a funeral, and buried the dog in a spot just a short walk from their new house near Denver. That night after the TCI jet landed in Denver, Malone hopped into his white SUV. Darth Vader was on his way to feed the cats.

Quietly but with purpose, Malone began buying up the two things cowboys crave most: cattle and land. By late 1999, Malone had collected enough of both to make him the largest individual landowner in Colorado and one of the 10 largest cattle operations in the United States.

If anything, Malone was carrying on a company tradition. For 20 years, TCI and Magness had owned and operated Cow Creek Valley, a 22,000-acre spread just north of the Colorado border in Wyoming. Magness had craved a ranch for years, and in 1981, doing business as the Silver Spur Land & Cattle Company, TCI had paid $1.3 million for the property. For 20 years, Magness and TCI got their money's worth out of Cow Creek Valley. It was both a working cattle ranch and the stage for TCI's meetings with its biggest shareholders, where often Malone, Barton, and TCI investors would get up and discuss a merger over bacon and scrambled eggs they cooked themselves. More than anything, Magness got a genuine kick out of fishing, riding, and resting a few weeks a year in a guest cabin he had remodeled into a house on the 80-acre South Ranch. He called it the Ponderosa. When the AT&T-TCI merger was struck, Malone bought the land from Liberty Media, as much for sentimental reasons as an investment, for $17 million.

Like Magness, Malone was a collector, an accumulator of assets. Magness had tutored Malone over the years about cattle, and occasionally Malone had jumped into farm chores with vigor. Now Malone owned more than 18,000 special hybrid Angus cattle, one of the biggest herds in the West. "He knows cattle," Thad York, general manager for Silver Spur Land & Cattle, told Malone's hometown paper, the *Rocky Mountain News*. "And what he doesn't know now, he will know before long. He's quick to catch on." Malone had already won the hard-earned respect of some of the nation's biggest cattle ranchers. "John Malone will definitely be a player," chimed in Chuck Lambert, chief economist for the National Cattlemen's Beef Association. The newspaper quickly christened Malone a "Beef Baron."

The economics of the cattle industry were compelling to Malone, and he spent hours mapping out his own theories about how to make it more profitable.

In addition to the economics of raising cattle, Malone immersed himself in the specifics of breeding. He loved the inherent efficiencies in hybrid vigor, the known improvements in growth or yield in one generation of hybrids over their parents. "The idea is to have [a] 1,000-pound cow producing a 550-pound calf at weaning. She is more efficient. The smaller the cow, the less grass she eats. If you get a 2,000-pound cow producing a 300-pound weaning calf, you are doing it the wrong way."

Malone removed much of the chance and guesswork from his cattle operations by overhauling the business with information technology. With advanced bar-code machinery and other tracing methods, Malone could track each cow's offspring, paternity, and growth rates, fine-tuning where necessary. All this was done on a grand scale.

ᙈᙈᙈ

But Malone wasn't buying land merely to raise cattle. As cerebral as he seemed to the outside world, there was a side of Malone that felt genuinely at peace in the natural world. Occasionally, he would take friends out on massive tracts of land he owned south of Denver; it was populated by elk, deer, and mountain goats. One afternoon, on a tour with Romrell, Gould, and Barton on four-wheel all-terrain vehicles, Malone left his comrades in a puff of dust. He led the pack to a brush-covered plateau that offered an extraordinary view of the Rockies some 20 miles away. Malone killed the engine and got off his four-wheeler, never looking back to see if his friends had followed. Gazing at the breathtaking panorama before him on a golden fall afternoon, he stared for 10 minutes before saying a word.

"I'm a collector of land, and the basic idea is to own land in pretty places that haven't been ruined yet and to not develop it," Malone said one afternoon in his ranch office. Choosing properties most worthy of saving was a challenge he found trickier than first appeared. Sometimes, a parcel of unspoiled land could quickly become surrounded by housing or other developments. "So you don't necessarily want to shoot your wad too early in this game, because you can't protect it all," he said. The elements of success in cable could also be applied to buying land: scale, timing and efficiency.

Almost all of the land and ranch purchases by Malone had a single element in common: conservation easements, which allow landowners to take charitable tax deductions if they opt never to develop a property. Often, the deals were a combination of public and private money. While the conservation easements created tax shelters for Malone, using easements to offset capital gains wasn't exactly cost-effective. "If your motive isn't conservation, then it's very inefficient," he said. "If your motive is tax-deferral or tax avoidance, it's crazy. Your motive's got to be, 'Hey, this is a beautiful piece of property, I'd like to protect it.'" Little wonder then, that he would later join the board of the Nature Conservancy, the world's largest conservation organization, which claimed a hand in helping "safeguard more than 12 million acres of natural habitat in the [United States]."

As early as 1995, Malone had begun buying parcels of land in Colorado, Wyoming, and New Mexico. Not long after, word spread that Malone was one of those rich absentee ranch owners, a familiar breed who shuns local businesses, hogs water during droughts, and overgrazes the land. And yet, for all the whispering about the new interloper, Malone paid fair prices and seemed to ingratiate himself with the locals—in part by having no development aspirations for the land.

Indeed, Malone drove around town in his truck and occasionally stopped by certain homes to ask folks if they were interested in selling. Malone politely sat down in the living rooms and front porches of many ranchers and farmers south of Denver, some of whom had no idea they were in direct negotiations with one of America's most powerful media moguls.

"I think he'll be a good steward of the land," said Bill Hudick, a lifetime Elbert resident who traded property with Malone. "He's a nice guy. He's a good neighbor."[1] In June 1997, Ronald Boone, an Elbert rancher, sold more than 500 acres to Malone for $455,645. "I turned him down a couple of times and then he upped it [the price] a little bit, and I thought, 'This is a once-in-a-lifetime chance.' So I sold it," Boone told the *Denver Post*.[2] "Then I turned around and leased it all back from him. I've got a lifetime residency. I'm running my cattle and doing my hay, same as always. It worked out good for me, I'm satisfied." Relative to local real estate values, Malone paid fair market value for the property, which sold for between $1,000 and $3,000 an acre.

In 1999, he picked up the pace, and bought five ranches totaling 256,900 acres in Colorado and Wyoming, paying about $75 million altogether. Malone's accumulated land in Colorado alone—more than 270,000 deeded and leased acres—made him the state's largest individual landowner.[3] One of his ranches was the Bijou Springs, part of the Bijou Basin, a pastoral setting that history books claim was first settled in the mid-1800s by homesteading pioneers, American Indians, and buffalo hunters. Aside from several houses, the property was home to a game reserve with 250 head of elk, deer, and some Rocky Mountain sheep, as well as a commercial hunting camp from which Malone collected fees from sportsmen hoping to bag a trophy.[4]

Malone loved the idea of small rural outposts so much, he nego-tiated the price on eight burial plots near land he owned (at a vol-ume discount, of course), which he then set aside for members of the immediate family. He managed to quickly ease minds and dis-solve misperceptions wherever he bought land, including Jackson County, where several of his ranch managers bought a half-dozen prize steers, sheep, and swine raised by 4-H Club youngsters and Future Farmers of America at the local North Park Fair. "He's pay-ing better than scale for ranch managers and hands, he's kept most of the people on, and he's keeping the rivers open for fish-ing," said Jim Dustin, owner of the local paper, the *Jackson County Star,* who described Malone as a "preservationist and not a tree-hugger."[5]

Malone even changed the way ranch jobs were structured, giving generous health insurance, retirement plans, college tuition, and a computer to every family. "We want to create an opportunity for those guys who have worked hard all their lives, but never had a lot," Malone said. "And we'd like to see their kids go to college."[6]

For all his buying in the West, though, Malone also was acquisi-tive in Maine, his second home. In the mid-1990s, using $1 million in funds donated by Malone, the Boothbay Region Land Trust bought the Ovens Mouth Preserve, a 146-acre stretch of land that abutted Malone's property. The land was the trust's largest pre-serve, comprising woods, lakes, meadows, and a 93-foot-span foot-bridge that arched over a salt marsh.

In July 2000, Malone bought more property in Maine, including some 7,500 acres of pristine shorefront on Spencer Lake, a favorite public fishing hole located in the middle of the Northern Forest Alliance's Western Mountains Wildland. The purchase, by the appropriately named Mosquito LLC, a Maine company formed by Malone, was valued at $10 million, or $1,330 an acre. The land was a complement to 8,000 acres he already owned on the southern part of the 1,800-acre lake, which he had bought from International Paper for nearly $3.5 million. Now he owned the entire shoreline. To many of the state's sportsmen, the 5-mile-long lake, known for its salmon fishing, had become a big pond for one rich guy overnight. "We can't have our boat launch, but he can have his own private playground," said George Smith, executive director of the Sport-man's Alliance of Maine.[7]

A few months later, in January 2001, Malone told the sports enthusiasts in Maine that he had decided to keep his property open to the public. A Malone representative told the state's Inland Fisheries and Wildlife Department that the public was welcome to use the 15,000 acres Malone owned for camping, fishing, hiking, and hunting. But Malone made clear that access would be denied if the land was abused. "He has said, 'I want the public to enjoy my land. All I ask is that my property be treated properly and I be treated courteously as the landowner,'" said Sgt. David Peppard of the fish and game department.[8]

A gate was built along an access road to the property, but it was never closed. "They put the gate in as a kind of symbol," Peppard said. "The ball is in the land users' court. No one is going to have anyone to blame but themselves if the gate is shut."[9] Besides keeping the land open, Malone replaced a dam on the outlet of Spencer Lake, which made it easier to use a boat launch upstream on Fish Pond. For his family's own getaway, Malone bought a seven-building lakeside complex known as the Falcon Lodge on a 900-acre tract in Maine's Unorganized Territory in 1996 in a bankruptcy proceeding for $850,000. By the summer of 2002, Malone seemed to be just getting warmed up, snapping up more than 53,000 acres on Maine's western edge, which included Frontier Forest, woods that extended to the border of Quebec.

Back in Colorado, Malone turned one of his largest acquisitions into a donation to fellow Colorado residents, viewable along Denver's Interstate 25, the black ribbon that split a sea of subdivision homes and commercial development. In February 2001, Malone inked a deal that would save a 21,000-acre open-space buffer between Denver and Colorado Springs. It was the last large open tract of land on the eastern slope of the Rocky Mountains, offering a sweeping, uninterrupted view of Pike's Peak and the Front Range, the snow-capped spine of mountains closest to Denver.

Malone bought the land, called Greenland Ranch, from Ed Gaylord, developer of the Grand Ole Opry in Tennessee and a majority owner in The Broadmoor hotel in Colorado Springs. The ranch was appraised at a value of $76.2 million. Gaylord agreed to sell it for $70 million, allowing the $6.2 million difference as a charitable tax deduction. With money from the state, county, and local land groups, Malone donated around $50 million to complete the purchase, believed to be the largest gift of its kind in Colorado history. The conservation easements Malone had obtained to complete the purchase guaranteed that Greenland Ranch would remain open space. But with public access open only to a portion, most of it would remain open only to its owner.

The work of Malone's mind—the never-ending days, the negotiations, the clashes, the fat profits, and the losses—had been fueled by nothing less than an absolute passion. Twenty-five years in the public spotlight had been enough. John Malone was finally ready to be alone.

ACKNOWLEDGMENTS

I first heard of John Malone in 1991, when I started writing about the cable TV industry for the *Wall Street Journal*. After six years of deciphering the rules, finances, and technology, I began to see the implausible story of an industry's birth. The career of Malone, better than anyone, reflected cable TV's mercurial ascent. I set out to show how America was wired with cable TV, to offer an accurate portrait of a man who profoundly influenced our modern media, and to understand what propels ordinary individuals to great heights. Readers will best decide whether those goals were realized.

Though this book is unauthorized, it was written with Malone's cooperation. His immediate family declined to talk with me, but beginning in 1997, Malone and I met in person a total of 23 times, almost always in his office in Denver. Only once did I join him on his boat, *Liberty*, where, unable to take notes because of choppy seas, I hugged a toilet below deck for six hours and retched. This book is the product of those conversations with Malone and his reflections on watershed events at Tele-Communications, Incorporated (TCI) and the cable industry.

All sources are identified in the "Notes" chapter, and all interviews are mine unless noted otherwise. Research is based on my notes, reportage and stories from the *Wall Street Journal*, and nearly 200 interviews with executives connected to the cable industry.

At TCI, Peter Barton gave me unique insights into Malone's deal making and personality. Leo Hindery helped with details of TCI's final

289

days and the AT&T merger, while Dob Bennett helped simplify Malone's more intricate financial transactions. Several of the company's old guard volunteered their time to piece together company history, including Steve Brett, Tom Elliott, Donne Fisher, Marvin Jones, Larry Romrell, J. C. Sparkman, Dan Shields, and Dave Willis. And the book benefited in various ways from other thoughtful sources connected to the cable industry, including: Ed Bleier, Bill Bresnan, Julian Brodsky, Bill Daniels, Barry Diller, Charles Dolan, Amos Hostetter, Reed Hundt, Glenn Jones, Gus Hauser, Gerald Levin, Marc Nathanson, Nick Nicholas, Brian and Ralph Roberts, Sumner Redstone, Stratford Smith, Ted Turner, and Tom Southwick.

The Cable Center in Denver was a historical treasure trove, and the staff there was as eager as it was efficient. John Accola helped track documents from Denver, and I am grateful to several financial analysts who guided me through insufferably complex TCI deals over the years, including Chris Dixon, Ray Katz, Dennis Lebowitz, John Reidy, Jessica Reif, John Tinker, and Tom Wolzien. At the *Wall Street Journal,* Laura Landro, my editor, encouraged me to pursue Malone's story, and the paper granted me a generous, extended leave.

I owe a big debt to the early readers: Johnnie Roberts, a former *Journal* scribe whose early help was indispensable; John Higgins, a veteran media editor blessed with an encyclopedic memory of the TV business; and Lamar Graham, managing editor at *Parade,* who talked me through two computer crashes and counseled me as loyally as he has since our days at the *Columbia Daily Tribune* in Missouri 15 years ago. I am particularly grateful to Dennis Kneale, a Brooklyn neighbor, managing editor of *Forbes,* and a former *Journal* editor of mine who was uniquely qualified to help edit this sprawling story. His suggestions were superb, his queries instructive, and his encouragement invaluable.

Despite more delays than I care to admit, Andrew Wylie, my agent, believed in the book from the start, and Jeanne Glasser at John Wiley & Sons recognized the importance of Malone's story.

I am indebted to my parents for their support, which came early and often. Finally, this book could not have happened without my wife, Mary, who never fails to inspire, humor, and heal me.

Mark Robichaux
Brooklyn
August 2002

NOTES

INTRODUCTION

1. Paul Kagan Associates, Inc., "Malone Magic Makes TCI Number One Stock of All Time," *Cable TV Investor,* 13 March 1998, p. 6.

CHAPTER 1

1. Malone interview.
2. 1974 TCI proxy statement
3. 1972 TCI Annual Report.
4. Charlotte Magness, Bob Magness' mother, author interview.
5. Charlotte Magness, author interview.
6. Bob Magness, Oral History, Cable Center.
7. Ibid.
8. "First Showing of Cable TV Slated for Friday Night." *Memphis Democrat,* 2 August 1956.
9. Bob Magness, oral history, Cable Center.
10. "Construction Underway on Television System." *Memphis Democrat,* 27 March 1956.
11. Parsons, Patrick, and Robert M. Frieden. *The Cable and Satellite Television Industries.* Boston: Allyn & Bacon, 1998, pp. 26, 27.
12. Ed Parsons, Oral History, Cable Center.
13. Bill Daniels, Oral History, Cable Center.
14. Bill Daniels, author interview.
15. Bob Magness, Oral History, Cable Center.

16. Parisi, Paula. "Brave New Television." *The Hollywood Reporter Salutes TCI on Its 25th Anniversary,* May 1994.
17. Larry Romrell, author interview.
18. Tom Elliott, author interview.
19. TCI memo to Ann Draper from Monica Payne.
20. Southwick, Thomas. *Distant Signals.* Overland Park, KS: Primedia Intertec, p. 26
21. Parsons, Patrick, and Robert M. Frieden. *The Cable and Satellite Television Industries.* Boston: Allyn & Bacon, 1998, p. 47.
22. Smith, Ralph Lee. *Wired Nation.* New York: Harper & Row, p. 40.
23. Sharon Magness, author interview. Romrell.

CHAPTER 2

1. Kahn, convicted in 1971, was transferred to the penitentiary at Eglin Air Force Base in Florida from Allenwood and released after serving 20 months. He vehemently denied he bribed the officials and argued that the payment was extortion to get a cable license.
2. Parsons, Frieden, *The Cable and Satellite Television Industries,* p. 50.
3. Malone, author interview.
4. Fred Andreae, author interview.
5. Gerald Bennington, author interview.
6. Malone, author interview.
7. Malone, author interview.
8. Malone, author interview.

CHAPTER 3

1. 1974 TCI Annual Report.
2. Malone, author interview.
3. Malone, author interview.
4. Internal TCI memo to Malone from Art Lee and Steve Schoen, 7 November 1973; Stephen Keating, *Cutthroat,* Boulder, CO: Johnson Printing, pp. 64–65.
5. Malone, author interview.
6. 1974 TCI Annual Report.
7. J. C. Sparkman, author interview.
8. Paul Kagan, author interview.
9. Malone, author interview.

CHAPTER 4

1. Charles Dolan, author interview.
2. Dolan, author interview.

3. Mair, George. *Inside HBO.* New York: Dodd, Mead & Co., p. 25.
4. Southwick, Thomas. *Distant Signals.* Overland Park, KS: Primedia Intertec, p. 118.
5. Malone, author interview.
6. 1975 TCI Annual Report.
7. Bibb, Porter. *Ted Turner: It Ain't As Easy As It Looks.* Boulder, CO: Johnson Books, 1993, 1997, p. 31.
8. "Cable TV:The Race to Plug In." *Business Week,* 8 December 1980, p. 63.
9. Parsons and Frieden, *The Cable and Satellite Television Industries.* p. 54.
10. "The Pay-TV Diet the Public Will Pay For." *Business Week,* 8 December 1980, p. 65.
11. "Cable TV: The Race to Plug In." *Business Week,* 8 December 1980.
12. Bruck, Connie. *Master of the Game.* New York: Simon & Schuster, 1994, p. 68.
13. "The Rise of American Pay TV." *The Economist,* 29 December 1978.
14. Smith, Ralph Lee. *Wired Nation,* Harper & Row, 1972.
15. "Cable TV: The Race To Plug In." *Business Week,* 8 December 1980.
16. Sykes, Charles J. "Wired In." *Milwaukee Magazine,* April 1982.
17. Bauer, Pat. "Free Shares of Cable TV Cost Its Users." *Washington Post,"* 14 September 1980.
18. Dawson, Fred. "The Franchise Story." *CableVision,* 19 May 1980.
19. Salmans, Sandra. "TCI's No. 1 Cable Strategy." *New York Times,* 19 October 1983.
20. *Community Communications Co. v City of Boulder, CO et. al.,* U.S. Court of Appeals, Tenth Circuit, 28 May 1980.
21. E.F.C. "Nasty, Nasty." *Forbes,* 6 April 1987.
22. Malone, author interview.
23. *Central Telecommunications Inc. v TCI Cablevision Inc. et al.* No 85-1805WM Brief of Appellee, U.S. Court of Appeals, 8th Circuit.
24. Ibid, Affidavit of Elmer Smalling.
25. Knowton, Christopher. "Want This Stock? It's up 91,000%." *Fortune,* 31 July 1989.
26. Roberts, Johnnie. "Cabal Cabal." *Wall Street Journal,* 27 January 1992.
27. Des Ruisseaux, Richard. "Cable Wars." *Louisville Courier Journal,* 16 August 1992.
28. Accola, John. "Town Blocked TCI Steamroller." *Denver Rocky Mountain News,* 13 December 1994.
29. Thomas W. Hazlett, director of the telecommunications policy program at the University of California, Davis. He served as chief economist of the FCC from 1991 to 1992.
30. NCTA; *The Cable and Satellite Television Industries.* Parsons, Frieden, p. 59.

CHAPTER 5

1. Ivey, Mark, Frances Seghers, and Matt Rothman. "The King of Cable TV—Meet the Man Who Makes the Networks Tremble." *Business Week*, 26 October 1987.
2. "Cable-TV Bidding War to Serve Big Cities Is Cooling Off." *Dow Jones News Service*, 1 April 1983.
3. Cohen, Laurie. "Cable-Television Firms and Cities Haggle over Franchises That Trail Expectations." *Wall Street Journal*, 28 December 1983.
4. Mahar, Maggie. "The Baby Bells vs. the Big Gorilla? Competition Threat Clouds Picture for Tele-Communications Inc." *Barron's*, 1 August 1988.
5. Richard Reiss newsletter.
6. "Malone Alone." *Channels*, June 1989.
7. Hoak, James, author interview.
8. Ivey, Mark, Frances Seghers, and Matt Rothman. "The King of Cable TV. Meet the Man Who Makes the Networks Tremble." *Business Week*, 26 October 1987.
9. Malone, author interview.
10. Mahar, Maggie. "The Baby Bells vs. the Big Gorilla?" *Barron's*, 1 August 1988.
11. Mahar, Maggie. "The Baby Bells vs. the Big Gorilla?" *Barron's*, 1 August 1988.
12. Powell, Bill. "Cable's Biggest Leaguer." *Newsweek*, 1 June 1997.
13. Landro, Laura. "Tele-Communications Sets Cable TV Agenda." *Wall Street Journal*, 11 February 1986.
14. Malone oral history. Cable Center.
15. Bibb, Porter. *Ted Turner: It Ain't as Easy as It Looks*. Boulder, CO: Johnson Books, 1993, 1997, p. 317.
16. Ted Turner, author interview.
17. The original TCI investment in Turner was made on June 3, 1987. At the time, TCI owned 65 percent of United Artists, which invested $75 million, more than 20 percent of United Cable, which invested $50 million, and Heritage, which invested $1.5 million, according to Liberty Media.
18. Peter Barton, author interview.
19. Ozanian, Michael K. "Yesterday's Darling." *FW*, 25 December 1990.
20. Knowton, Christopher. "Want This Stock? It's up 91,000%." *Fortune*, 31 July 1989.
21. Ivey, Mark. "The King of Cable TV." *Business Week*, 26 October 1987.
22. "Video Programming Distribution and Cable Television: Current Policy Issues and Recommendations." U.S. Dept. of Commerce, June 1988.
23. Malone, author interview.
24. Malone, author interview.

25. Prenuptual agreement between Sharon Costello and Bob Magness, dated 16 March 1989.

26. Knowton, Christopher. "Want This Stock? It's up 91,000%." *Fortune,* 31 July 1989.

27. Knowton, Christopher. "Want This Stock? It's up 91,000%." *Fortune,* 31 July 1989. Information based on Paul Kagan Associates, Inc., comparing the lows of stocks 20 years earlier to closing prices in April 1989.

CHAPTER 6

1. Myerson, Allen R. "A Merger of Giants." *New York Times,* 14 October 1993.

2. Kupfer, Andrew. "The No. 1 in Cable Has Big Plans." *Fortune,* 28 June 1993

3. This encounter was taken from C-Span video of Malone's testimony before the subcommittee on Communications, U.S. Senate Committee on Commerce, Science, and Transportation, 16 November 1989.

4. Halonen, Doug. "Cable Gets More Flak on the Hill." *Electronic Media,* 10 November 1989.

5. The most widely cited figure at the time was from a General Accounting Office study that stated the price of the most popular tier of basic rate service increased from $11.71 per month in November 1986 to $18.84 in April of 1991, an increase of 61 percent.

6. Malone, author interview.

7. Herndon, Keith. "TCI Boss a Key Force in Cable TV." *Atlanta Journal and Constitution,* 22 February 1987.

8. Ainslie, Peter. "Malone Alone." *Channels,* June 1989.

9. Malone, author interview.

10. Dedrick, Jay. "City Asks TCI to End Increase in Cable Rates." *News Record,* 3 May 1990.

11. *TCI Cablevision v. City of Gillette,* US District Court, Wyoming, No 90-CV-1043J.

12. Statement of Roy M. Speer, Chairman and CEO, Home Shopping Network, Inc. before the U.S. Senate Subcommittee on Communications, 14 March, 1991.

13. Roberts, Johnnie. "Cable Cabal: How Giant TCI Uses Self-Dealing, Hardball to Dominate Market." *Wall Street Journal,* 27 January 1992.

14. Landro, Laura. "Tele-Communications' Big Spinoff Plan to Test Business Acumen of John Malone." *Wall Street Journal,* 22 January 1990.

15. Landro, Laura. "Tele-Communications' Big Spinoff Plan to Test Business Acumen of John Malone." *Wall Street Journal,* 22 January 1990.

16. Malone, author interview.

17. Malone, author interview.

18. Palmeri, Christoper. "What Price Liberty?" *Forbes,* 1 April 1991.

19. Malone, author interview.

20. Malone, author interview.

21. Hazlett, Thomas. "Regulating Cable Television Rates: An Economic Analysis." Institute of Government Affairs, University of California, Davis, July 1994.

22. Camire, Dennis. "Congress Approves Cable Bill; Hands Bush A Political Slap." *Gannet News Service,* 5 October 1992.

23. CBS Chairman Laurnce Tisch cited this estimate in testimony before Congress, a figure repeated often by Jim Mooney of the NCTA.

24. Robichaux, Mark. "Scrambled Picture: How Cable TV Firms Raised Rates in Wake of Law to Curb Them." *Wall Street Journal,* 28 September 1993.

25. Huey, John, and Andrew Kupfer, "What That Merger Means For You," *Fortune,* 15 November 1993.

CHAPTER 7

1. Robichaux, Mark. "Tele-Communications to Unveil Plan to Rewire Cable Systems for $2 billion." *Wall Street Journal,* 12 April 1993.

2. Pearl, Daniel, and Mark Robichaux. "Bell Atlantic Cleared to Offer Video Programs." *Wall Street Journal,* 25 August 1993.

3. Hazlett, Thomas W. "Regulating Cable Television Rates: An Economic Analysis." Program on Telecommunications Policy, Institute of Government Affairs, University of California, Davis, July 1994.

4. Robichaux, Mark. "Scrambled Picture: How Cable TV Firms Raised Rates in Wake of Law to Curb Them." *Wall Street Journal,* 28 September 1993.

5. Hazlett, Thomas W. "Regulating Cable Television Rates: An Economic Analysis." Institute of Government Affairs, University of California, Davis, July 1994.

6. Robichaux, Mark. "TCI Offers Apology to FCC for Memo on Cable Rate Rules." *Wall Street Journal,* 17 November 1993.

7. Letter from John Malone to James Quello, dated 13 December 1993.

8. Roberts, Johnnie L., and Mark Robichaux. "Diller Bets on Home Shopping Future." *Wall Street Journal,* 11 December 1992.

CHAPTER 8

1. Auletta, Ken. *The Highwaymen: Warriors of the Information Superhighway.* New York: Random House, 1997, pp. 46, 47. This list first appeared in a superb profile of Malone by Auletta in the 7 February 1994 issue of the *New Yorker.*

2. Malone, author interview.

3. Keller, John J. "Free At Last: How Raymond Smith Cut the Apron Strings of Sclerotic Ma Bell." *Wall Street Journal,* 12 December 1993. Smith's background is based on this profile.
4. Malone, author interview.
5. Malone, author interview.
6. Statement of John C. Malone, President and CEO, Tele-Communications Inc. before the Subcommittee on Antitrust, Monopolies, and Business Rights, Committee on the Judiciary, United States Senate, 16 December 1993.
7. Statement of John C. Malone, President and CEO, Tele-Communications Inc. before the Subcommittee on Antitrust, Monopolies, and Business Rights, Committee on the Judiciary, United States Senate, 16 December 1993.
8. Higgins, John M. "Cable Ops Score Big in Teleport Deal." *Broadcasting & Cable,* 12 January 1998.
9. Greenwald, John. "Disconnected." *Time,* 7 March 1994.
10. Robichaux, Mark. "The FCC's Rate Cuts Will Slow Traffic on Information Superhighway." *Wall Street Journal,* 25 February 1994.
11. Sugawara, Sandra, and Paul Farhi. "Ripples Spread form Megamerger's End." *Washington Post,* 25 February 1994.
12. Greenwald, John. "Disconnected." *Time,* 7 March 1994.
13. Malone, author interview.
14. Malone, author interview.
15. Kline, David. "Align and Conquer." *Wired,* February 1995.
16. Greenwald, John. "Disconnected." *Time,* 7 March 1994.
17. Kline, David. "Align and Conquer." *Wired,* February 1995.
18. Kline, David. "Align and Conquer." *Wired,* February 1995.
19. Kline, David. "Align and Conquer." *Wired,* February 1995.

CHAPTER 9

1. Loomis, Carol J., and Andrew Kupfer. "High Noon for John Malone." *Fortune,* 13 January 1997.
2. Liberty Media.
3. Shapiro, Eben. "Viacom Agrees to Spin Off, Then Sell Its Cable Systems." *Wall Street Journal,* 26 July 1995.
4. Accola, John. "Government Stalks Cable Colossus TCI." *Denver Rocky Mountain News,* 11 December 1994.
5. Beem, Edgar Allen. "Cable Baron John Malone Is Bullish on Boothbay." *Maine Times,* 22 July 1994.
6. Auletta, Ken. "John Malone: Flying Solo." *New Yorker,* 7 February 1994.
7. Eisenmann, Thomas R. "Structure and Strategy: Explaining Consolidation in the U.S. Cable Television Industry." Thesis, Harvard University Graduate School of Business Administration, 1997.

8. Shapiro, Eben, and David D. Kirkpatrick. "TCI's 3rd-Period Preliminary Results Disappoint Already-Wary Wall Street." *Wall Street Journal,* 25 October 1996.

9. Malone, author interview.

10. Robichaux, Mark. "Highway of Hype." *Wall Street Journal,* 29 November 1993.

11. Colman, Price. "Malone Retakes the Point." *Broadcasting and Cable,* 28 October 1996. Malone's quotes and disposition were confirmed by several attending analysts.

12. Robichaux, Mark. "Bad Call: Malone Says TCI Push into Phones, Internet Isn't Working for Now." *Wall Street Journal,* 2 February 1997.

13. Malone, author interview.

14. Quillen, Ed. "Someday TCI May Indeed Show Us What We're Really Looking For." *Denver Post,* 18 February 1997.

15. Lesly, Elizabeth, Gail DeGeorge, and Ronald Grover. "Sumner's Last Stand." *Business Week,* 3 March 1997.

16. Malone, author interview.

17. Malone, author interview.

18. Kirkpatrick, David. "TCI Instructs Its Suppliers to Halt Their Shipments." *Wall Street Journal,* 25 October 1996.

19. Fessler, Karen. "Investors, Customers Lose Patience with TCI." *New Haven Register,* 3 November 1996.

CHAPTER 10

1. Robichaux, Mark. "New President Hopes to Speed Change at TCI." *Wall Street Journal,* 10 February 1997.

2. Hindery, author interview.

3. Kerver, Tom, "Leo's Crown." *Cablevision,* 28 November 1994.

4. Reese, Jennifer, *Stanford Business Magazine of Graduate School of Business,* March 1998.

5. "Malone and Hindery: The Road to Recovery?" *Multichannel News,* 5 May 1997.

6. Paul Gould, author interview.

7. Bell, Emily. "Rival Master of the Universe." *The Observer,* 26 May 1996.

8. Malone, author interview.

9. Testimony of Rupert Murdoch, chairman and chief executive of News Corp. before the U.S. Senate Commerce, Science, and Transportation, 10 April 1997.

10. Malone, author interview.

11. Lippman, John, Mark Robichaux, and Bryan Gruley. "No Liftoff: So Far, Murdoch's Bid to Enter Satellite TV in U.S. Goes Nowhere." *Wall Street Journal,* 15 May 1997.

12. *U.S. v. Primestar, TCI, et al.,* U.S. District of Columbia, filed 12 May 1998.
13. *U.S. v. Primestar, TCI, et al.*
14. Lippman, John, Mark Robichaux, and Bryan Gruley. "No Liftoff: So Far, Murdoch's Bid to Enter Satellite TV in U.S. Goes Nowhere." *Wall Street Journal,* 15 May 1997.
15. Robichaux, Mark. "Echostar Chief Must Build Link to Murdoch." *Wall Street Journal,* 26 February 1997.
16. Lippman, John. Interview with Padden.
17. Robichaux, Mark. "News Corp., Echostar Plan May Unravel," *Wall Street Journal,* 29 April 1997.

CHAPTER 11

1. Peter Barton, author interview.
2. Larry Romrell, author interview.
3. Malone, author interview.
4. Malone, author interview.
5. *Kim Magness and Gary Magness v. Donne F. Fisher, Daniel Ritchie, TCI, John Malone in the matter of the Estate of Bob Magness,* Arapahoe County, Colorado, Case No. 96 PR 944, Div. 3, 29 October 1997.
6. Affidavit and Notice of Revocation. Cherry Hills, CO: Cherry Hills Police Department, 6 June 1994.
7. "Bonds of $100,000 Each Set for Four in Heroin Probe." *Denver Post,* 13 April 1973.
8. Fisher, author interview.
9. *Kim Magness and Gary Magness v Donne F. Fisher, Daniel Ritchie, TCI, John Malone in the matter of the Estate of Bob Magness,* Arapahoe County, CO, Case No. 96 PR 944, Div. 3, 29 October 1997.
10. Accola, John. "The Magness Mess How a Tycoon's blunder triggered Colorado's Nastiest Estate Battle." *Rocky Mountain News,* 14 December 1997.
11. Sharon Magness, author interview.
12. Petition for Removal of Personal Representatives in the Matter of the Estate of Bob Magness, Case No. 96 PR944., Div. 3 Arapahoe County, CO. 11 September 1997.
13. Letter from Steven Rattner of Lazard Freres to Donne Fisher and Dan Ritchie, dated 16 June 1997.

CHAPTER 12

1. Leo Hindery, author interview.
2. Brian Roberts, author interview.
3. Brian Roberts, author interview.
4. Brian Roberts, author interview.

5. Grover, Ron, "Malone: Wheeling, Dealing, and Rallying." *Business Week,* 4 September 1997.
6. Brian Roberts, author interview.
7. Brian Roberts, author interview.
8. Karlga, Rich. "Silicon Valley's Politics of Envy." *Wall Street Journal,* 20 October 1997.
9. Malone, author interview.
10. Malone, author interview.
11. Malone, author interview.
12. Desmond, Edward. "Malone Again." *Fortune,* 16 February 1998.
13. Taken from "Broadband Revolution," an address Malone gave to students at the Yale School of Organization and Management on 9 November 1993.
14. Malone, author interview.

CHAPTER 13

1. Accola, John, and Rebecca Cantwell. "Magness Estate Fight Over." *Rocky Mountain News,* 6 January 1998.
2. *Kenneth Steiner v John Malone, et al. and TCI,* Case No. 16130NC, Court of Chancery of the State of Delaware, filed 8 January 1998.
3. Accola, John. "TCI Chief Giving His Fortune to Education." *Rocky Mountain News,* 13 January 1998.
4. Waldman, Peter. "AT&T's Plan to Sell Newspaper Ads Fuel to a Salt Lake Feud." *Wall Street Journal,* 6 October 2000.
5. Elmstrom, Peter. "Mike Armstrong's Strong Showing." *Business Week,* 25 January 1999.
6. Malone, author interview.
7. TCI owned 39 percent of the @Home stock, but 72 percent of the shareholder votes.
8. Cauley, Leslie. "AT&T to Acquire TCI for $37.3 Billion—Agreement Paves the Way For Long-Distance Firm to Pursue Local Market." *Wall Street Journal,* 25 June 1998.
9. Sloan, Allan. "John Malone's $170 Million Prize: TCI Deal to Get Higher Price for 'B' Shares Gives Chairman Added Profit." *Washington Post,* 30 June 1998.

CHAPTER 14

1. Nouse, Dale. "Give Me Liberty." *Showboats International,* January 1997.
2. Cauley, Leslie. "AT&T's Attempt to Spin Off Liberty Media Encounters Snag." *Wall Street Journal,* 12 June 2001.
3. Nelson, Brett. "The Inside Track." *Forbes,* 18 October 1999.

4. Mehta, Stephanie N. "Connected: The AT&T-TCI Linkup." *Wall Street Journal,* 25 June 1998.
5. Malone, author interview.
6. Malone, author interview.
7. Malone, author interview.
8. Malone, author interview.
8. Malone, author interview.
9. Hindery, author interview.
10. Hindery, author interview.
11. Cho, Joshua. "AT&T's Strategy is Fixed." *Cable World,* 13 December 1999.
12. Cauley, Leslie. "Hung Up: Armstrong's Vision of AT&T Cable Empire Unravels on the Ground." *Wall Street Journal,* 18 October 2000.
13. Higgins, John M. "Leo Makes His Break." *Broadcasting and Cable,* 11 October 1999.
14. AT&T initially paid almost $100 billion for TCI and MediaOne, but sold some nonstrategic assets, which brought the net figure closer to $80 billion.
15. Malone, author interview.
16. Cauley, Leslie. "Hung Up: Armstrong's Vision of AT&T Cable Empire Unravels on the Ground." *Wall Street Journal,* 18 October 2000.
17. Higgins, John M. "Break Up AT&T?" *Broadcasting,* 18 September 2000.
18. Caulk, Steve. "Cable Mogul Prepares for Spinoff from AT&T." *Rocky Mountain News,* 4 August 2001.
19. Liberty Media.
20. Malone, author interview.

CHAPTER 15

1. Ridgway, Nicole. "A Family Affair." *Forbes,* 27 November 2000.
2. Liberty Media.
3. Mehta, Stephanie N. "The Island of Dr. Malone." *Fortune,* 24 July 2000.
4. Gordon Crawford, author interview.

EPILOGUE

1. Emery, Erin. "TCI Chief Extends Territory Malone Buys Elbert Acreage over Three Years." *Denver Post,* 26 April 1998.
2. Emery, Erin. "TCI Chief Extends Territory Malone Buys Elbert Acreage over Three Years." *Denver Post,* 26 April 1998.

3. Frazier, Deborah. "Malone Moving from Cable to Cattle." *Denver Rocky Mountain News,* 18 September 1999. In addition to deeded land, leases include state and federal grazing permits that are transferred as a part of a ranch sale.

4. Laden, Rich. "Cable TV Magnate Buys Historic Bijou Ranch/Malone Completes $35 Million Deal." *The Gazette,* 7 May 1999.

5. Frazier, Deborah. "Malone Moving from Cable to Cattle." *Denver Rocky Mountain News,* 18 September 1999.

6. Malone, author interview.

7. Young, Susan. "The Man Who Bought a Lake." *Bangor Daily News,* 27 November 2000.

8. Adams, Glenn. "Colorado Billionaire Opens Maine Preserve to Public." *Associated Press,* 11 January 2001.

9. Ibid.

INDEX